D1515711

MARK TWAIN'S
The Mysterious Stranger
and the Critics

edited by
John S. Tuckey
Purdue University

Wadsworth Publishing Company, Inc.
Belmont, California

L. C. Cat. Card No.: 68–11086

Printed in the United States of America by American Book–Stratford Press, Inc.

PREFACE

The Mysterious Stranger is a work of particular interest to students as well as to more advanced scholars. With its unique boy-angel character, ironically called Satan, its evocative description of the dream-steeped Eseldorf setting, its impressive symbolic representation of the human condition, its satire and its notable passage on the use of laughter as a weapon, and its startling conclusion, the story is one of much intrinsic appeal. Differing in theme, mood, and philosophy from most of Mark Twain's earlier and better-known writings, *The Mysterious Stranger* represents the work of his later period and is generally considered his most important literary creation of that period.

This novella has, moreover, come to be regarded as an important key to an understanding of Mark Twain's later life and work. It has already received much critical attention and seems certain to receive much more. There are some extraordinary and intriguing textual problems. For example, it is now clear that Albert Bigelow Paine and Frederick A. Duneka, who edited the story as it was published six years after Mark Twain's death, actually wrote into the tale a character—the astrologer—who did not appear at all in the manuscript as Mark Twain had written it; they also deleted thousands of Mark Twain's own words. With such extensive changes, their editing amounted to unsanctioned coauthorship. The resulting problems will challenge the best students and engage the efforts of scholars for a long time to come.

For the text of *The Mysterious Stranger* I have followed the 1916 edition of Paine and Duneka. I have, however, corrected an obvious misprint: in Chapter 8, "victors" has been supplied in place of "victims," making a sentence read, "Next came the Hebraic wars, and we saw the victors massacre the survivors . . ." I have also annotated the text to give some indication of the ways in which the 1916 edition differs from the manuscripts upon which it was based. In my essay *"The Mysterious Stranger:* Mark Twain's Texts and the Paine-Duneka Edition," included in the "Text and Structure" section, I have considered some of the textual problems—among them our lack of any other completed, coherent version of the story to replace the Paine-Duneka edition.

Within each section containing critical articles, the order of presentation is chronological, by date of publication. The authors' own titles have generally been used for the selections; in a few instances I have supplied titles and have mentioned the original titles in footnotes. Page numbers of the original sources of the articles are shown by raised numbers within brackets. Where a word division occurs at the end of a page in the source, the number follows the complete word. Where page references have been made to *The Mysterious Stranger* as published elsewhere than in this book, they have been allowed to stand. Scrupulosity in documentation has seemed preferable to editorial tampering for the sake of minor convenience; presumably those who read and use the articles will have become familiar enough with *The Mysterious Stranger* to locate cited passages readily. An effort has been made to hold to a minimum deletions of irrelevant matter; use of "From" at the beginning of the first footnote to a selection indicates that some part of the total work has been omitted, and internal omissions are further shown by ellipses (. . .).

In preparing this book I have drawn upon what I have learned by working in the Mark Twain Papers collection at the University of California, Berkeley. For the opportunity to make these studies I am grateful to the Mark Twain Estate, to its former literary editor Henry Nash Smith, and to its present one, Frederick Anderson. For permission to reprint works included in this volume, I offer warm thanks to the authors and publishers of the various articles; to Harper & Row, Publishers, who control publication rights for *The Mysterious Stranger;* to James M. Cox, who was especially kind in letting me use a climactic chapter from his *Mark Twain: The Fate of Humor* almost immediately after the publication of that book; to the Purdue Research Foundation, which holds copyright on my book *Mark Twain and Little Satan: The Writing of "The Mysterious Stranger";* and to Maurice Beebe, for encouraging me to prepare this book and for making available his valuable editorial expertise.

J. S. T.

CONTENTS

CHRONOLOGY: Samuel L. Clemens (Mark Twain)

1835   Born November 30 at Florida, Missouri.

1839   Moved with family to Hannibal, Missouri.

1847   Father died March 24.

1848–53   Printer for Hannibal newspapers.

1853–57   Printer in St. Louis; New York; Philadelphia; Keokuk, Iowa; Cincinnati.

1857–61   Cub pilot and pilot of steamboats on the Mississippi.

1861   After the closing of the river in April by the outbreak of the Civil War, served in the Missouri militia for several weeks in the spring or early summer. Departed with brother Orion for the Nevada Territory, leaving St. Joseph, Missouri, by stagecoach on July 26.

1861–62   Prospector for silver and gold in the Nevada Territory.

1862–64   Reporter and correspondent for the Virginia City *Territorial Enterprise.*

1864–66   Reporter and free-lance writer for San Francisco periodicals. Returned briefly to prospecting in the Tuolumne district of California, December 1864 to February 1865.

1866   Traveled to Sandwich Islands (Hawaii) as correspondent for the Sacramento *Union.* Departed for New York in December.

1866–67   New York correspondent for the San Francisco *Alta California.*

1867   *Quaker City* voyage to Europe and Palestine as correspondent for the *Alta California,* June to November.

1869   *The Innocents Abroad* published.

1870   Married Olivia Langdon of Elmira, New York, February 2. Editor of Buffalo *Express.*

1870   Son, Langdon, born November 7.

1871   Leased the Hooker house on Forest Street in Hartford, Connecticut, in October. Lecture tours.

1872   Daughter, Susy, born March 19. *Roughing It* published. Lecture tour in England. Langdon Clemens died June 2.

1873   *The Gilded Age* published. Lecture tour in England.

1874   Daughter, Clara, born June 8. Moved into new home on Farmington Avenue, Hartford, in April.

1875   *Sketches, New and Old* published.

1876   *The Adventures of Tom Sawyer* published.

1878–79   Traveled in Europe.

1880   *A Tramp Abroad* published. Daughter, Jean, born July 26.

1882   *The Prince and the Pauper* published.

1883   *Life on the Mississippi* published.

1884   Established publishing firm, Charles L. Webster and Company.

1884–85   Lecture tour with George W. Cable.

1885   *Adventures of Huckleberry Finn* published.

1889   *A Connecticut Yankee in King Arthur's Court* published.

1891–95   Lived in Europe, making occasional business trips to the United States.

1894   Bankruptcy of Charles L. Webster and Company. *Pudd'nhead Wilson* published.

1895–96   Lecture tour around the world.

1896   Susy Clemens died August 18 in the Hartford home, of meningitis. *Personal Recollections of Joan of Arc* published.

1897   At London in June and at Weggis, Switzerland, in July and August, made notes for the writing of *The Mysterious Stranger*. After moving to Vienna in September, began initial draft, which quickly became the "Eseldorf" version. Wrote some 95 pages of the "Eseldorf" manuscript between November 1897 and January 1898. *Following the Equator* published.

1898   Wrote story "The Great Dark" (unfinished) at Kaltenleutgeben, near Vienna, in August 1898. At Vienna in November and December wrote the "Hannibal" version of *The Mysterious Stranger*.

1899   At London and at Sanna, Sweden, wrote part of a novel *Which Was It?* (the "George Harrison story," unfinished). Between May and October continued the "Eseldorf" manuscript.

1900   At Dollis Hill House, London, wrote the remaining part of the "Eseldorf" manuscript in June, July, and August. Returned to America in October.

1902–03   Continued work on *Which Was It?* Began composition of the "Print Shop" version of *The Mysterious Stranger*.

1904   At Florence, Italy, continued composition of "Print Shop" version, writing more than three hundred additional manuscript pages between January and June, including the "dream-ending" fragment that was used to conclude the posthumously published story as edited by Albert B. Paine and Frederick A. Duneka.

1904   Olivia Langdon Clemens died June 5 at Florence.

1904   Left Florence June 20 to return to the United States.

1905   Wrote *Three Thousand Years among the Microbes* (unfinished novel) between May 20 and June 23, at Dublin, New Hampshire. Continued composition of "Print Shop" version, late June to mid-July.

1908   Moved into new home, Stormfield, near Redding, Connecticut, on June 18. Composed an additional chapter of the "Print Shop" version.

1909   Jean Clemens died December 24 at Stormfield.

1910   Died April 21 at Stormfield.

PART ONE/THE TEXT

The Mysterious Stranger

MARK TWAIN (SAMUEL L. CLEMENS)

Chapter 1

IT WAS IN 1590—WINTER.[1] AUSTRIA WAS FAR AWAY FROM THE WORLD, AND asleep; it was still the Middle Ages in Austria, and promised to remain so forever. Some even set it away back centuries upon centuries and said that by the mental and spiritual clock it was still the Age of Belief in Austria. But they meant it as a compliment, not a slur, and it was so taken, and we were all proud of it. I remember it well, although I was only a boy; and I remember, too, the pleasure it gave me.

Yes, Austria was far from the world, and asleep, and our village was in the middle of that sleep, being in the middle of Austria. It drowsed in peace in the deep privacy of a hilly and woodsy solitude where news from the world hardly ever came to disturb its dreams, and was infinitely content. At its front flowed the tranquil river, its surface painted with cloud-forms and the reflections of drifting arks and stone-boats; behind it rose the woody steeps to the base of the lofty precipice; from the top of the precipice frowned a vast castle, its long stretch of towers and bastions mailed in vines; beyond the river, a league to the left, was a tumbled expanse of forest-clothed hills cloven by winding gorges where the sun never penetrated; and to the right a precipice overlooked the river, and between it and the hills just spoken of lay a far-reaching plain dotted with little homesteads nested among orchards and shade trees.[2]

"The Mysterious Stranger" from *The Mysterious Stranger and Other Stories* by Mark Twain. Copyright 1916 by Harper & Brothers; renewed 1944 by Clara Clemens Gabrilowitsch. Reprinted by permission of Harper & Row, Publishers.

[1] In the Mark Twain holograph, manuscript DV 327 in the Mark Twain Papers (hereafter MTP) at the General Library, University of California at Berkeley, Mark Twain at first indicated May of 1702 as the time of action. Later he deleted that date and moved the time back to the winter of 1490. Finally, in a typescript prepared under his direction (DV 327a, MTP), he struck out "1490" and inserted "1590."

[2] In composing this setting, Mark Twain closely followed a passage from his notebook (unpublished), dated July 25, 1897, in which he describes the scenery at the Swiss village of Weggis, beside Lake Lucerne, where he was staying at the time.

The whole region for leagues around was the hereditary property of a prince, whose servants kept the castle always in perfect condition for occupancy, but neither he nor his family came there oftener than once in five years. When they came it was as if the lord of the world had arrived, and had brought all the glories of its kingdoms along; and when they went they left a calm behind which was like the deep sleep which follows an orgy.

Eseldorf[3] was a paradise for us boys. We were not overmuch pestered with schooling. Mainly we were trained to be good Christians; to revere the Virgin, the Church, and the saints above everything. Beyond these matters we were not required to know much; and, in fact, not allowed to. Knowledge was not good for the common people, and could make them discontented with the lot which God had appointed for them, and God would not endure discontentment with His plans. We had two priests. One of them, Father Adolf, was a very zealous and strenuous priest, much considered.[4]

There may have been better priests, in some ways, than Father Adolf, but there was never one in our commune who was held in more solemn and awful respect. This was because he had absolutely no fear of the Devil. He was the only Christian I have ever known of whom that could be truly said. People stood in deep dread of him on that account; for they thought that there must be something supernatural about him, else he could not be so bold and so confident. All men speak in bitter disapproval of the Devil, but they do it reverently, not flippantly; but Father Adolf's way was very different; he called him by every name he could lay his tongue to, and it made everyone shudder that heard him; and often he would even speak of him scornfully and scoffingly; then the people crossed themselves and went quickly out of his presence, fearing that something fearful might happen.

Father Adolf had actually met Satan face to face more than once,

---

[3] In his working notes, Mark Twain first designated the village as "Hasenfeld" ("Rabbitfield"), then changed the name to "Eseldorf" ("Assville" or "Donkeytown").

[4] As Mark Twain actually wrote the story, Father Adolf is a bad priest, the villain who falsely accuses Father Peter of stealing from him, gives false testimony at the trial, and commits many other evil deeds. Many changes were made in the story by Albert Bigelow Paine, Twain's official biographer and literary executor, and Frederick A. Duneka, then general manager of Harper & Brothers, who edited the manuscript for posthumous publication. Much of the derogatory characterization of Father Adolf was cut out of the tale. Furthermore, the editors invented one character, the astrologer, who does not appear in the tale as Twain wrote it, and attributed to him many of the bad priest's misdeeds that could not be left out without destroying the plot. For a fuller discussion of the composition of *The Mysterious Stranger* and of the editing by Paine and Duneka, see the selection from *Mark Twain and Little Satan* that is reprinted in this book.

and defied him. This was known to be so. Father Adolf said it himself. He never made any secret of it, but spoke it right out. And that he was speaking true there was proof in at least one instance, for on that occasion he quarreled with the enemy, and intrepidly threw his bottle at him; and there, upon the wall of his study, was the ruddy splotch where it struck and broke.

But it was Father Peter, the other priest, that we all loved best and were sorriest for. Some people charged him with talking around in conversation that God was all goodness and would find a way to save all his poor human children. It was a horrible thing to say, but there was never any absolute proof that Father Peter said it; and it was out of character for him to say it, too, for he was always good and gentle and truthful. He wasn't charged with saying it in the pulpit, where all the congregation could hear and testify, but only outside, in talk; and it is easy for enemies to manufacture *that*. Father Peter had an enemy and a very powerful one, the astrologer who lived in a tumbled old tower up the valley, and put in his nights studying the stars. Every one knew he could foretell wars and famines, though that was not so hard, for there was always a war and generally a famine somewhere. But he could also read any man's life through the stars in a big book he had, and find lost property, and everyone in the village except Father Peter stood in awe of him. Even Father Adolf, who had defied the Devil, had a wholesome respect for the astrologer when he came through our village wearing his tall, pointed hat and his long, flowing robe with stars on it, carrying his big book, and a staff which was known to have magic power. The bishop himself sometimes listened to the astrologer, it was said, for, besides studying the stars and prophesying, the astrologer made a great show of piety, which would impress the bishop, of course.

But Father Peter took no stock in the astrologer. He denounced him openly as a charlatan—a fraud with no valuable knowledge of any kind, or powers beyond those of an ordinary and rather inferior human being, which naturally made the astrologer hate Father Peter and wish to ruin him. It was the astrologer, as we all believed, who originated the story about Father Peter's shocking remark and carried it to the bishop. It was said that Father Peter had made the remark to his niece, Marget, though Marget denied it and implored the bishop to believe her and spare her old uncle from poverty and disgrace. But the bishop wouldn't listen. He suspended Father Peter indefinitely, though he wouldn't go so far as to excommunicate him on the evidence of only one witness; and now Father Peter had been out a couple of years, and our other priest, Father Adolf, had his flock.

Those had been hard years for the old priest and Marget. They had been favorites, but of course that changed when they came under the shadow of the bishop's frown. Many of their friends fell away entirely, and the rest became cool and distant. Marget was a lovely girl of eighteen when the trouble came, and she had the best head in the village, and the most in it. She taught the harp, and earned all her clothes and pocket money by her own industry. But her scholars fell off one by one now; she was forgotten when there were dances and parties among the youth of the village; the young fellows stopped coming to the house, all except Wilhelm Meidling—and he could have been spared; she and her uncle were sad and forlorn in their neglect and disgrace, and the sunshine was gone out of their lives. Matters went worse and worse, all through the two years. Clothes were wearing out, bread was harder and harder to get. And now, at last, the very end was come. Solomon Isaacs had lent all the money he was willing to put on the house, and gave notice that to-morrow he would foreclose.

Chapter II

Three of us boys were always together, and had been so from the cradle, being fond of one another from the beginning, and this affection deepened as the years went on—Nikolaus Bauman, son of the principal judge of the local court; Seppi Wohlmeyer, son of the keeper of the principal inn, the "Golden Stag," which had a nice garden, with shade trees reaching down to the riverside, and pleasure boats for hire; and I was the third—Theodor Fischer, son of the church organist, who was also leader of the village musicians, teacher of the violin, composer, tax-collector of the commune, sexton, and in other ways a useful citizen, and respected by all. We knew the hills and the woods as well as the birds knew them; for we were always roaming them when we had leisure—at least, when we were not swimming or boating or fishing, or playing on the ice or sliding down hill.

And we had the run of the castle park, and very few had that. It was because we were pets of the oldest servingman in the castle—Felix Brandt; and often we went there, nights, to hear him talk about old times and strange things, and to smoke with him (he taught us that) and to drink coffee; for he had served in the wars, and was at the siege of Vienna; and there, when the Turks were defeated and driven away, among the captured things were bags of coffee, and the Turkish prisoners explained the character of it and how to make a pleasant drink out of it, and now he always kept coffee by him, to drink himself and also to astonish the ignorant with. When it stormed he kept us all night; and while it thundered and lightened outside he told us about ghosts and horrors of every kind, and of battles and murders and mutilations, and such things, and made it pleasant and cozy inside; and he told these things from his own experience largely. He had seen many ghosts in his time, and witches and enchanters, and once he was lost in a fierce storm at midnight in the mountains, and by the glare of the lightning had seen the Wild Huntsman rage on the blast with his specter dogs chasing after him through the driving cloud-rack. Also he had seen an incubus once, and several times he had seen the great bat that sucks the blood from the necks of people while they are asleep, fanning them softly with its wings and so keeping them drowsy till they die.

He encouraged us not to fear supernatural things, such as ghosts, and said they did no harm, but only wandered about because they were lonely and distressed and wanted kindly notice and compassion; and in time we learned not to be afraid, and even went down with him in the night to the haunted chamber in the dungeons of the castle. The ghost appeared only once, and it went by very dim to the sight and floated noiseless through the air, and then disappeared; and we scarcely trembled, he had taught us so well. He said it came up sometimes in the night and woke him by passing its clammy hand over his face, but it did him no hurt; it only wanted sympathy and notice. But the strangest thing was that he had seen angels—actual angels out of heaven—and had talked with them. They had no wings, and wore clothes, and talked and looked and acted just like any natural person, and you would never know them for angels except for the wonderful things they did which a mortal could not do, and the way they suddenly disappeared while you were talking with them, which was also a thing which no mortal could do. And he said they were pleasant and cheerful, not gloomy and melancholy, like ghosts.

It was after that kind of a talk one May night[5] that we got up next morning and had a good breakfast with him and then went down and crossed the bridge and went away up into the hills on the left to a woody hill-top which was a favorite place of ours, and there we stretched out on the grass in the shade to rest and smoke and talk over these strange things, for they were in our minds yet, and impressing us. But we couldn't smoke, because we had been heedless and left our flint and steel behind.

Soon there came a youth strolling toward us through the trees, and he sat down and began to talk in a friendly way, just as if he knew us. But we did not answer him, for he was a stranger and we were not used to strangers and were shy of them. He had new and good clothes on, and was handsome and had a winning face and a pleasant voice, and was easy and graceful and unembarrassed, not slouchy and awkward and diffident, like other boys. We wanted to be friendly with him, but didn't know how to begin. Then I thought of the pipe, and wondered if it would be taken as kindly meant if I offered it to him. But I remembered that we had no fire, so I was sorry and disappointed. But he looked up bright and pleased, and said:

[5] Mark Twain at first planned to have the action begin in May (see note 1), and in fact it does here.

"Fire? Oh, that is easy; I will furnish it."

I was so astonished I couldn't speak; for I had not said anything. He took the pipe and blew his breath on it, and the tobacco glowed red, and spirals of blue smoke rose up. We jumped up and were going to run, for that was natural; and we did run a few steps, although he was yearningly pleading for us to stay, and giving us his word that he would not do us any harm, but only wanted to be friends with us and have company. So we stopped and stood, and wanted to go back, being full of curiosity and wonder, but afraid to venture. He went on coaxing, in his soft, persuasive way; and when we saw that the pipe did not blow up and nothing happened, our confidence returned by little and little, and presently our curiosity got to be stronger than our fear, and we ventured back—but slowly, and ready to fly at any alarm.

He was bent on putting us at ease, and he had the right art; one could not remain doubtful and timorous where a person was so earnest and simple and gentle, and talked so alluringly as he did; no, he won us over, and it was not long before we were content and comfortable and chatty, and glad we had found this new friend. When the feeling of constraint was all gone we asked him how he had learned to do that strange thing, and he said he hadn't learned it at all; it came natural to him—like other things—other curious things.

"What ones?"

"Oh, a number; I don't know how many."

"Will you let us see you do them?"

"Do—please!" the others said.

"You won't run away again?"

"No—indeed we won't. Please do. Won't you?"

"Yes, with pleasure; but you mustn't forget your promise, you know."

We said we wouldn't, and he went to a puddle and came back with water in a cup which he had made out of a leaf, and blew upon it and threw it out, and it was a lump of ice the shape of the cup. We were astonished and charmed, but not afraid any more; we were very glad to be there, and asked him to go on and do some more things. And he did. He said he would give us any kind of fruit we liked, whether it was in season or not. We all spoke at once:

"Orange!"

"Apple!"

"Grapes!"

"They are in your pockets," he said, and it was true. And they were of the best, too, and we ate them and wished we had more, though none of us said so.

"You will find them where those came from," he said, "and everything else your appetites call for; and you need not name the thing you wish; as long as I am with you, you have only to wish and find."

And he said true. There was never anything so wonderful and so interesting. Bread, cakes, sweets, nuts—whatever one wanted, it was there. He ate nothing himself, but sat and chatted, and did one curious thing after another to amuse us. He made a tiny toy squirrel out of clay, and it ran up a tree and sat on a limb overhead and barked down at us. Then he made a dog that was not much larger than a mouse, and it treed the squirrel and danced about the tree, excited and barking, and was as alive as any dog could be. It frightened the squirrel from tree to tree and followed it up until both were out of sight in the forest. He made birds out of clay and set them free, and they flew away, singing.

At last I made bold to ask him to tell us who he was.

"An angel," he said, quite simply, and set another bird free and clapped his hands and made it fly away.

A kind of awe fell upon us when we heard him say that, and we were afraid again; but he said we need not be troubled, there was no occasion for us to be afraid of an angel, and he liked us, anyway. He went on chatting as simply and unaffectedly as ever; and while he talked he made a crowd of little men and women the size of your finger, and they went diligently to work and cleared and leveled off a space a couple of yards square in the grass and began to build a cunning little castle in it, the women mixing the mortar and carrying it up the scaffoldings in pails on their heads, just as our work-women have always done, and the men laying the courses of masonry—five hundred of these toy people swarming briskly about and working diligently and wiping the sweat off their faces as natural as life. In the absorbing interest of watching those five hundred little people make the castle grow step by step and course by course, and take shape and symmetry, that feeling and awe soon passed away and we were quite comfortable and at home again. We asked if we might make some people, and he said yes, and told Seppi to make some cannon for the walls, and told Nikolaus to make some halberdiers, with breastplates and greaves and helmets, and I was to make some cavalry, with horses, and in allotting these tasks he called us by our names, but did not say how he knew them. Then Seppi asked him what his own name was, and he said, tranquilly, "Satan," and held out a chip and caught a little woman on it who was falling from the scaffolding and put her back where she belonged, and said, "She is an idiot to step backward like that and not notice what she is about."

It caught us suddenly, that name did, and our work dropped out of our hands and broke to pieces—a cannon, a halberdier, and a horse. Satan laughed, and asked what was the matter. I said, "Nothing, only it seemed a strange name for an angel." He asked why.

"Because it's—it's—well, it's his name, you know."

"Yes—he is my uncle."

He said it placidly, but it took our breath for a moment and made our hearts beat. He did not seem to notice that, but mended our halberdiers and things with a touch, handing them to us finished, and said, "Don't you remember?—he was an angel himself, once."

"Yes—it's true," said Seppi; "I didn't think of that."

"Before the Fall he was blameless."

"Yes," said Nikolaus, "he was without sin."

"It is a good family—ours," said Satan; "there is not a better. He is the only member of it that has ever sinned."

I should not be able to make anyone understand how exciting it all was. You know that kind of quiver that trembles around through you when you are seeing something so strange and enchanting and wonderful that it is just a fearful joy to be alive and look at it; and you know how you gaze, and your lips turn dry and your breath comes short, but you wouldn't be anywhere but there, not for the world. I was bursting to ask one question—I had it on my tongue's end and could hardly hold it back—but I was ashamed to ask it; it might be a rudeness. Satan set an ox down that he had been making, and smiled up at me and said:

"It wouldn't be a rudeness, and I should forgive it if it was. Have I seen him? Millions of times. From the time that I was a little child a thousand years old I was his second favorite among the nursery angels of our blood and lineage—to use a human phrase—yes, from that time until the Fall, eight thousand years, measured as you count time."

"Eight—thousand!"

"Yes." He turned to Seppi, and went on as if answering something that was in Seppi's mind: "Why, naturally I look like a boy, for that is what I am. With us what you call time is a spacious thing; it takes a long stretch of it to grow an angel to full age." There was a question in my mind, and he turned to me and answered it, "I am sixteen thousand years old—counting as you count." Then he turned to Nikolaus and said: "No, the Fall did not affect me nor the rest of the relationship. It was only he that I was named for who ate of the fruit of the tree and then beguiled the man and the woman with it. We others are still ignorant of sin; we are not able to commit it; we are without blemish, and shall abide in that estate always. We—" Two of the little workmen were quarreling, and in buzzing little bumblebee voices they were cursing and swearing at each other; now came blows and blood; then they locked themselves together in a life-and-death struggle. Satan reached out his hand and crushed the life out of them with his fingers, threw them away, wiped the red from his fingers on his handkerchief, and went on talking where he had left off: "We cannot do wrong; neither have we any disposition to do it, for we do not know what it is."

It seemed a strange speech, in the circumstances, but we barely noticed that, we were so shocked and grieved at the wanton murder he had committed—for murder it was, that was its true name, and it was without palliation or excuse, for the men had not wronged him in any way. It made us miserable, for we loved him, and had thought him so noble and so beautiful and gracious, and had honestly believed he was an angel; and to have him do this cruel thing—ah, it lowered him so, and we had had such pride in him. He went right on talking, just as if nothing had happened, telling about his travels, and the interesting things he had seen in the big worlds of our solar systems and of other solar systems far away in the remotenesses of space, and about the customs of the immortals that inhabit them, somehow fascinating us, enchanting us, charming us in spite of the pitiful scene that was now under our eyes, for the wives of the little dead men had found the crushed and shapeless bodies and were crying over them, and sobbing and lamenting, and a priest was kneeling there with his hands crossed upon his breast, praying; and crowds and crowds of pitying friends were massed about them, reverently uncovered, with their bare heads bowed, and many with the tears running down—a scene which Satan paid no attention to until the small noise of the weeping and praying began to annoy him, then he reached out and took the heavy board seat out of our swing and brought it down and mashed all those people into the earth just as if they had been flies, and went on talking just the same.

An angel, and kill a priest! An angel who did not know how to do wrong, and yet destroys in cold blood hundreds of helpless poor men and women who had never done him any harm! It made us sick to see that awful deed, and to think that none of those poor creatures was prepared except the priest, for none of them had ever heard a mass or seen a church. And we were witnesses; we had seen these murders done and it was our duty to tell, and let the law take its course.

But he went on talking right along, and worked his enchantments upon us again with that fatal music of his voice. He made us forget everything; we could only listen to him, and love him, and be his slaves, to do with us as he would. He made us drunk with the joy of being with him, and of looking into the heaven of his eyes, and of feeling the ecstasy that thrilled along our veins from the touch of his hand.

Chapter III

The Stranger had seen everything, he had been everywhere, he knew everything, and he forgot nothing. What another must study, he learned at a glance; there were no difficulties for him. And he made things live before you when he told about them. He saw the world made; he saw Adam created; he saw Samson surge against the pillars and bring the temple down in ruins about him; he saw Caesar's death; he told of the daily life in heaven; he had seen the damned writhing in the red waves of hell; and he made us see all these things, and it was as if we were on the spot and looking at them with our own eyes. And we felt them, too, but there was no sign that they were anything to him beyond mere entertainments. Those visions of hell, those poor babes and women and girls and lads and men shrieking and supplicating in anguish—why, we could hardly bear it, but he was as bland about it as if it had been so many imitation rats in an artificial fire.

And always when he was talking about men and women here on the earth and their doings—even their grandest and sublimest—we were secretly ashamed, for his manner showed that to him they and their doings were of paltry poor consequence; often you would think he was talking about flies, if you didn't know. Once he even said, in so many words, that our people down here were quite interesting to him, notwithstanding they were so dull and ignorant and trivial and conceited, and so diseased and rickety, and such a shabby, poor, worthless lot all around.[6] He said it in a quite matter-of-course way and without bitterness, just as a person might talk about bricks or manure or any other thing that was of no consequence and hadn't feelings. I could see he meant no offense, but in my thoughts I set it down as not very good manners.

"Manners!" he said. "Why, it is merely the truth, and truth is good manners; manners are a fiction. The castle is done. Do you like it?"

Any one would have been obliged to like it. It was lovely to look at, it was so shapely and fine, and so cunningly perfect in all its particulars, even to the little flags waving from the turrets. Satan said we must put the artillery in place now, and station the halberdiers and display the cavalry. Our men and horses were a spectacle to see, they were so little like what they were intended for; for, of course, we had no art in making such things. Satan said they were the worst he had seen; and when he touched them and made them alive, it was just ridiculous the way they acted, on account of their legs not being of uniform lengths. They reeled and sprawled around as if they were drunk, and endangered everybody's lives around them, and finally fell over and lay helpless and kicking. It made us all laugh, though it was a shameful thing to see. The guns were charged with dirt, to fire a salute, but they were so crooked and so badly made that they all burst when they went off, and killed some of the gunners and crippled the others. Satan said we would have a storm now, and an earthquake, if we liked, but we must stand off a piece, out of danger. We wanted to call the people away, too, but he said never mind them; they were of no consequence, and we could make more, some time or other, if we needed them.

A small storm-cloud began to settle down black over the castle, and the miniature lightning and thunder began to play, and the ground to quiver, and the wind to pipe and wheeze, and the rain to fall, and all the people flocked into the castle for shelter. The cloud settled down

[6] In this passage and in some later ones, Mark Twain closely followed parts of his essay "The Lowest Animal," which he had written during the summer and fall of 1896; see Paul Baender, "The Date of Mark Twain's 'The Lowest Animal,'" *American Literature*, XXXVI (May 1964), 174–179.

blacker and blacker, and one could see the castle only dimly through it; the lightning blazed out flash upon flash and pierced the castle and set it on fire, and the flames shone out red and fierce through the cloud, and the people came flying out, shrieking, but Satan brushed them back, paying no attention to our begging and crying and imploring; and in the midst of the howling of the wind and volleying of the thunder the magazine blew up, the earthquake rent the ground wide, and the castle's wreck and ruin tumbled into the chasm, which swallowed it from sight, and closed upon it, with all that innocent life, not one of the five hundred poor creatures escaping. Our hearts were broken; we could not keep from crying.

"Don't cry," Satan said; "they were of no value."

"But they are gone to hell!"

"Oh, it is no matter; we can make plenty more."

It was of no use to try to move him; evidently he was wholly without feeling, and could not understand. He was full of bubbling spirits, and as gay as if this were a wedding instead of a fiendish massacre. And he was bent on making us feel as he did, and of course his magic accomplished his desire. It was no trouble to him; he did whatever he pleased with us. In a little while we were dancing on that grave, and he was playing to us on a strange, sweet instrument which he took out of his pocket; and the music—but there is no music like that, unless perhaps in heaven, and that was where he brought it from, he said. It made one mad, for pleasure; and we could not take our eyes from him, and the looks that went out of our eyes came from our hearts, and their dumb speech was worship. He brought the dance from heaven, too, and the bliss of paradise was in it.

Presently he said he must go away on an errand. But we could not bear the thought of it, and clung to him, and pleaded with him to stay; and that pleased him, and he said so, and said he would not go yet, but would wait a little while and we would sit down and talk a few minutes longer; and he told us Satan was only his real name, and he was to be known by it to us alone, but he had chosen another one to be called by in the presence of others; just a common one, such as people have—Philip Traum.

It sounded so odd and mean for such a being! But it was his decision, and we said nothing; his decision was sufficient.

We had seen wonders this day; and my thoughts began to run on the pleasure it would be to tell them when I got home, but he noticed those thoughts, and said:

"No, all these matters are a secret among us four. I do not mind your trying to tell them, if you like, but I will protect your tongues, and nothing of the secret will escape from them."

It was a disappointment, but it couldn't be helped, and it cost us a sigh or two. We talked pleasantly along, and he was always reading our thoughts and responding to them, and it seemed to me that this was the most wonderful of all the things he did, but he interrupted my musings and said:

"No, it would be wonderful for you, but it is not wonderful for me. I am not limited like you. I am not subject to human conditions. I can measure and understand your human weaknesses, for I have studied them; but I have none of them. My flesh is not real, although it would seem firm to your touch; my clothes are not real; I am a spirit. Father Peter is coming." We looked around, but did not see any one. "He is not in sight yet, but you will see him presently."

"Do you know him, Satan?"

"No."

"Won't you talk with him when he comes? He is not ignorant and dull, like us, and he would so like to talk with you. Will you?"

"Another time, yes, but not now. I must go on my errand after a little. There he is now; you can see him. Sit still, and don't say anything."[7]

We looked up and saw Father Peter approaching through the chestnuts. We three were sitting together in the grass, and Satan sat in front of us in the path. Father Peter came slowly along with his head down, thinking, and stopped within a couple of yards of us and took off his hat and got out his silk handkerchief, and stood there mopping his face and looking as if he were going to speak to us, but he didn't. Presently he muttered, "I can't think what brought me here; it seems as if I were in my study a minute ago—but I suppose I have been dreaming along for an hour and have come all this stretch without noticing; for I am not myself in these troubled days." Then he went mumbling along to himself and walked straight through Satan, just as if nothing were there. It made us catch our breath to see it. We had the impulse to cry out, the way you nearly always do when a startling thing happens, but something mysteriously restrained us and we remained quiet, only breathing fast. Then the trees hid Father Peter after a little, and Satan said:

"It is as I told you—I am only a spirit."

"Yes, one perceives it now," said Nikolaus, "but we are not spirits. It is plain he did not see you, but were we invisible, too? He looked at us, but he didn't seem to see us."

---

[7] Beginning with what follows, Mark Twain inserted nineteen pages of a first draft of what became the "Eseldorf" version. He at first used an American setting. These pages, originally numbered 12, 16–18, 20, 20–32 (two pages numbered 20), and 34, were included in the "Eseldorf" version (DV 327) as pages 53, 56–72, and 74. In the inserted parts the name "Huck" was, before revision, used in place of "Nikolaus," and the names "Pole" and "Tom Andrews"—which identify persons whom young Samuel Clemens had known in Hannibal, Missouri—appeared in place of "Seppi" and "Wilhelm Meidling." The good clergyman was called not "Father Peter" but "Mr. Block" and was represented as a Presbyterian minister. In its earliest form, *The Mysterious Stranger* thus had a Hannibalesque locale.

"No, none of us was visible to him, for I wished it so."

It seemed almost too good to be true, that we were actually seeing these romantic and wonderful things, and that it was not a dream. And there he sat, looking just like anybody—so natural and simple and charming, and chatting along again the same as ever, and—well, words cannot make you understand what we felt. It was an ecstasy; and an ecstasy is a thing that will not go into words; it feels like music, and one cannot tell about music so that another person can get the feeling of it. He was back in the old ages once more now, and making them live before us. He had seen so much, so much! It was just a wonder to look at him and try to think how it must seem to have such experience behind one.

But it made you seem sorrowfully trivial, and the creature of a day, and such a short and paltry day, too. And he didn't say anything to raise up your drooping pride—no, not a word. He always spoke of men in the same old indifferent way—just as one speaks of bricks and manure-piles and such things; you could see that they were of no consequence to him, one way or the other. He didn't mean to hurt us, you could see that; just as we don't mean to insult a brick when we disparage it; a brick's emotions are nothing to us; it never occurs to us to think whether it has any or not.

Once when he was bunching the most illustrious kings and conquerors and poets and prophets and pirates and beggars together—just a brick-pile—I was shamed into putting in a word for man, and asked him why he made so much difference between men and himself. He had to struggle with that a moment; he didn't seem to understand how I could ask such a strange question. Then he said:

"The difference between man and me? The difference between a mortal and an immortal? between a cloud and a spirit?" He picked up a wood-louse that was creeping along a piece of bark: "What is the difference between Caesar and this?"

I said, "One cannot compare things which by their nature and by the interval between them are not comparable."

"You have answered your own question," he said. "I will expand it. Man is made of dirt—I saw him made. I am not made of dirt. Man is a museum of diseases, a home of impurities; he comes to-day and is gone to-morrow; he begins as dirt and departs as stench; I am of the aristocracy of the Imperishables. And man has the *Moral Sense*. You understand? He has the *Moral Sense*. That would seem to be difference enough between us, all by itself."

He stopped there, as if that settled the matter. I was sorry, for at that time I had but a dim idea of what the Moral Sense was. I merely knew that we were proud of having it, and when he talked like that about it, it wounded me, and I felt as a girl feels who thinks her dearest finery is being admired and then overhears strangers making fun of it. For a while we were all silent, and I, for one, was depressed. Then Satan began to chat again, and soon he was sparkling along in such a cheerful and vivacious vein that my spirits rose once more. He told some very cunning things that put us in a gale of laughter; and when he was telling about the time that Samson tied the torches to the foxes' tails and set them loose in the Philistines' corn, and Samson sitting on the fence slapping his thighs and laughing, with the tears running down his cheeks, and lost his balance and fell off the fence, the memory of that picture got him to laughing, too, and we did have a most lovely and jolly time. By and by he said:

"I am going on my errand now."

"Don't!" we all said. "Don't go; stay with us. You won't come back."

"Yes, I will; I give you my word."

"When? To-night? Say when."

"It won't be long. You will see."

"We like you."

"And I you. And as a proof of it I will show you something fine to see. Usually when I go I merely vanish; but now I will dissolve myself and let you see me do it."

He stood up, and it was quickly finished. He thinned away and thinned away until he was a soap-bubble, except that he kept his shape. You could see the bushes through him as clearly as you see things through a soap-bubble, and all over him played and flashed the delicate iridescent colors of the bubble, and along with them was that thing shaped like a window-sash which you always see on the globe of the bubble. You have seen a bubble strike the carpet and lightly bound along two or three times before it bursts. He did that. He sprang—touched the grass—bounded—floated along—touched again —and so on, and presently exploded—puff! and in his place was vacancy.

It was a strange and beautiful thing to see. We did not say anything, but sat wondering and dreaming and blinking; and finally Seppi roused up and said, mournfully sighing:

"I suppose none of it has happened."

Nikolaus sighed and said about the same.

I was miserable to hear them say it, for it was the same cold fear that was in my own mind. Then we saw poor old Father Peter wandering along back, with his head bent down, searching the ground. When he was pretty close to us he looked up and saw us, and said, "How long have you been here, boys?"

"A little while, Father."

"Then it is since I came by, and maybe you can help me. Did you come up by the path?"

"Yes, Father."

"That is good. I came the same way. I have lost my wallet. There wasn't much in it, but a very little is much to me, for it was all I had. I suppose you haven't seen anything of it?"

"No, Father, but we will help you hunt."

"It is what I was going to ask you. Why, here it is!"

We hadn't noticed it; yet there it lay, right where Satan stood when he began to melt—if he did melt and it wasn't a delusion. Father Peter picked it up and looked very much surprised.

"It is mine," he said, "but not the contents. This is fat; mine was flat; mine was light; this is heavy." He opened it; it was stuffed as full as it could hold with gold coins. He let us gaze our fill; and of course we did gaze, for we had never seen so much money at one time before. All our mouths came open to say "Satan did it!" but nothing came out. There it was, you see—we couldn't tell what Satan didn't want told; he had said so himself.

"Boys, did you do this?"

It made us laugh. And it made him laugh, too, as soon as he thought what a foolish question it was.

"Who has been here?"

Our mouths came open to answer, but stood so for a moment, because we couldn't say "Nobody," for it wouldn't be true, and the right word didn't seem to come; then I thought of the right one, and said it:

"Not a human being."

"That is so," said the others, and let their mouths go shut.

"It is not so," said Father Peter, and looked at us very severely. "I came by here a while ago, and there was no one here, but that is nothing; some one has been here since. I don't mean to say that the person didn't pass here before you came, and I don't mean to say you saw him, but someone did pass, that I know. On your honor—you saw no one?"

"Not a human being."

"That is sufficient; I know you are telling me the truth."

He began to count the money on the path, we on our knees eagerly helping to stack it in little piles.

"It's eleven hundred ducats odd!" he said. "Oh dear! if it were only mine—and I need it so!" and his voice broke and his lips quivered.

"It is yours, sir!" we all cried out at once, "every heller!"

"No—it isn't mine. Only four ducats are mine; the rest ...!" He fell to dreaming, poor old soul, and caressing some of the coins in his hands, and forgot where he was, sitting there on his heels with his old gray head bare; it was pitiful to see. "No," he said, waking up, "it isn't mine. I can't account for it. I think some enemy ... it must be a trap."

Nikolaus said: "Father Peter, with the exception of the astrologer[8] you haven't a real enemy in the village—nor Marget, either. And not

[8] Here, as throughout the story, the references to the astrologer were supplied by the editors. Mark Twain actually wrote, "with the exception of Father Adolf ..."

even a half-enemy that's rich enough to chance eleven hundred ducats
to do you a mean turn. I'll ask you if that's so or not?"

He couldn't get around that argument, and it cheered him up.
"But it isn't mine, you see—it isn't mine, in any case."

He said it in a wistful way, like a person that wouldn't be sorry,
but glad, if anybody would contradict him.

"It is yours, Father Peter, and we are witness to it. Aren't we,
boys?"

"Yes, we are—and we'll stand by it, too."

"Bless your hearts, you do almost persuade me; you do, indeed.
If I had only a hundred-odd ducats of it! The house is mortgaged
for it, and we've no home for our heads if we don't pay tomorrow.
And that four ducats is all we've got in the—"

"It's yours, every bit of it, and you've got to take it—we are bail
that it's all right. Aren't we, Theodor? Aren't we, Seppi?"

We two said yes, and Nikolaus stuffed the money back into the
shabby old wallet and made the owner take it. So he said he would
use two hundred of it, for his house was good enough security for
that, and would put the rest at interest till the rightful owner came for
it; and on our side we must sign a paper showing how he got the
money—a paper to show to the villagers as proof that he had not got
out of his troubles dishonestly.

Chapter IV

It made immense talk next day, when Father Peter paid Solomon
Isaacs in gold and left the rest of the money with him at interest. Also,
there was a pleasant change; many people called at the house to congratulate him, and a number of cool old friends became kind and
friendly again; and, to top all, Marget was invited to a party.

And there was no mystery; Father Peter told the whole circumstance just as it happened, and said he could not account for it, only
it was the plain hand of Providence, so far as he could see.

One or two shook their heads and said privately it looked more
like the hand of Satan; and really that seemed a surprisingly good
guess for ignorant people like that. Some came slyly buzzing around
and tried to coax us boys to come out and "tell the truth"; and
promised they wouldn't ever tell, but only wanted to know for their
own satisfaction, because the whole thing was so curious. They even
wanted to buy the secret, and pay money for it; and if we could have
invented something that would answer—but we couldn't; we hadn't
the ingenuity, so we had to let the chance go by, and it was a pity.

We carried that secret around without any trouble, but the other
one, the big one, the splendid one, burned the very vitals of us, it was
so hot to get out and we so hot to let it out and astonish people with it.
But we had to keep it in; in fact, it kept itself in. Satan said it would,

and it did. We went off every day and got to ourselves in the woods so that we could talk about Satan, and really that was the only subject we thought of or cared anything about; and day and night we watched for him and hoped he would come, and we got more and more impatient all the time. We hadn't any interest in the other boys any more, and wouldn't take part in their games and enterprises. They seemed so tame, after Satan; and their doings so trifling and commonplace after his adventures in antiquity and the constellations, and his miracles and meltings and explosions, and all that.

During the first day we were in a state of anxiety on account of one thing, and we kept going to Father Peter's house on one pretext or another to keep track of it. That was the gold coin; we were afraid it would crumble and turn to dust, like fairy money. If it did— But it didn't. At the end of the day no complaint had been made about it, so after that we were satisfied that it was real gold, and dropped the anxiety out of our minds.

There was a question which we wanted to ask Father Peter, and finally we went there the second evening, a little diffidently, after drawing straws, and I asked it as casually as I could, though it did not sound as casual as I wanted, because I didn't know how:

"What is the Moral Sense, sir?"

He looked down, surprised, over his great spectacles, and said, "Why, it is the faculty which enables us to distinguish good from evil."

It threw some light, but not a glare, and I was a little disappointed, also to some degree embarrassed. He was waiting for me to go on, so, in default of anything else to say, I asked, "Is it valuable?"

"Valuable? Heavens, lad, it is the one thing that lifts man above the beasts that perish and makes him heir to immortality!"

This did not remind me of anything further to say, so I got out, with the other boys, and we went away with that indefinite sense you have often had of being filled but not fatted. They wanted me to explain, but I was tired.

We passed out through the parlor, and there was Marget at the spinnet teaching Marie Lueger. So one of the deserting pupils was back; and an influential one, too; the others would follow. Marget jumped up and ran and thanked us again, with tears in her eyes—this was the third time—for saving her and her uncle from being turned into the street, and we told her again we hadn't done it; but that was her way, she never could be grateful enough for anything a person did for her; so we let her have her say. And as we passed through the garden, there was Wilhelm Meidling sitting there waiting, for it was getting toward the edge of the evening, and he would be asking Marget to take a walk along the river with him when she was done with the lesson. He was a young lawyer, and succeeding fairly well and working his way along, little by little. He was very fond of Marget, and she of him. He had not deserted along with the others, but had stood his ground all through. His faithfulness was not lost on Marget and her uncle. He hadn't so very much talent, but he was handsome and good, and these are a kind of talents themselves and help along. He asked us how the lesson was getting along, and we told him it was about done. And maybe it was so; we didn't know anything about it, but we judged it would please him, and it did, and didn't cost us anything.

Chapter V

On the fourth day comes the astrologer from his crumbling old tower up the valley, where he had heard the news, I reckon. He had a private talk with us, and we told him what we could, for we were mightily in dread of him. He sat there studying and studying awhile to himself; then he asked:

"How many ducats did you say?"

"Eleven hundred and seven, sir."

Then he said, as if he were talking to himself: "It is ver-y singular. Yes . . . very strange. A curious coincidence." Then he began to ask questions, and went over the whole ground from the beginning, we answering. By and by he said: "Eleven hundred and six ducats. It is a large sum."

"Seven," said Seppi, correcting him.

"Oh, seven, was it? Of course a ducat more or less isn't of consequence, but you said eleven hundred and six before."

It would not have been safe for us to say he was mistaken, but we knew he was. Nikolaus said, "We ask pardon for the mistake, but we meant to say seven."

"Oh, it is no matter, lad; it was merely that I noticed the discrepancy. It is several days, and you cannot be expected to remember precisely. One is apt to be inexact when there is no particular circumstance to impress the count upon the memory."

"But there was one, sir," said Seppi, eagerly.

"What was it, my son?" asked the astrologer, indifferently.

"First, we all counted the piles of coin, each in turn, and all made it the same—eleven hundred and six. But I had slipped one out, for fun, when the count began, and now I slipped it back and said, 'I think there is a mistake—there are eleven hundred and seven; let us count again.' We did, and of course I was right. They were astonished; then I told how it came about."

The astrologer asked us if this was so, and we said it was.

"That settles it," he said. "I know the thief now. Lads, the money was stolen."

Then he went away, leaving us very much troubled, and wondering what he could mean. In about an hour we found out; for by that time it was all over the village that Father Peter had been arrested for stealing a great sum of money from the astrologer. Everybody's tongue was loose and going. Many said it was not in Father Peter's character and must be a mistake; but the others shook their heads and said misery and want could drive a suffering man to almost anything. About one detail there were no differences; all agreed that Father Peter's account of how the money came into his hands was just about unbelievable—it had such an impossible look. They said it might have come into the astrologer's hands in some such way, but into Father Peter's, never! Our characters began to suffer now. We were Father Peter's only witnesses; how much did he probably pay us to back up his fantastic tale? People talked that kind of talk to us pretty freely and frankly, and were full of scoffings when we begged them to believe really we had told only the truth. Our parents were harder on us than anyone else. Our fathers said we were disgracing our families, and they commanded us to purge ourselves of our lie, and there was no limit to their anger when we continued to say we had spoken true. Our mothers cried over us and begged us to give back our bribe and get back our honest names and save our families from shame, and come out and honorably confess. And at last we were so worried and harassed that we tried to tell the whole thing, Satan and all—but no, it wouldn't come out. We were hoping and longing all the time that Satan would come and help us out of our trouble, but there was no sign of him.

Within an hour after the astrologer's talk with us, Father Peter was in prison and the money sealed up and in the hands of the officers of the law. The money was in a bag, and Solomon Isaacs said he had not touched it since he had counted it; his oath was taken that it was the same money, and that the amount was eleven hundred and seven ducats. Father Peter claimed trial by the ecclesiastical court, but our other priest, Father Adolf, said an ecclesiastical court hadn't jurisdiction over a suspended priest. The bishop upheld him. That settled it; the case would go to trial in the civil court. The court would not sit for some time to come. Wilhelm Meidling would be Father Peter's lawyer and do the best he could, of course, but he told us privately that a weak case on his side and all the power and prejudice on the other made the outlook bad.

So Marget's new happiness died a quick death. No friends came to condole with her, and none were expected; an unsigned note withdrew her invitation to the party. There would be no scholars to take lessons. How could she support herself? She could remain in the house, for the mortgage was paid off, though the government and not poor Solomon Isaacs had the mortgage money in its grip for the present. Old Ursula, who was cook, chambermaid, housekeeper, laundress, and everything else for Father Peter, and had been Marget's nurse in earlier years, said God would provide. But she said that from habit, for she was a good Christian. She meant to help in the providing, to make sure, if she could find a way.

We boys wanted to go and see Marget and show friendliness for her, but our parents were afraid of offending the community and wouldn't let us. The astrologer was going around inflaming everybody against Father Peter, and saying he was an abandoned thief and had stolen eleven hundred and seven gold ducats from him. He said he knew he was a thief from that fact, for it was exactly the sum he had lost and which Father Peter pretended he had "found."

In the afternoon of the fourth day after the catastrophe old Ursula appeared at our house and asked for some washing to do, and begged my mother to keep this secret, to save Marget's pride, who would stop this project if she found it out, yet Marget had not enough to eat and was growing weak. Ursula was growing weak herself, and showed it; and she ate of the food that was offered her like a starving person, but could not be persuaded to carry any home, for Marget would not eat charity food. She took some clothes down to the stream to wash them, but we saw from the window that handling the bat was too much for her strength; so she was called back and a trifle of money offered her, which she was afraid to take lest Marget should suspect; then she took it, saying she would explain that she found it in the road. To keep it from being a lie and damning her soul, she got me to drop it while she watched; then she went along by there and found it, and exclaimed with surprise and joy, and picked it up and went her way. Like the rest of the village, she could tell every-day lies fast enough and without taking any precautions against fire and brimstone on their account; but this was a new kind of lie, and it had a dangerous look because she hadn't had any practice in it. After a week's practice it wouldn't have given her any trouble. It is the way we are made.

I was in trouble, for how would Marget live? Ursula could not find a coin in the road every day—perhaps[9] not even a second one. And I was ashamed, too, for not having been near Marget, and she so in need of friends; but that was my parents' fault, not mine, and I couldn't help it.

I was walking along the path, feeling very downhearted, when a most cheery and tingling freshening-up sensation went rippling through me, and I was too glad for any words, for I knew by that sign that Satan was by. I had noticed it before. Next moment he was alongside of me and I was telling him all my trouble and what had been happening to Marget and her uncle. While we were talking we

[9] Here Mark Twain resumed work upon the "Eseldorf" version, in the spring of 1899, after having laid it aside for more than a year. Almost certainly he had written the preceding part, pages 1–85 of the holograph, between November 1897 and January 1898. During that period he had also written nearly all of the trial scene, on pages at first numbered 84–93. These latter pages were also put aside and were not inserted in the manuscript until he had reached, some two and one-half years later, Chapter 10; they were then repaginated 377–386.

turned a curve and saw old Ursula resting in the shade of a tree, and she had a lean stray kitten in her lap and was petting it. I asked her where she got it, and she said it came out of the woods and followed her; and she said it probably hadn't any mother or any friends and she was going to take it home and take care of it. Satan said:

"I understand you are very poor. Why do you want to add another mouth to feed? Why don't you give it to some rich person?"

Ursula bridled at this and said: "Perhaps you would like to have it. You must be rich, with your fine clothes and quality airs." Then she sniffed and said: "Give it to the rich—the idea! The rich don't care for anybody but themselves; it's only the poor that have feeling for the poor, and help them. The poor and God. God will provide for this kitten."

"What makes you think so?"

Ursula's eyes snapped with anger. "Because I know it!" she said. "Not a sparrow falls to the ground without His seeing it."

"But it falls, just the same. What good is seeing it fall?"

Old Ursula's jaws worked, but she could not get any word out for the moment, she was so horrified. When she got her tongue she stormed out, "Go about your business, you puppy, or I will take a stick to you!"

I could not speak, I was so scared. I knew that with his notions about the human race Satan would consider it a matter of no consequence to strike her dead, there being "plenty more"; but my tongue stood still, I could give her no warning. But nothing happened; Satan remained tranquil—tranquil and indifferent. I suppose he could not be insulted by Ursula any more than the king could be insulted by a tumblebug. The old woman jumped to her feet when she made her remark, and did it as briskly as a young girl. It had been many years since she had done the like of that. That was Satan's influence; he was a fresh breeze to the weak and the sick, wherever he came. His presence affected even the lean kitten, and it skipped to the ground and began to chase a leaf. This surprised Ursula, and she stood looking at the creature and nodding her head wonderingly, her anger quite forgotten.

"What's come over it?" she said. "Awhile ago it could hardly walk."

"You have not seen a kitten of that breed before," said Satan.

Ursula was not proposing to be friendly with the mocking stranger, and she gave him an ungentle look and retorted: "Who asked you to come here and pester me, I'd like to know? And what do you know about what I've seen and what I haven't seen?"

"You haven't seen a kitten with the hair-spines on its tongue pointing to the front, have you?"

"No—nor you, either."

"Well, examine this one and see."

Ursula was become pretty spry, but the kitten was spryer, and she could not catch it, and had to give it up. Then Satan said:

"Give it a name, and maybe it will come."

Ursula tried several names, but the kitten was not interested.

"Call it Agnes. Try that."

The creature answered to the name and came. Ursula examined its tongue. "Upon my word, it's true!" she said. "I have not seen this kind of a cat before. Is it yours?"

"No."

"Then how did you know its name so pat?"

"Because all cats of that breed are named Agnes; they will not answer to any other."

Ursula was impressed. "It is the most wonderful thing!" Then a shadow of trouble came into her face, for her superstitions were aroused, and she reluctantly put the creature down, saying: "I suppose I must let it go; I am not afraid—no, not exactly that, though the priest—well, I've heard people—indeed, many people . . . And, besides, it is quite well now and can take care of itself." She sighed, and turned to go, murmuring: "It is such a pretty one, too, and would be such company—and the house is so sad and lonesome these troubled days. . . . Miss Marget so mournful and just a shadow, and the old master shut up in jail."

"It seems a pity not to keep it," said Satan.

Ursula turned quickly—just as if she were hoping someone would encourage her.

"Why?" she asked, wistfully.

"Because this breed brings luck."

"Does it? Is it true? Young man, do you know it to be true? How does it bring luck?"

"Well, it brings money, anyway."

Ursula looked disappointed. "Money? A cat bring money? The idea! You could never sell it here; people do not buy cats here; one can't even give them away." She turned to go.

"I don't mean sell it. I mean have an income from it. This kind is called the Lucky Cat. Its owner finds four silver groschen in his pocket every morning."

I saw the indignation rising in the old woman's face. She was insulted. This boy was making fun of her. That was her thought. She thrust her hands into her pockets and straightened up to give him a piece of her mind. Her temper was all up, and hot. Her mouth came open and let out three words of a bitter sentence, . . . then it fell silent, and the anger in her face turned to surprise or wonder or fear, or something, and she slowly brought out her hands from her pocket and opened them and held them so. In one was my piece of money, in the other lay four silver groschen. She gazed a little while, perhaps to see if the groschen would vanish away; then she said, fervently:

"It's true—it's true—and I'm ashamed and beg forgiveness, O dear master and benefactor!" And she ran to Satan and kissed his hand, over and over again, according to the Austrian custom.

In her heart she probably believed it was a witch-cat and an agent of the Devil; but no matter, it was all the more certain to be able to keep its contract and furnish a daily good living for the family, for in matters of finance even the piousest of our peasants would have more confidence in an arrangement with the Devil than with an archangel. Ursula started homeward, with Agnes in her arms, and I said I wished I had her privilege of seeing Marget.

Then I caught my breath, for we were there. There in the parlor, and Marget standing looking at us, astonished. She was feeble and pale, but I knew that those conditions would not last in Satan's atmosphere, and it turned out so. I introduced Satan—that is, Philip Traum—and we sat down and talked. There was no constraint. We were simple folk, in our village, and when a stranger was a pleasant person we were soon friends. Marget wondered how we got in without her hearing us. Traum said the door was open, and we walked in and waited until she should turn around and greet us. This was not true; no door was open; we entered through the walls or the roof or down the chimney, or somehow; but no matter, what Satan wished a person to believe, the person was sure to believe, and so Marget was quite satisfied with that explanation. And then the main part of her mind was on Traum, anyway; she couldn't keep her eyes off him, he was so beautiful. That gratified me, and made me proud. I hoped he would show off some, but he didn't. He seemed only interested in being friendly and telling lies. He said he was an orphan. That made Marget pity him. The water came into her eyes. He said he had never known his mamma; she passed away while he was a young thing; and said his papa was in shattered health, and had no property to speak of—in fact, none of any earthly value—but he had an uncle in business down in the tropics, and he was very well off and had a monopoly, and it was from this uncle that he drew his support. The very mention of a kind uncle was enough to remind Marget of her own, and her eyes filled again. She said she hoped their two uncles would meet, some day. It made me shudder. Philip said he hoped so, too; and that made me shudder again.

"Maybe they will," said Marget. "Does your uncle travel much?"

"Oh yes, he goes all about; he has business everywhere."[10]

And so they went on chatting, and poor Marget forgot her sor-

[10] The holograph has here a passage of about one hundred words in which Satan speaks of his uncle's trading in "soles" and also reveals that French is the official language of his uncle's domain. This passage also appears, uncanceled, in the typescript, which was used as the printer's copy for the first ten chapters of *The Mysterious Stranger*. Probably the material was deleted by Paine or Duneka while the story was in proof.

row for one little while, anyway. It was probably the only really bright and cheery hour she had known lately. I saw she liked Philip, and I knew she would. And when he told her he was studying for the ministry I could see that she liked him better than ever. And then, when he promised to get her admitted to the jail so that she could see her uncle, that was the capstone. He said he would give the guards a little present, and she must always go in the evening after dark, and say nothing, "but just show this paper and pass in, and show it again when you come out"—and he scribbled some queer marks on the paper and gave it to her, and she was ever so thankful, and right away was in a fever for the sun to go down; for in that old, cruel time prisoners were not allowed to see their friends, and sometimes they spent years in the jails without ever seeing a friendly face. I judged that the marks on the paper were an enchantment, and that the guards would not know what they were doing, nor have any memory of it afterward; and that was indeed the way of it. Ursula put her head in at the door now and said:

"Supper's ready, miss." Then she saw us and looked frightened, and motioned me to come to her, which I did, and she asked if we had told about the cat. I said no, and she was relieved, and said please don't; for if Miss Marget knew, she would think it was an unholy cat and would send for a priest and have its gifts all purified out of it, and then there wouldn't be any more dividends. So I said we wouldn't tell, and she was satisfied. Then I was beginning to say good-by to Marget, but Satan interrupted and said, ever so politely—well, I don't remember just the words, but anyway he as good as invited himself to supper, and me, too. Of course Marget was miserably embarrassed, for she had no reason to suppose there would be half enough for a sick bird. Ursula heard him, and she came straight into the room, not a bit pleased. At first she was astonished to see Marget looking so fresh and rosy, and said so; then she spoke up in her native tongue, which was Bohemian, and said—as I learned afterward—"Send him away, Miss Marget; there's not victuals enough."

Before Marget could speak, Satan had the word, and was talking back at Ursula in her own language—which was a surprise to her, and for her mistress, too. He said, "Didn't I see you down the road a while ago?"

"Yes, sir."

"Ah, that pleases me; I see you remember me." He stepped to her and whispered: "I told you it is a Lucky Cat. Don't be troubled; it will provide."

That sponged the slate of Ursula's feelings clean of its anxieties, and a deep, financial joy shone in her eyes. The cat's value was augmenting. It was getting full time for Marget to take some sort of notice of Satan's invitation, and she did it in the best way, the honest way that was natural to her. She said she had little to offer, but that we were welcome if we would share it with her.

We had supper in the kitchen, and Ursula waited at table. A small fish was in the frying pan, crisp and brown and tempting, and one could see that Marget was not expecting such respectable food as this. Ursula brought it, and Marget divided it between Satan and me, declining to take any of it herself; and was beginning to say she did not care for fish to-day, but she did not finish the remark. It was because she noticed that another fish had appeared in the pan. She looked surprised, but did not say anything. She probably meant to inquire of Ursula about this later. There were other surprises: flesh and game and wines and fruits—things which had been strangers in that house lately; but Marget made no exclamations, and now even looked unsurprised, which was Satan's influence, of course. Satan talked right along, and was entertaining, and made the time pass pleasantly and cheerfully; and although he told a good many lies, it was no harm in him, for he was only an angel and did not know any better. They do not know right from wrong; I knew this, because I remembered what he had said about it. He got on the good side of Ursula. He praised her to Marget, confidentially, but speaking just loud enough for Ursula to hear. He said she was a fine woman, and he hoped some day to bring her and his uncle together. Very soon Ursula was mincing and simpering around in a ridiculous girly way, and smoothing out her gown and prinking at herself like a foolish old hen, and all the time pretending she was not hearing what Satan was saying. I was ashamed, for it showed us to be what Satan considered us, a silly race and trivial. Satan said his uncle entertained a great deal, and to have a clever woman presiding over the festivities would double the attractions of the place.

"But your uncle is a gentleman, isn't he?" asked Marget.

"Yes," said Satan, indifferently; "some even call him a Prince, out of compliment, but he is not bigoted; to him personal merit is everything, rank nothing."

My hand was hanging down by my chair; Agnes came along and licked it; by this act a secret was revealed. I started to say, "It is all a mistake; this is just a common, ordinary cat; the hair-needles on her tongue point inward, not outward." But the words did not come, because they couldn't. Satan smiled upon me, and I understood.

When it was dark Marget took food and wine and fruit, in a basket, and hurried away to the jail, and Satan and I walked toward my home. I was thinking to myself that I should like to see what the inside of the jail was like; Satan overheard the thought, and the next moment we were in the jail. We were in the torture-chamber, Satan said. The rack was there, and the other instruments, and there was a smoky lantern or two hanging on the walls and helping to make the place look dim and dreadful. There were people there—and executioners—but as they took no notice of us, it meant that we were invisible. A young man lay bound, and Satan said he was suspected of being a heretic, and the executioners were about to inquire into it. They asked the man to confess to the charge, and he said he could not, for it was not true. Then they drove splinter after splinter under his nails, and he shrieked with the pain. Satan was not disturbed, but I could not endure it, and had to be whisked out of there. I was faint and sick, but the fresh air revived me, and we walked toward my home. I said it was a brutal thing.

"No, it was a human thing. You should not insult the brutes by such a misuse of that word; they have not deserved it," and he went on talking like that. "It is like your paltry race—always lying, always claiming virtues which it hasn't got, always denying them to the higher animals, which alone possess them. No brute ever does a cruel thing—that is the monopoly of those with the Moral Sense. When a brute inflicts pain he does it innocently; it is not wrong; for him there is no such thing as wrong. And he does not inflict pain for the pleasure of inflicting it—only man does that. Inspired by that mongrel Moral Sense of his! A sense whose function is to distinguish between right and wrong, with liberty to choose which of them he will do. Now what advantage can he get out of that? He is always choosing, and in nine cases out of ten he prefers the wrong. There shouldn't be any wrong; and without the Moral Sense there couldn't be any. And yet he is such an unreasoning creature that he is not able to perceive that the Moral Sense degrades him to the bottom layer of animated beings and is a shameful possession. Are you feeling better? Let me show you something."

Chapter VI

In a moment we were in a French Village. We walked through a great factory of some sort, where men and women and little children were toiling in heat and dirt and a fog of dust; and they were clothed in rags, and drooped at their work, for they were worn and half starved, and weak and drowsy. Satan said:

"It is some more Moral Sense. The proprietors are rich, and very holy; but the wage they pay to these poor brothers and sisters of theirs is only enough to keep them from dropping dead with hunger. The work-hours are fourteen per day, winter and summer—from six in the morning till eight at night—little children and all. And they walk to and from the pigsties which they inhabit—four miles each way, through mud and slush, rain, snow, sleet, and storm, daily, year in and year out. They get four hours of sleep. They kennel together, three families in a room, in unimaginable filth and stench; and disease comes, and they die off like flies. Have they committed a crime, these mangy things? No. What have they done, that they are punished so? Nothing at all, except getting themselves born into your foolish race. You have seen how they treat a misdoer there in the jail; now you see how they treat the innocent and the worthy. Is your race logical? Are these ill-smelling innocents better off than that heretic? Indeed, no; his punishment is trivial compared with theirs. They broke him on the wheel and smashed him to rags and pulp after we left, and he is dead now, and free of your precious race; but these poor slaves here—why, they have been dying for years, and some of them will not escape from life for years to come. It is the Moral Sense which teaches the factory proprietors the difference between right and wrong—you perceive the result. They think themselves better than dogs. Ah, you are such an illogical, unreasoning race! And paltry—oh, unspeakably!"

Then he dropped all seriousness and just overstrained himself making fun of us, and deriding our pride in our warlike deeds, our great heroes, our imperishable fames, our mighty kings, our ancient aristocracies, our venerable history—and laughed and laughed till it was enough to make a person sick to hear him; and finally he sobered a little and said, "But, after all, it is not all ridiculous; there is a sort of pathos about it when one remembers how few are your days, how childish your pomps, and what shadows you are!"

Presently all things vanished suddenly from my sight, and I knew what it meant. The next moment we were walking along in our village; and down toward the river I saw the twinkling lights of the Golden Stag. Then in the dark I heard a joyful cry:

"He's come again!"

It was Seppi Wohlmeyer. He had felt his blood leap and his spirits rise in a way that could mean only one thing, and he knew Satan was near, although it was too dark to see him. He came to us, and we walked along together, and Seppi poured out his gladness like water. It was as if he were a lover and had found his sweetheart who had been lost. Seppi was a smart and animated boy, and had enthusiasm and expression, and was a contrast to Nikolaus and me. He was full of the last new mystery, now—the disappearance of Hans Oppert, the village loafer. People were beginning to be curious about it, he said. He did not say anxious—curious was the right word, and strong enough. No one had seen Hans for a couple of days.

"Not since he did that brutal thing, you know," he said.

"What brutal thing?" It was Satan that asked.

"Well, he is always clubbing his dog, which is a good dog, and his only friend, and is faithful, and loves him, and does no one any harm; and two days ago he was at it again, just for nothing—just for pleasure—and the dog was howling and begging, and Theodor and I begged, too, but he threatened us, and struck the dog again with all his might and knocked one of his eyes out, and he said to us, 'There,

I hope you are satisfied now; that's what you have got for him by your damned meddling'—and he laughed, the heartless brute." Seppi's voice trembled with pity and anger. I guessed what Satan would say, and he said it.

"There is that misused word again—that shabby slander. Brutes do not act like that, but only men."

"Well, it was inhuman, anyway."

"No, it wasn't, Seppi; it was human—quite distinctly human. It is not pleasant to hear you libel the higher animals by attributing to them dispositions which they are free from, and which are found nowhere but in the human heart. None of the higher animals is tainted with the disease called the Moral Sense. Purify your language, Seppi; drop those lying phrases out of it."

He spoke pretty sternly—for him—and I was sorry I hadn't warned Seppi to be more particular about the word he used. I knew how he was feeling. He would not want to offend Satan; he would rather offend all his kin. There was an uncomfortable silence, but relief soon came, for that poor dog came along now, with his eye hanging down, and went straight to Satan, and began to moan and mutter brokenly, and Satan began to answer in the same way, and it was plain that they were talking together in the dog language. We all sat down in the grass, in the moonlight, for the clouds were breaking away now, and Satan took the dog's head in his lap and put the eye back in its place, and the dog was comfortable, and he wagged his tail and licked Satan's hand, and looked thankful and said the same; I knew he was saying it, though I did not understand the words. Then the two talked together a bit, and Satan said:

"He says his master was drunk."

"Yes, he was," said we.

"And an hour later he fell over the precipice there beyond the Cliff Pasture."

"We know the place; it is three miles from here."

"And the dog has been often to the village, begging people to go there, but he was only driven away and not listened to."

We remembered it, but hadn't understood what he wanted.

"He only wanted help for the man who had misused him, and he thought only of that, and has had no food nor sought any. He has watched by his master two nights. What do you think of your race? Is heaven reserved for it, and this dog ruled out, as your teachers tell you? Can your race add anything to this dog's stock of morals and magnanimities?" He spoke to the creature, who jumped up, eager and happy, and apparently ready for orders and impatient to execute them. "Get some men; go with the dog—he will show you that carrion; and take a priest along to arrange about insurance, for death is near."

With the last word he vanished, to our sorrow and disappointment. We got the men and Father Adolf, and we saw the man die.

Nobody cared but the dog; he mourned and grieved, and licked the dead face, and could not be comforted. We buried him where he was, and without a coffin, for he had no money, and no friend but the dog. If we had been an hour earlier the priest would have been in time to send that poor creature to heaven, but now he was gone down into the awful fires, to burn forever. It seemed·such a pity that in a world where so many people have difficulty to pūt in their time, one little hour could not have been spared for this poor creature who needed it so much, and to whom it would have made the difference between eternal joy and eternal pain. It gave an appalling idea of the value of an hour, and I thought I could never waste one again without remorse and terror. Seppi was depressed and grieved, and said it must be so much better to be a dog and not run such awful risks. We took this one home with us and kept him for our own. Seppi had a very good thought as we were walking along, and it cheered us up and made us feel much better. He said the dog had forgiven the man that had wronged him so, and maybe God would accept that absolution.

There was a very dull week, now, for Satan did not come, nothing much was going on, and we boys could not venture to go and see Marget, because the nights were moonlit and our parents might find us out if we tried. But we came across Ursula a couple of times taking a walk in the meadows beyond the river to air the cat, and we learned from her that things were going well. She had natty new clothes on and bore a prosperous look. The four groschen a day were arriving without a break, but were not being spent for food and wine and such things—the cat attended to all that.

Marget was enduring her forsakenness and isolation fairly well, all things considered, and was cheerful, by help of Wilhelm Meidling. She spent an hour or two every night in the jail with her uncle, and had fattened him up with the cat's contributions. But she was curious to know more about Philip Traum, and hoped I would bring him again. Ursula was curious about him herself, and asked a good many questions about his uncle. It made the boys laugh, for I had told them the nonsense Satan had been stuffing her with. She got no satisfaction out of us, our tongues being tied.

Ursula gave us a small item of information: money being plenty now, she had taken on a servant to help about the house and run errands. She tried to tell it in a commonplace, matter-of-course way, but she was so set up by it and so vain of it that her pride in it leaked out pretty plainly. It was beautiful to see her veiled delight in this grandeur, poor old thing, but when we heard the name of the servant we wondered if she had been altogether wise; for although we were young, and often thoughtless, we had fairly good perception on some matters. This boy was Gottfried Narr, a dull, good creature, with no harm in him and nothing against him personally; still, he was under a cloud, and properly so, for it had not been six months since a social blight had mildewed the family—his grandmother had been burned as a witch. When that kind of a malady is in the blood it does not always come out with just one burning. Just now was not a good time for Ursula and Marget to be having dealings with a member of such a family, for the witch-terror had risen higher during the past year than it had ever reached in the memory of the oldest villagers. The mere mention of a witch was almost enough to frighten us out of our wits. This was natural enough, because of late years there were more kinds of witches than there used to be; in old times it had been only old women, but of late years they were of all ages—even children of eight and nine; it was getting so that anybody might turn out to be a familiar of the Devil—age and sex hadn't anything to do with it. In our little region we had tried to extirpate the witches, but the more of them we burned the more of the breed rose up in their places.

Once, in a school for girls only ten miles away, the teachers found that the back of one of the girls was all red and inflamed, and they were greatly frightened, believing it to be the Devil's marks. The girl was scared, and begged them not to denounce her, and said it was only fleas; but of course it would not do to let the matter rest there. All the girls were examined, and eleven out of the fifty were badly marked, the rest less so. A commission was appointed, but the eleven only cried for their mothers and would not confess. Then they were shut up, each by herself, in the dark, and put on black bread and water for ten days and nights; and by that time they were haggard and wild, and their eyes were dry and they did not cry any more, but only sat and mumbled, and would not take the food. Then one of them confessed, and said they had often ridden through the air on broomsticks to the witches' Sabbath, and in a bleak place high up in the mountains had danced and drunk and caroused with several hundred other witches and the Evil One, and all had conducted themselves in a scandalous way and had reviled the priests and blasphemed God. That is what she said—not in narrative form, for she was not able to remember any of the details without having them called to her mind one after the other; but the commission did that, for they knew just what questions to ask, they being all written down for the use of witch-commissioners two centuries before. They asked, "Did you do so and so?" and she always said yes, and looked weary and tired, and took no interest in it. And so when the other ten heard that this one confessed, they confessed, too, and answered yes to the questions. Then they were burned at the stake all together, which was just and right; and everybody went from all the countryside to see it. I went, too; but when I saw that one of them was a bonny, sweet girl I used to play with, and looked so pitiful there chained to the stake, and her mother crying over her and devouring her with kisses and clinging around her neck, and saying, "Oh, my God! oh, my God!" it was too dreadful, and I went away.

It was bitter cold weather when Gottfried's grandmother was burned. It was charged that she had cured bad headaches by kneading the person's head and neck with her fingers—as she said—but really by the Devil's help, as everybody knew. They were going to examine her, but she stopped them, and confessed straight off that her power was from the Devil. So they appointed to burn her next morning, early, in our market square. The officer who was to prepare the fire was there first, and prepared it. She was there next—brought by the constables, who left her and went to fetch another witch. Her family did not come with her. They might be reviled, maybe stoned, if the people were excited. I came, and gave her an apple. She was squatting at the fire, warming herself and waiting; and her old lips and hands were blue with the cold. A stranger came next. He was a traveler, passing through; and he spoke to her gently, and, seeing nobody but me there to hear, said he was sorry for her. And he asked if what she confessed was true, and she said no. He looked surprised and still more sorry then, and asked her:

"Then why did you confess?"

"I am old and very poor," she said, "and I work for my living. There was no way but to confess. If I hadn't they might have set me free. That would ruin me, for no one would forget that I had been suspected of being a witch, and so I would get no more work, and wherever I went they would set the dogs on me. In a little while I would starve. The fire is best; it is soon over. You have been good to me, you two, and I thank you."

She snuggled closer to the fire, and put out her hands to warm them, the snow-flakes descending soft and still on her old gray head and making it white and whiter. The crowd was gathering now, and an egg came flying and struck her in the eye, and broke and ran down her face. There was a laugh at that.

I told Satan all about the eleven girls and the old woman, once, but it did not affect him. He only said it was the human race, and what the human race did was of no consequence. And he said he had seen it made; and it was not made of clay; it was made of mud—part of it was, anyway. I knew what he meant by that—the Moral Sense. He saw the thought in my head, and it tickled him and made him laugh. Then he called a bullock out of a pasture and petted it and talked with it, and said:

"There—he wouldn't drive children mad with hunger and fright and loneliness, and then burn them for confessing to things invented for them which had never happened. And neither would he break the hearts of innocent, poor old women and make them afraid to trust themselves among their own race; and he would not insult them in their death-agony. For he is not besmirched with the Moral Sense, but is as the angels are, and knows no wrong, and never does it."

Lovely as he was, Satan could be cruelly offensive when he chose;

and he always chose when the human race was brought to his attention. He always turned up his nose at it, and never had a kind word for it.[11]

Well, as I was saying, we boys doubted if it was a good time for Ursula to be hiring a member of the Narr family. We were right. When the people found it out they were naturally indignant. And, moreover, since Marget and Ursula hadn't enough to eat themselves, where was the money coming from to feed another mouth? That is what they wanted to know; and in order to find out they stopped avoiding Gottfried and began to seek his society and have sociable conversations with him. He was pleased—not thinking any harm and not seeing the trap—and so he talked innocently along, and was no discreeter than a cow.

"Money!" he said; "they've got plenty of it. They pay me two groschen a week, besides my keep. And they live on the fat of the land, I can tell you; the prince himself can't beat their table."

This astonishing statement was conveyed by the astrologer to Father Adolf on a Sunday morning when he was returning from mass. He was deeply moved, and said:

"This must be looked into."

He said there must be witchcraft at the bottom of it, and told the villagers to resume relations with Marget and Ursula in a private and unostentatious way, and keep both eyes open. They were told to keep their own counsel, and not rouse the suspicions of the household. The villagers were at first a bit reluctant to enter such a dreadful place, but the priest said they would be under his protection while there, and no harm could come to them, particularly if they carried a trifle of holy water along and kept their beads and crosses handy. This satisfied them and made them willing to go; envy and malice made the baser sort even eager to go.

And so poor Marget began to have company again, and was as pleased as a cat. She was like 'most anybody else—just human, and happy in her prosperities and not averse from showing them off a little; and she was humanly grateful to have the warm shoulder turned to her and be smiled upon by her friends and the village again; for of all the hard things to bear, to be cut by your neighbors and left in contemptuous solitude is maybe the hardest.

The bars were down, and we could all go there now, and we did—our parents and all—day after day. The cat began to strain herself. She provided the top of everything for those companies, and in abundance—among them many a dish and many a wine which they

[11] In the lower margin of the typescript at this point (p. 66), Mark Twain planned some revisions that he never made: the boys were to accompany Satan on a visit to an asteroid and also to some immense world in another planetary system. Presumably Satan would have found occasion for further comparisons unflattering to mankind.

had not tasted before and which they had not even heard of except at second-hand from the prince's servants. And the tableware was much above ordinary, too.

Marget was troubled at times, and pursued Ursula with questions to an uncomfortable degree; but Ursula stood her ground and stuck to it that it was Providence, and said no word about the cat. Marget knew that nothing was impossible to Providence, but she could not help having doubts that this effort was from there, though she was afraid to say so, lest disaster come of it. Witchcraft occurred to her, but she put the thought aside, for this was before Gottfried joined the household, and she knew Ursula was pious and a bitter hater of witches. By the time Gottfried arrived Providence was established, un-shakably intrenched, and getting all the gratitude. The cat made no murmur, but went on composedly improving in style and prodigality by experience.

In any community, big or little, there is always a fair proportion of people who are not malicious or unkind by nature, and who never do unkind things except when they are overmastered by fear, or when their self-interest is greatly in danger, or some such matter as that. Eseldorf had its proportion of such people, and ordinarily their good and gentle influence was felt, but these were not ordinary times—on account of the witch-dread—and so we did not seem to have any gentle and compassionate hearts left, to speak of. Every person was frightened at the unaccountable state of things at Marget's house, not doubting that witchcraft was at the bottom of it, and fright frenzied their reason. Naturally there were some who pitied Marget and Ursula for the danger that was gathering about them, but naturally they did not say so; it would not have been safe. So the others had it all their own way, and there was none to advise the ignorant girl and the foolish woman and warn them to modify their doings. We boys wanted to warn them, but we backed down when it came to the pinch, being afraid. We found that we were not manly enough nor brave enough to do a generous action when there was a chance that it could get us into trouble. Neither of us confessed this poor spirit to the others, but did as other people would have done—dropped the subject and talked about something else. And I knew we all felt mean, eating and drink-ing Marget's fine things along with those companies of spies, and petting her and complimenting her with the rest, and seeing with self-reproach how foolishly happy she was, and never saying a word to put her on her guard. And, indeed, she was happy, and as proud as a princess, and so grateful to have friends again. And all the time these people were watching with all their eyes and reporting all they saw to Father Adolf.

But he couldn't make head or tail of the situation. There must be an enchanter somewhere on the premises, but who was it? Marget was not seen to do any jugglery, nor was Ursula, nor yet Gottfried; and still the wines and dainties never ran short, and a guest could not call for a thing and not get it. To produce these effects was usual enough with witches and enchanters—that part of it was not new; but to do it without any incantations, or even any rumblings or earthquakes or lightnings or apparitions—that was new, novel, wholly irregular. There was nothing in the books like this. Enchanted things were always unreal. Gold turned to dirt in an unenchanted atmosphere, food withered away and vanished. But this test failed in the present case. The spies brought samples: Father Adolf prayed over them, exorcised them, but it did no good; they remained sound and real, they yielded to natural decay only, and took the usual time to do it.

Father Adolf was not merely puzzled, he was also exasperated; for these evidences very nearly convinced him—privately—that there was no witchcraft in the matter. It did not wholly convince him, for this could be a new kind of witchcraft. There was a way to find out as to this: if this prodigal abundance of provender was not brought in from the outside, but produced on the premises, there was witchcraft, sure.

Chapter VII

Marget announced a party, and invited forty people; the date for it was seven days away. This was a fine opportunity. Marget's house stood by itself, and it could be easily watched. All the week it was watched night and day. Marget's household went out and in as usual, but they carried nothing in their hands, and neither they nor others brought anything to the house. This was ascertained. Evidently rations for forty people were not being fetched. If they were furnished any sustenance it would have to be made on the premises. It was true that Marget went out with a basket every evening, but the spies ascertained that she always brought it back empty.

The guests arrived at noon and filled the place. Father Adolf followed; also, after a little, the astrologer, without invitation. The spies had informed him that neither at the back nor the front had any parcels been brought in. He entered, and found the eating and drinking going on finely, and everything progressing in a lively and festive way. He glanced around and perceived that many of the cooked delicacies and all of the native and foreign fruits were of a perishable character, and he also recognized that these were fresh and perfect. No apparitions, no incantations, no thunder. That settled it. This was witchcraft. And not only that, but of a new kind—a kind never dreamed of before. It was a prodigious power, an illustrious power; he resolved to discover its secret. The announcement of it would resound throughout the world, penetrate to the remotest lands, paralyze all the nations with amazement—and carry his name with it, and make him renowned forever. It was a wonderful piece of luck, a splendid piece of luck; the glory of it made him dizzy.

All the house made room for him; Marget politely seated him; Ursula ordered Gottfried to bring a special table for him. Then she decked it and furnished it, and asked for his orders.

"Bring me what you will," he said.

The two servants brought supplies from the pantry, together with white wine and red—a bottle of each. The astrologer, who very likely had never seen such delicacies before, poured out a beaker of red wine, drank it off, poured another, then began to eat with a grand appetite.

I was not expecting Satan, for it was more than a week since I had seen or heard of him, but now he came in—I knew it by the feel, though people were in the way and I could not see him. I heard him apologizing for intruding; and he was going away, but Marget urged him to stay, and he thanked her and stayed. She brought him along, introducing him to the girls, and to Meidling, and to some of the elders; and there was quite a rustle of whispers: "It's the young stranger we hear so much about and can't get sight of, he is away so much." "Dear, dear, but he is beautiful—what is his name?" "Philip Traum." "Ah, it fits him!" (You see, "Traum" is German for "Dream.") "What does he do?" "Studying for the ministry, they say." "His face is his fortune—he'll be a cardinal some day." "Where is his home?" "Away down somewhere in the tropics, they say—has a rich uncle down there." And so on. He made his way at once; everybody was anxious to know him and talk with him. Everybody noticed how cool and fresh it was, all of a sudden, and wondered at it, for they could see that the sun was beating down the same as before, outside, and the sky was clear of clouds, but no one guessed the reason, of course.

The astrologer had drunk his second beaker;[12] he poured out a third. He set the bottle down, and by accident overturned it. He seized it before much was spilled, and held it up to the light, saying, "What a pity—it is royal wine." Then his face lighted with joy or triumph, or something, and he said, "Quick! Bring a bowl."

It was brought—a four-quart one. He took up that two-pint bottle and began to pour; went on pouring, the red liquor gurgling and gushing into the white bowl and rising higher and higher up its sides, everybody staring and holding their breath—and presently the bowl was full to the brim.

"Look at the bottle," he said, holding it up; "it is full yet!" I glanced at Satan, and in that moment he vanished. Then Father Adolf

[12] As Mark Twain wrote the story, it is of course Father Adolf who drinks the beakers of wine and then, prompted by Satan, performs in a way that makes him appear to be indeed possessed. And in a following passage, which was deleted by Paine and Duneka, Mark Twain relates that although the people feel that the bad priest should be denounced to the witch commission no one is brave enough to take such action.

rose up, flushed and excited, crossed himself, and began to thunder in his great voice, "This house is bewitched and accursed!" People began to cry and shriek and crowd toward the door. "I summon this detected household to—"

His words were cut off short. His face became red, then purple, but he could not utter another sound. Then I saw Satan, a transparent film, melt into the astrologer's body; then the astrologer put up his hand, and apparently in his own voice said, "Wait—remain where you are." All stopped where they stood. "Bring a funnel!" Ursula brought it, trembling and scared, and he stuck it in the bottle and took up the great bowl and began to pour the wine back, the people gazing and dazed with astonishment, for they knew the bottle was already full before he began. He emptied the whole of the bowl into the bottle, then smiled out over the room, chuckled, and said, indifferently: "It is nothing—anybody can do it! With my powers I can even do much more."

A frightened cry burst out everywhere. "Oh, my God, he is possessed!" and there was a tumultuous rush for the door which swiftly emptied the house of all who did not belong in it except us boys and Meidling. We boys knew the secret, and would have told it if we could, but we couldn't. We were very thankful to Satan for furnishing that good help at the needful time.

Marget was pale, and crying; Meidling looked kind of petrified; Ursula the same; but Gottfried was the worst—he couldn't stand, he was so weak and scared. For he was of a witch family, you know, and it would be bad for him to be suspected. Agnes came loafing in, looking pious and unaware, and wanted to rub up against Ursula and be petted, but Ursula was afraid of her and shrank away from her, but pretending she was not meaning any incivility, for she knew very well it wouldn't answer to have strained relations with that kind of a cat. But we boys took Agnes and petted her, for Satan would not have befriended her if he had not had a good opinion of her, and that was indorsement enough for us. He seemed to trust anything that hadn't the Moral Sense.

Outside, the guests, panic-stricken, scattered in every direction and fled in a pitiable state of terror; and such a tumult as they made with their running and sobbing and shrieking and shouting that soon all the village came flocking from their houses to see what had happened, and they thronged the street and shouldered and jostled one another in excitement and fright; and then Father Adolf appeared, and they fell apart in two walls like the cloven Red Sea, and presently down this lane the astrologer came striding and mumbling, and where he passed the lanes surged back in packed masses, and fell silent with awe, and their eyes stared and their breasts heaved, and several women fainted; and when he was gone by the crowd swarmed together and followed him at a distance, talking excitedly and asking questions and finding out the facts. Finding out the facts and passing them on to others, with improvements—improvements which soon enlarged the bowl of wine to a barrel, and made the one bottle hold it all and yet remain empty to the last.

When the astrologer reached the market-square he went straight to a juggler, fantastically dressed, who was keeping three brass balls in the air, and took them from him and faced around upon the approaching crowd and said: "This poor clown is ignorant of his art. Come forward and see an expert perform."

So saying, he tossed the balls up one after another and set them whirling in a slender bright oval in the air, and added another, then another and another, and soon—no one seeing whence he got them—adding, adding, adding, the oval lengthening all the time, his hands moving so swiftly that they were just a web or a blur and not distinguishable as hands; and such as counted said there were now a hundred balls in the air. The spinning great oval reached up twenty feet in the air and was a shining and glinting and wonderful sight. Then he folded his arms and told the balls to go on spinning without his help—and they did it. After a couple of minutes he said, "There, that will do," and the oval broke and came crashing down, and the balls scattered abroad and rolled every whither. And wherever one of them came the people fell back in dread, and no one would touch it. It made him laugh, and he scoffed at the people and called them cowards and old women. Then he turned and saw the tightrope, and said foolish people were daily wasting their money to see a clumsy and ignorant varlet degrade that beautiful art; now they should see the work of a master. With that he made a spring into the air and lit firm on his feet on the rope. Then he hopped the whole length of it back and forth on one foot, with his hands clasped over his eyes; and next he began to throw somersaults, both backward and forward, and threw twenty-seven.

The people murmured, for the astrologer was old, and always before had been halting of movement and at times even lame, but he was nimble enough now and went on with his antics in the liveliest manner. Finally he sprang lightly down and walked away, and passed up the road and around the corner and disappeared. Then that great, pale, silent, solid crowd drew a deep breath and looked into one another's faces as if they said: "Was it real? Did you see it, or was it only I—and I was dreaming?" Then they broke into a low murmur of talking, and fell apart in couples, and moved toward their homes, still talking in that awed way, with faces close together and laying a hand on an arm and making other such gestures as people make when they have been deeply impressed by something.

We boys followed behind our fathers, and listened, catching all we could of what they said; and when they sat down in our house and continued their talk they still had us for company. They were in a sad mood, for it was certain, they said, that disaster for the village must follow this awful visitation of witches and devils. Then my father remembered that Father Adolf had been struck dumb at the moment of his denunciation.

"They have not ventured to lay their hands upon an anointed servant of God before," he said; "and how they could have dared it this time I cannot make out, for he wore his crucifix. Isn't it so?"

"Yes," said the others, "we saw it."

"It is serious, friends, it is very serious. Always before, we had a protection. It has failed."

The others shook, as with a sort of chill, and muttered those words over—"It has failed." "God has forsaken us."

"It is true," said Seppi Wohlmeyer's father; "there is nowhere to look for help."

"The people will realize this," said Nikolaus's father, the judge, "and despair will take away their courage and their energies. We have indeed fallen upon evil times."

He sighed, and Wohlmeyer said, in a troubled voice: "The report of it all will go about the country, and our village will be shunned as being under the displeasure of God. The Golden Stag will know hard times."

"True, neighbor," said my father; "all of us will suffer—all in repute, many in estate. And, good God!—"

"What is it?"

"That can come—to finish us!"

"Name it—um Gottes Willen!"

"The Interdict!"

It smote like a thunderclap, and they were like to swoon with the terror of it. Then the dread of this calamity roused their energies, and they stopped brooding and began to consider ways to avert it. They discussed this, that, and the other way, and talked till the afternoon was far spent, then confessed that at present they could arrive at no decision. So they parted sorrowfully, with oppressed hearts which were filled with bodings.

While they were saying their parting words I slipped out and set my course for Marget's house to see what was happening there. I met many people, but none of them greeted me. It ought to have been surprising, but it was not, for they were so distraught with fear and dread that they were not in their right minds, I think; they were white and haggard, and walked like persons in a dream, their eyes open but seeing nothing, their lips moving but uttering nothing, and worriedly clasping and unclasping their hands without knowing it.

At Marget's it was like a funeral. She and Wilhelm sat together on the sofa, but said nothing, and not even holding hands. Both were steeped in gloom, and Marget's eyes were red from the crying she had been doing. She said:

"I have been begging him to go, and come no more, and so save himself alive. I cannot bear to be his murderer. This house is bewitched, and no inmate will escape the fire. But he will not go, and he will be lost with the rest."

Wilhelm said he would not go; if there was danger for her, his place was by her, and there he would remain. Then she began to cry again, and it was all so mournful that I wished I had stayed away. There was a knock, now, and Satan came in, fresh and cheery and beautiful, and brought that winy atmosphere of his and changed the whole thing. He never said a word about what had been happening, nor about the awful fears which were freezing the blood in the hearts of the community, but began to talk and rattle on about all manner of gay and pleasant things; and next about music—an artful stroke which cleared away the remnant of Marget's depression and brought her spirits and her interests broad awake. She had not heard anyone talk so well and so knowingly on that subject before, and she was so uplifted by it and so charmed that what she was feeling lit up her face and came out in her words; and Wilhelm noticed it and did not look as pleased as he ought to have done. And next Satan branched off into poetry, and recited some, and did it well, and Marget was charmed again; and again Wilhelm was not as pleased as he ought to have been, and this time Marget noticed it and was remorseful.[13]

I fell asleep to pleasant music that night—the patter of rain upon the panes and the dull growling of distant thunder.[14] Away in the night Satan came and roused me and said: "Come with me. Where shall we go?"

"Anywhere—so it is with you."

Then there was a fierce glare of sunlight, and he said, "This is China."

That was a grand surprise, and made me sort of drunk with vanity and gladness to think I had come so far—so much, much farther than anybody else in our village, including Bartel Sperling, who had such a great opinion of his travels. We buzzed around over that empire for more than half an hour, and saw the whole of it. It was wonderful, the spectacles we saw; and some were beautiful, others too horrible to think. For instance— However, I may go into that by and by, and also why Satan chose China for this excursion instead of another place;

[13] Here the editors cut more than seven thousand words out of Mark Twain's story (DV 327a, pp. 81–111). The deleted section mainly concerns the love-rivalry of Wilhelm Meidling and a brewer named Joseph Fuchs (Mark Twain seems to have intended changing his last name to Schultz) with the young Satan, who captivates the girls Marget and Lilly. By leaving out this material, Paine and Duneka sustained the sardonic tone of the tale in a way that Mark Twain evidently did not intend.

[14] After writing the foregoing part, Mark Twain seems to have laid the manuscript aside (probably in October 1899), but to have resumed composition in the following summer, beginning with "I fell asleep . . ."

it would interrupt my tale to do it now. Finally we stopped flitting and lit.

We sat upon a mountain commanding a vast landscape of mountain-range and gorge and valley and plain and river, with cities and villages slumbering in the sunlight, and a glimpse of blue sea on the farther verge. It was a tranquil and dreamy picture, beautiful to the eye and restful to the spirit. If we could only make a change like that whenever we wanted to, the world would be easier to live in than it is, for change of scene shifts the mind's burdens to the other shoulder and banishes old, shop-worn wearinesses from mind and body both.

We talked together, and I had the idea of trying to reform Satan and persuade him to lead a better life. I told him about all those things he had been doing, and begged him to be more considerate and stop making people unhappy. I said I knew he did not mean any harm, but that he ought to stop and consider the possible consequences of a thing before launching it in that impulsive and random way of his; then he would not make so much trouble. He was not hurt by this plain speech; he only looked amused and surprised, and said:

"What? I do random things? Indeed, I never do. I stop and consider possible consequences? Where is the need? I know what the consequences are going to be—always."

"Oh, Satan, then how could you do these things?"

"Well, I will tell you, and you must understand if you can. You belong to a singular race. Every man is a suffering-machine and a happiness-machine combined. The two functions work together harmoniously, with a fine and delicate precision, on the give-and-take principle. For every happiness turned out in the one department the other stands ready to modify it with a sorrow or a pain—maybe a dozen. In most cases the man's life is about equally divided between happiness and unhappiness. When this is not the case the unhappiness predominates—always; never the other. Sometimes a man's make and disposition are such that his misery-machine is able to do nearly all the business. Such a man goes through life almost ignorant of what happiness is. Everything he touches, everything he does, brings a misfortune upon him. You have seen such people? To that kind of a person life is not an advantage, is it? It is only a disaster. Sometimes for an hour's happiness a man's machinery makes him pay years of misery. Don't you know that? It happens every now and then. I will give you a case or two presently. Now the people of your village are nothing to me—you know that, don't you?"

I did not like to speak out too flatly, so I said I had suspected it.

"Well, it is true that they are nothing to me. It is not possible that they should be. The difference between them and me is abysmal, immeasurable. They have no intellect."

"No intellect?"

"Nothing that resembles it. At a future time I will examine what man calls his mind and give you the details of that chaos, then you will see and understand. Men have nothing in common with me—there is no point of contact; they have foolish little feelings and foolish little vanities and impertinences and ambitions; their foolish little life is but a laugh, a sigh, and extinction; and they have no sense. Only the Moral Sense. I will show you what I mean. Here is a red spider, not so big as a pin's head. Can you imagine an elephant being interested in him—caring whether he is happy or isn't, or whether he is wealthy or poor, or whether his sweetheart returns his love or not, or whether his mother is sick or well, or whether he is looked up to in society or not, or whether his enemies will smite him or his friends desert him, or whether his hopes will suffer blight or his political ambitions fail, or whether he shall die in the bosom of his family or neglected and despised in a foreign land? These things can never be important to the elephant; they are nothing to him; he cannot shrink his sympathies to the microscopic size of them. Man is to me as the red spider is to the elephant. The elephant has nothing against the spider—he cannot get down to that remote level; I have nothing against man. The elephant is indifferent; I am indifferent. The elephant would not take the trouble to do the spider an ill turn; if he took the notion he might do him a good turn, if it came in his way and cost nothing. I have done men good service, but no ill turns.

"The elephant lives a century, the red spider a day; in power, intellect, and dignity the one creature is separated from the other by a distance which is simply astronomical. Yet in these, as in all qualities, man is immeasurably further below me than is the wee spider below the elephant.

"Man's mind clumsily and tediously and laboriously patches little trivialities together and gets a result—such as it is. My mind creates! Do you get the force of that? Creates anything it desires—and in a moment. Creates without material. Creates fluids, solids, colors—anything, everything—out of the airy nothing which is called Thought. A man imagines a silk thread, imagines a machine to make it, imagines a picture, then by weeks of labor embroiders it on canvas with the thread. I think the whole thing, and in a moment it is before you—created.

"I think a poem, music, the record of a game of chess—anything—and it is there. This is the immortal mind—nothing is beyond its reach. Nothing can obstruct my vision; the rocks are transparent to me, and darkness is daylight. I do not need to open a book; I take the whole of its contents into my mind at a single glance, through the cover; and in a million years I could not forget a single word of it, or its place in the volume. Nothing goes on in the skull of man, bird, fish, insect, or other creature which can be hidden from me. I pierce the learned man's brain with a single glance, and the treasures which cost him threescore years to accumulate are mine; he can forget, and he does forget, but I retain.

"Now, then, I perceive by your thoughts that you are understanding me fairly well. Let us proceed. Circumstances might so fall out that the elephant could like the spider—supposing he can see it—but he could not love it. His love is for his own kind—for his equals. An angel's love is sublime, adorable, divine, beyond the imagination of man—infinitely beyond it! But it is limited to his own august order. If it fell upon one of your race for only an instant, it would consume its object to ashes. No, we cannot love men, but we can be harmlessly indifferent to them; we can also like them, sometimes. I like you and the boys, I like Father Peter, and for your sakes I am doing all these things for the villagers."

He saw that I was thinking a sarcasm, and he explained his position.

"I have wrought well for the villagers, though it does not look like it on the surface. Your race never know good fortune from ill. They are always mistaking the one for the other. It is because they cannot see into the future. What I am doing for the villagers will bear good fruit some day; in some cases to themselves; in others, to unborn generations of men. No one will ever know that I was the cause, but it will be none the less true, for all that. Among you boys you have a game: you stand a row of bricks on end a few inches apart; you push a brick, it knocks its neighbor over, the neighbor knocks over the next brick—and so on till all the row is prostrate. That is human life. A child's first act knocks over the initial brick, and the rest will follow inexorably. If you could see into the future, as I can, you would see everything that was going to happen to that creature; for nothing can change the order of its life after the first event has determined it. That is, nothing will change it, because each act unfailingly begets an act, that act begets another, and so on to the end, and the seer can look forward down the line and see just when each act is to have birth, from cradle to grave."

"Does God order the career?"

"Foreordain it? No. The man's circumstances and environment order it. His first act determines the second and all that follow after. But suppose, for argument's sake, that the man should skip one of these acts; an apparently trifling one, for instance; suppose that it had been appointed that on a certain day, at a certain hour and minute, and second and fraction of a second he should go to the well, and he didn't go. That man's career would change utterly, from that moment; thence to the grave it would be wholly different from the career which his first act as a child had arranged for him. Indeed, it might be that if he had gone to the well he would have ended his career on a throne, and that omitting to do it would set him upon a career that would lead to beggary and a pauper's grave. For instance: if at any time—say in boyhood—Columbus had skipped the triflingest little link in the chain of acts projected and made inevitable by his first childish act, it would have changed his whole subsequent life, and he would have become a priest and died obscure in an Italian village, and America would not have been discovered for two centuries afterward. I know this. To skip any one of the billion acts in Columbus's chain would have wholly changed his life. I have examined his billion of possible careers, and in only one of them occurs the discovery of America. You people do not suspect that all of your acts are of one size and importance, but it is true; to snatch at an appointed fly is as big with fate for you as in any other appointed act—"

"As the conquering of a continent, for instance?"

"Yes. Now, then, no man ever does drop a link—the thing has never happened! Even when he is trying to make up his mind as to whether he will do a thing or not, that itself is a link, an act, and has its proper place in his chain; and when he finally decides an act, that also was the thing which he was absolutely certain to do. You see, now, that a man will never drop a link in his chain. He cannot. If he made up his mind to try, that project would itself be an unavoidable link—a thought bound to occur to him at that precise moment, and made certain by the first act of his babyhood."

It seemed so dismal!

"He is a prisoner for life," I said sorrowfully, "and cannot get free."

"No, of himself he cannot get away from the consequences of his first childish act. But I can free him."

I looked up wistfully.

"I have changed the careers of a number of your villagers."

I tried to thank him, but found it difficult, and let it drop.

"I shall make some other changes. You know that little Lisa Brandt?"

"Oh yes, everybody does. My mother says she is so sweet and so lovely that she is not like any other child. She says she will be the pride of the village when she grows up; and its idol, too, just as she is now."

"I shall change her future."

"Make it better?" I asked.

"Yes. And I will change the future of Nikolaus."

I was glad, this time, and said, "I don't need to ask about his case; you will be sure to do generously by him."

"It is my intention."

Straight off I was building that great future of Nicky's in my imagination, and had already made a renowned general of him and hofmeister at the court, when I noticed that Satan was waiting for me to get ready to listen again. I was ashamed of having exposed my cheap imaginings to him, and was expecting some sarcasms, but it did not happen. He proceeded with his subject:

"Nicky's appointed life is sixty-two years."

"That's grand!" I said.

"Lisa's, thirty-six. But, as I told you, I shall change their lives and those ages. Two minutes and a quarter from now Nikolaus will wake out of his sleep and find the rain blowing in. It was appointed that he should turn over and go to sleep again. But I have appointed that he shall get up and close the window first. That trifle will change his career entirely. He will rise in the morning two minutes later than the chain of his life had appointed him to rise. By consequence, thenceforth nothing will ever happen to him in accordance with the details of the old chain." He took out his watch and sat looking at it a few moments, then said: "Nikolaus has risen to close the window. His life is changed, his new career has begun. There will be consequences."

It made me feel creepy; it was uncanny.

"But for this change certain things would happen twelve days from now. For instance, Nikolaus would save Lisa from drowning. He would arrive on the scene at exactly the right moment—four minutes past ten, the long-ago appointed instant of time—and the water would be shoal, the achievement easy and certain. But he will arrive some seconds too late, now; Lisa will have struggled into deeper water. He will do his best, but both will drown."

"Oh, Satan! oh, dear Satan!" I cried, with the tears rising in my eyes, "save them! Don't let it happen. I can't bear to lose Nikolaus, he is my loving playmate and friend; and think of Lisa's poor mother!"

I clung to him and begged and pleaded, but he was not moved. He made me sit down again, and told me I must hear him out.

"I have changed Nikolaus's life, and this has changed Lisa's. If I had not done this, Nikolaus would save Lisa, then he would catch cold from his drenching; one of your race's fantastic and desolating scarlet fevers would follow, with pathetic after-effects; for forty-six years he would lie in his bed a paralytic log, deaf, dumb, blind, and praying night and day for the blessed relief of death. Shall I change his life back?"

"Oh no! Oh, not for the world! In charity and pity leave it as it is."

"It is best so. I could not have changed any other link in his life and done him so good a service. He had a billion possible careers, but not one of them was worth living; they were charged full with miseries and disasters. But for my intervention he would do his brave deed twelve days from now—a deed begun and ended in six minutes—and get for all reward those forty-six years of sorrow and suffering I told you of. It is one of the cases I was thinking of a while ago when I said that sometimes an act which brings the actor an hour's happiness and self-satisfaction is paid for—or punished—by years of suffering."

I wondered what poor little Lisa's early death would save her from. He answered the thought:

"From ten years of pain and slow recovery from an accident, and then from nineteen years' pollution, shame, depravity, crime, ending with death at the hands of the executioner. Twelve days hence she will die; her mother would save her life if she could. Am I not kinder than her mother?"

"Yes—oh, indeed yes; and wiser."

"Father Peter's case is coming on presently. He will be acquitted, through unassailable proofs of his innocence."

"Why, Satan, how can that be? Do you really think it?"

"Indeed, I know it. His good name will be restored, and the rest of his life will be happy."

"I can believe it. To restore his good name will have that effect."

"His happiness will not proceed from that cause. I shall change his life that day, for his good. He will never know his good name has been restored."

In my mind—and modestly—I asked for particulars, but Satan paid no attention to my thought. Next, my mind wandered to the astrologer, and I wondered where he might be.

"In the moon," said Satan, with a fleeting sound which I believed was a chuckle. "I've got him on the cold side of it, too. He doesn't know where he is, and is not having a pleasant time; still, it is good enough for him, a good place for his star studies. I shall need him presently; then I shall bring him back and possess him again. He has a long and cruel and odious life before him, but I will change that, for I have no feeling against him and am quite willing to do him a kindness. I think I shall get him burned."

He had such strange notions of kindness! But angels are made so, and do not know any better. Their ways are not like our ways; and, besides, human beings are nothing to them; they think they are only freaks. It seemed to me odd that he should put the astrologer so far away; he could have dumped him in Germany just as well, where he would be handy.

"Far away?" said Satan. "To me no place is far away; distance does not exist for me. The sun is less than a hundred million miles from here, and the light that is falling upon us has taken eight minutes to come; but I can make that flight, or any other, in a fraction of time so minute that it cannot be measured by a watch. I have but to think the journey, and it is accomplished."

I held out my hand and said, "The light lies upon it; think it into a glass of wine, Satan."

He did it. I drank the wine.

"Break the glass," he said.

I broke it.

"There—you see it is real. The villagers thought the brass balls were magic stuff and as perishable as smoke. They were afraid to touch them. You are a curious lot—your race. But come along; I have business. I will put you to bed." Said and done. Then he was gone; but his voice came back to me through the rain and darkness saying, "Yes, tell Seppi, but no other."

It was the answer to my thought.

Chapter VIII

Sleep would not come. It was not because I was proud of my travels and excited about having been around the big world to China, and feeling contemptuous of Bartel Sperling, "the traveler," as he called himself, and looked down upon us others because he had been to Vienna once and was the only Eseldorf boy who had made such a journey and seen the world's wonders. At another time that would have kept me awake, but it did not affect me now. No, my mind was filled with Nikolaus, my thoughts ran upon him only, and the good days we had seen together at romps and frolics in the woods and the fields and the river in the long summer days, and skating and sliding in the winter when our parents thought we were in school. And now he was going out of this young life, and the summers and winters would come and go, and we others would rove and play as before, but his place would be vacant; we should see him no more. To-morrow he would not suspect, but would be as he had always been, and it would shock me to hear him laugh, and see him do lightsome and frivolous things, for to me he would be a corpse, with waxen hands and dull eyes, and I should see the shroud around his face; and next day he would not suspect, nor the next, and all the time his handful of days would be wasting swiftly away and that awful thing coming nearer and nearer, his fate closing steadily around him and no one knowing it but Seppi and me. Twelve days—only twelve days. It was awful to think of. I noticed that in my thoughts I was not calling him by his familiar names, Nick and Nicky, but was speaking of him by his full name, and reverently, as one speaks of the dead. Also, as incident after incident of our comradeship came thronging into my mind out of the past, I noticed that they were mainly cases where I had wronged him or hurt him, and they rebuked me and reproached me, and my heart was wrung with remorse, just as it is when we remember our unkindnesses to friends who have passed beyond the veil, and we wish we could have them back again, if only for a moment, so that we could go on our knees to them and say, "Have pity, and forgive."

Once when we were nine years old he went a long errand of nearly two miles for the fruiterer, who gave him a splendid big apple for reward, and he was flying home with it, almost beside himself with astonishment and delight, and I met him, and he let me look at the apple, not thinking of treachery, and I ran off with it, eating it as I ran, he following me and begging; and when he overtook me I offered him the core, which was all that was left; and I laughed. Then he turned away, crying, and said he had meant to give it to his little sister. That smote me, for she was slowly getting well of a sickness, and it would have been a proud moment for him, to see her joy and surprise and have her caresses. But I was ashamed to say I was ashamed, and only said something rude and mean, to pretend I did not care, and he made no reply in words, but there was a wounded look in his face as he turned away toward his home which rose before me many times in after years, in the night, and reproached me and made me ashamed again. It had grown dim in my mind, by and by, then it disappeared; but it was back now, and not dim.

Once at school, when we were eleven, I upset my ink and spoiled four copy-books, and was in danger of severe punishment; but I put it upon him, and he got the whipping.

And only last year I had cheated him in a trade, giving him a large fishhook which was partly broken through for three small sound ones. The first fish he caught broke the hook, but he did not know I was blamable, and he refused to take back one of the small hooks which my conscience forced me to offer him, but said, "A trade is a trade; the hook was bad, but that was not your fault."

No, I could not sleep. These little, shabby wrongs upbraided me and tortured me, and with a pain much sharper than one feels when the wrongs have been done to the living. Nikolaus was living, but no matter; he was to me as one already dead. The wind was still moaning about the eaves, the rain still pattering upon the panes.

In the morning I sought out Seppi and told him. It was down by the river. His lips moved, but he did not say anything, he only looked dazed and stunned, and his face turned very white. He stood like that a few moments, the tears welling into his eyes, then he turned away and I locked my arm in his and we walked along thinking, but not speaking. We crossed the bridge and wandered through the meadows and up among the hills and the woods, and at last the talk came and flowed freely, and it was all about Nikolaus and was a recalling of the life we had lived with him. And every now and then Seppi said, as if to himself:

"Twelve days!—less than twelve days."

We said we must be with him all the time; we must have all of him we could; the days were precious now. Yet we did not go to seek him. It would be like meeting the dead, and we were afraid. We did not say it, but that was what we were feeling. And so it gave us a shock when we turned a curve and came upon Nikolaus face to face. He shouted, gaily:

"Hi-hi! What is the matter? Have you seen a ghost?"

We couldn't speak, but there was no occasion, he was willing to talk for us all, for he had just seen Satan and was in high spirits about it. Satan had told him about our trip to China, and he had begged Satan to take him a journey, and Satan had promised. It was to be a far journey, and wonderful and beautiful; and Nikolaus had begged him to take us, too, but he said no, he would take us some day, maybe, but not now. Satan would come for him on the 13th, and Nikolaus was already counting the hours, he was so impatient.

That was the fatal day. We were already counting the hours, too.

We wandered many a mile, always following paths which had been our favorites from the days when we were little, and always we talked about the old times. All the blitheness was with Nikolaus; we others could not shake off our depression. Our tone toward Nikolaus was so strangely gentle and tender and yearning that he noticed it, and was pleased; and we were constantly doing him deferential little offices of courtesy, and saying. "Wait, let me do that for you," and that pleased him, too. I gave him seven fish-hooks—all I had—and made him take them; and Seppi gave him his new knife and a humming-top painted red and yellow—atonements for swindles practiced upon him formerly, as I learned later, and probably no longer remembered by Nikolaus now. These things touched him, and he could not have believed that we loved him so; and his pride in it and gratefulness for it cut us to the heart, we were so undeserving of them. When we parted at last, he was radiant, and said he had never had such a happy day.

As we walked along homeward, Seppi said, "We always prized him, but never so much as now, when we are going to lose him."

Next day and every day we spent all of our spare time with Nikolaus; and also added to it time which we (and he) stole from work and other duties, and this cost the three of us some sharp scoldings, and some threats of punishment. Every morning two of us woke with a start and a shudder, saying, as the days flew along, "Only ten days left"; "only nine days left"; "only eight"; "only seven." Always it was narrowing. Always Nikolaus was gay and happy, and always puzzled because we were not. He wore his invention to the bone trying to invent ways to cheer us up, but it was only a hollow success; he could see that our jollity had no heart in it, and that the laughs we broke into came up against some obstruction or other and suffered damage and decayed into a sigh. He tried to find out what the matter was, so that he could help us out of our trouble or make it lighter by sharing it with us; so we had to tell many lies to deceive him and appease him.

But the most distressing thing of all was that he was always making plans, and often they went beyond the 13th! Whenever that happened it made us groan in spirit. All his mind was fixed upon finding some way to conquer our depression and cheer us up; and at last, when he had but three days to live, he fell upon the right idea and was jubilant over it—a boys-and-girls' frolic and dance in the woods, up there where we first met Satan, and this was to occur on the 14th. It was ghastly, for that was his funeral day. We couldn't venture to protest; it would only have brought a "Why?" which we could not answer. He wanted us to help him invite his guests, and we did it—one can refuse nothing to a dying friend. But it was dreadful, for really we were inviting them to his funeral.

It was an awful eleven days; and yet, with a lifetime stretching back between to-day and then, they are still a grateful memory to me, and beautiful. In effect they were days of companionship with one's sacred dead, and I have known no comradeship that was so close or so precious. We clung to the hours and the minutes, counting them as they wasted away, and parting with them with that pain and bereavement which a miser feels who sees his hoard filched from him coin by coin by robbers and is helpless to prevent it.

When the evening of the last day came we stayed out too long; Seppi and I were in fault for that; we could not bear to part with Nikolaus; so it was very late when we left him at his door. We lingered near awhile, listening; and that happened which we were fearing. His father gave him the promised punishment, and we heard his shrieks. But we listened only a moment, then hurried away, remorseful for this thing which we had caused. And sorry for the father, too; our thought being, "If he only knew—if he only knew!"

In the morning Nikolaus did not meet us at the appointed place, so we went to his home to see what the matter was. His mother said:

"His father is out of all patience with these goings-on, and will not have any more of it. Half the time when Nick is needed he is not to be found; then it turns out that he has been gadding around with you two. His father gave him a flogging last night. It always grieved me before, and many's the time I have begged him off and saved him, but this time he appealed to me in vain, for I was out of patience myself."

"I wish you had saved him just this one time," I said, my voice trembling a little; "it would ease a pain in your heart to remember it some day."

She was ironing at the time, and her back was partly toward me. She turned about with a startled or wondering look in her face and said, "What do you mean by that?"

I was not prepared, and didn't know anything to say; so it was awkward, for she kept looking at me; but Seppi was alert and spoke up:

"Why, of course it would be pleasant to remember, for the very reason we were out so late was that Nikolaus got to telling how good you are to him, and how he never got whipped when you were by to save him; and he was so full of it, and we were so full of the interest of it, that none of us noticed how late it was getting."

"Did he say that? Did he?" and she put her apron to her eyes.

"You can ask Theodor—he will tell you the same."

"It is a dear, good lad, my Nick," she said. "I am sorry I let him get whipped; I will never do it again. To think—all the time I was sitting here last night, fretting and angry at him, he was loving me and praising me! Dear, dear, if we could only know! Then we shouldn't ever go wrong; but we are only poor, dumb beasts groping around and making mistakes. I sha'n't ever think of last night without a pang."

She was like all the rest; it seemed as if nobody could open a mouth, in these wretched days, without saying something that made us shiver. They were "groping around," and did not know what true, sorrowfully true things they were saying by accident.

Seppi asked if Nikolaus might go out with us.

"I am sorry," she answered, "but he can't. To punish him further, his father doesn't allow him to go out of the house to-day."

We had a great hope! I saw it in Seppi's eyes. We thought, "If he cannot leave the house, he cannot be drowned." Seppi asked, to make sure:

"Must he stay in all day, or only the morning?"

"All day. It's such a pity, too; it's a beautiful day, and he is so unused to being shut up. But he is busy planning his party, and maybe that is company for him. I do hope he isn't too lonesome."

Seppi saw that in her eye which emboldened him to ask if we might go up and help him pass his time.

"And welcome!" she said, right heartily. "Now I call that real friendship, when you might be abroad in the fields and the woods, having a happy time. You are good boys, I'll allow that, though you don't always find satisfactory ways of improving it. Take these cakes—for yourselves—and give him this one, from his mother."

The first thing we noticed when we entered Nikolaus's room was the time—a quarter to 10. Could that be correct? Only such a few minutes to live! I felt a contraction at my heart. Nikolaus jumped up and gave us a glad welcome. He was in good spirits over his plannings for his party and had not been lonesome.

"Sit down," he said, "and look at what I've been doing. And I've finished a kite that you will say is a beauty. It's drying, in the kitchen; I'll fetch it."

He had been spending his penny savings in fanciful trifles of various kinds, to go as prizes in the games, and they were marshaled with fine and showy effect upon the table. He said:

"Examine them at your leisure while I get mother to touch up the kite with her iron if it isn't dry enough yet."

Then he tripped out and went clattering downstairs, whistling.

We did not look at the things; we couldn't take any interest in anything but the clock. We sat staring at it in silence, listening to the ticking, and every time the minute hand jumped we nodded recognition—one minute fewer to cover in the race for life or for death. Finally Seppi drew a deep breath and said:

"Two minutes to ten. Seven minutes more and he will pass the death-point. Theodor, he is going to be saved! He's going to—"

"Hush! I'm on needles. Watch the clock and keep still."

Five minutes more. We were panting with the strain and the excitement. Another three minutes, and there was a footstep on the stair.

"Saved!" And we jumped up and faced the door.

The old mother entered, bringing the kite. "Isn't it a beauty?" she said. "And, dear me, how he has slaved over it—ever since daylight, I think, and only finished it awhile before you came." She stood it against the wall, and stepped back to take a view of it. "He drew the pictures his own self, and I think they are very good. The church isn't so very good, I'll have to admit, but look at the bridge—anyone can recognize the bridge in a minute. He asked me to bring it up. . . . Dear me! it's seven minutes past ten, and I—"

"But where is he?"

"He? Oh, he'll be here soon; he's gone out a minute."

"Gone out?"

"Yes. Just as he came downstairs little Lisa's mother came in and said the child had wandered off somewhere, and as she was a little uneasy I told Nikolaus to never mind about his father's orders—go and look her up. . . . Why, how white you two do look! I do believe you are sick. Sit down; I'll fetch something. That cake has disagreed with you. It is a little heavy, but I thought—"

She disappeared without finishing her sentence, and we hurried at once to the back window and looked toward the river. There was a great crowd at the other end of the bridge, and people were flying toward that point from every direction.

"Oh, it is all over—poor Nikolaus! Why, oh, why did she let him get out of the house!"

"Come away," said Seppi, half sobbing, "come quick—we can't bear to meet her; in five minutes she will know."

But we were not to escape. She came upon us at the foot of the stairs, with her cordials in her hands, and made us come in and sit down and take the medicine. Then she watched the effect, and it did not satisfy her; so she made us wait longer, and kept upbraiding herself for giving us the unwholesome cake.

Presently the thing happened which we were dreading. There was a sound of tramping and scraping outside, and a crowd came solemnly in, with heads uncovered, and laid the two drowned bodies on the bed.

"Oh, my God!" that poor mother cried out, and fell on her knees, and put her arms about her dead boy and began to cover the wet face with kisses. "Oh, it was I that sent him, and I have been his death. If I had obeyed, and kept him in the house, this would not have happened. And I am rightly punished; I was cruel to him last night, and him begging me, his own mother, to be his friend."

And so she went on and on, and all the women cried, and pitied her, and tried to comfort her, but she could not forgive herself and could not be comforted, and kept on saying if she had not sent him out he would be alive and well now, and she was the cause of his death.

It shows how foolish people are when they blame themselves for anything they have done. Satan knows, and he said nothing happens that your first act hasn't arranged to happen and made inevitable; and so, of your own motion you can't ever alter the scheme or do a thing that will break a link. Next we heard screams, and Frau Brandt came wildly plowing and plunging through the crowd with her dress in disorder and hair flying loose, and flung herself upon her dead child with moans and kisses and pleadings and endearments; and by and by she rose up almost exhausted with her outpourings of passionate emotion, and clenched her fist and lifted it toward the sky, and her tear-drenched face grew hard and resentful, and she said:

"For nearly two weeks I have had dreams and presentiments and warnings that death was going to strike what was most precious to me, and day and night and night and day I have groveled in the dirt before Him praying Him to have pity on my innocent child and save it from harm—and here is His answer!"

Why, He had saved it from harm—but she did not know.

She wiped the tears from her eyes and cheeks, and stood awhile gazing down at the child and caressing its face and its hair with her hands; then she spoke again in that bitter tone: "But in His hard heart is no compassion. I will never pray again."

She gathered her dead child to her bosom and strode away, the crowd falling back to let her pass, and smitten dumb by the awful words they had heard. Ah, that poor woman! It is as Satan said, we do not know good fortune from bad, and are always mistaking the one for the other. Many a time since I have heard people pray to God to spare the life of sick persons, but I have never done it.

Both funerals took place at the same time in our little church next day. Everybody was there, including the party guests. Satan was there, too; which was proper, for it was on account of his efforts that the funerals had happened. Nikolaus had departed this life without absolution, and a collection was taken up for masses, to get him out of purgatory. Only two-thirds of the required money was gathered, and the parents were going to try to borrow the rest, but Satan furnished it. He told us privately that there was no purgatory, but he had contributed in order that Nikolaus's parents and their friends might be saved from worry and distress. We thought it very good of him, but he said money did not cost him anything.

At the graveyard the body of little Lisa was seized for debt by a carpenter to whom the mother owed fifty groschen for work done the year before. She had never been able to pay this, and was not able now. The carpenter took the corpse home and kept it four days in his cellar, the mother weeping and imploring about his house all the time; then he buried it in his brother's cattle-yard, without religious ceremonies. It drove the mother wild with grief and shame, and she forsook her work and went daily about the town, cursing the carpenter and blaspheming the laws of the emperor and the church, and it was pitiful to see. Seppi asked Satan to interfere, but he said the carpenter and the rest were members of the human race and were acting quite neatly for that species of animal. He would interfere if he found a horse acting in such a way, and we must inform him when we came across that kind of horse doing that kind of a human thing, so that he could stop it. We believed this was sarcasm, for of course there wasn't any such horse.

But after a few days we found that we could not abide that poor woman's distress, so we begged Satan to examine her several possible careers, and see if he could not change her, to her profit, to a new one. He said the longest of her careers as they now stood gave her forty-two years to live, and her shortest one twenty-nine, and that both were charged with grief and hunger and cold and pain. The only improvement he could make would be to enable her to skip a certain three minutes from now; and he asked us if he should do it. This was such a short time to decide in that we went to pieces with nervous excitement, and before we could pull ourselves together and ask for particulars he said the time would be up in a few more seconds; so then we gasped out, "Do it!"

"It is done," he said; "she was going around a corner; I have turned her back; it has changed her career."

"Then what will happen, Satan?"

"It is happening now. She is having words with Fischer, the weaver. In his anger Fischer will straightway do what he would not have done but for this accident. He was present when she stood over her child's body and uttered those blasphemies."

"What will he do?"

"He is doing it now—betraying her. In three days she will go to the stake."

We could not speak; we were frozen with horror, for if we had not meddled with her career she would have been spared this awful fate. Satan noticed these thoughts, and said:

"What you are thinking is strictly human-like—that is to say, foolish. The woman is advantaged. Die when she might, she would go to heaven. By this prompt death she gets twenty-nine years more of heaven than she is entitled to, and escapes twenty-nine years of misery here."

A moment before we were bitterly making up our minds that

we would ask no more favors of Satan for friends of ours, for he did not seem to know any way to do a person a kindness but by killing him, but the whole aspect of the case was changed now, and we were glad of what we had done and full of happiness in the thought of it.

After a little I began to feel troubled about Fischer, and asked, timidly, "Does this episode change Fischer's life-scheme, Satan?"

"Change it? Why, certainly. And radically. If he had not met Frau Brandt awhile ago he would die next year, thirty-four years of age. Now he will live to be ninety, and have a pretty prosperous and comfortable life of it, as human lives go."

We felt a great joy and pride in what we had done for Fischer, and were expecting Satan to sympathize with this feeling; but he showed no sign, and this made us uneasy. We waited for him to speak, but he didn't; so, to assuage our solicitude we had to ask him if there was any defect in Fischer's good luck. Satan considered the question a moment, then said, with some hesitation:

"Well, the fact is, it is a delicate point. Under his several former possible life-careers he was going to heaven."

We were aghast. "Oh, Satan! and under this one—"

"There, don't be so distressed. You were sincerely trying to do him a kindness; let that comfort you."

"Oh, dear, dear, that cannot comfort us. You ought to have told us what we were doing, then we wouldn't have acted so."

But it made no impression on him. He had never felt a pain or a sorrow, and did not know what they were, in any really informing way. He had no knowledge of them except theoretically—that is to say, intellectually. And of course that is no good. One can never get any but a loose and ignorant notion of such things except by experience. We tried our best to make him comprehend the awful thing that had been done and how we were compromised by it, but he couldn't seem to get hold of it. He said he did not think it important where Fischer went to; in heaven he would not be missed, there were "plenty there." We tried to make him see that he was missing the point entirely; that Fischer, and not other people, was the proper one to decide about the importance of it; but it all went for nothing; he said he did not care for Fischer—there were plenty more Fischers.

The next minute Fischer went by on the other side of the way, and it made us sick and faint to see him, remembering the doom that was upon him, and we the cause of it. And how unconscious he was that anything had happened to him! You could see by his elastic step and his alert manner that he was well satisfied with himself for doing that hard turn for poor Frau Brandt. He kept glancing back over his shoulder expectantly. And, sure enough, pretty soon Frau Brandt followed after, in charge of the officers and wearing jingling chains. A mob was in her wake, jeering and shouting, "Blasphemer and heretic!" and some among them were neighbors and friends of her happier days. Some were trying to strike her, and the officers were not taking as much trouble as they might to keep them from it.

"Oh, stop them, Satan!" It was out before we remembered that he could not interrupt them for a moment without changing their whole after-lives. He puffed a little puff toward them with his lips and they began to reel and stagger and grab at the empty air; then they broke apart and fled in every direction, shrieking, as if in intolerable pain. He had crushed a rib of each of them with that little puff. We could not help asking if their life-chart was changed.

"Yes, entirely. Some have gained years, some have lost them. Some few will profit in various ways by the change, but only that few."

We did not ask if we had brought poor Fischer's luck to any of them. We did not wish to know. We fully believed in Satan's desire to do us kindnesses, but we were losing confidence in his judgment. It was at this time that our growing anxiety to have him look over our life-charts and suggest improvements began to fade out and give place to other interests.

For a day or two the whole village was a chattering turmoil over Frau Brandt's case and over the mysterious calamity that had overtaken the mob, and at her trial the place was crowded. She was easily convicted of her blasphemies, for she uttered those terrible words again and said she would not take them back. When warned that she was imperiling her life, she said they could take it in welcome, she did not want it, she would rather live with the professional devils in perdition than with these imitators in the village. They accused her of breaking all those ribs by witchcraft, and asked her if she was not a witch? She answered scornfully:

"No. If I had that power would any of you holy hypocrites be alive five minutes? No; I would strike you all dead. Pronounce your sentence and let me go; I am tired of your society."

So they found her guilty, and she was excommunicated and cut off from the joys of heaven and doomed to the fires of hell; then she was clothed in a coarse robe and delivered to the secular arm, and conducted to the market-place, the bell solemnly tolling the while. We saw her chained to the stake, and saw the first film of blue smoke rise on the still air. Then her hard face softened, and she looked upon the packed crowd in front of her and said, with gentleness:

"We played together once, in long-agone days when we were innocent little creatures. For the sake of that, I forgive you."

We went away then, and did not see the fires consume her, but we heard the shrieks, although we put our fingers in our ears. When they ceased we knew she was in heaven, notwithstanding the excommunication; and we were glad of her death and not sorry that we had brought it about.

One day, a little while after this, Satan appeared again. We were always watching out for him, for life was never very stagnant when he was by. He came upon us at that place in the woods where we had first met him. Being boys, we wanted to be entertained; we asked him to do a show for us.

"Very well," he said. "Would you like to see a history of the progress of the human race?—its development of that product which it calls civilization?"

We said we should.

So, with a thought, he turned the place into the Garden of Eden, and we saw Abel praying by his altar; then Cain came walking toward him with his club, and did not seem to see us, and would have stepped on my foot if I had not drawn it in. He spoke to his brother in a language which we did not understand; then he grew violent and threatening, and we knew what was going to happen, and turned away our heads for the moment; but we heard the crash of the blows and heard the shrieks and the groans; then there was silence, and we saw Abel lying in his blood and gasping out his life, and Cain standing over him and looking down at him, vengeful and unrepentant.

Then the vision vanished, and was followed by a long series of unknown wars, murders, and massacres. Next we had the Flood, and the Ark tossing around in the stormy waters, with lofty mountains in the distance showing veiled and dim through the rain. Satan said:

"The progress of your race was not satisfactory. It is to have another chance now."

The scene changed, and we saw Noah overcome with wine.

Next, we had Sodom and Gomorrah, and "the attempt to discover two or three respectable persons there," as Satan described it. Next, Lot and his daughters in the cave.

Next came the Hebraic wars, and we saw the victors massacre the survivors and their cattle, and save the young girls alive and distribute them around.

Next we had Jael; and saw her slip into the tent and drive the nail into the temple of her sleeping guest; and we were so close that when the blood gushed out it trickled in a little, red stream to our feet, and we could have stained our hands in it if we had wanted to.

Next we had Egyptian wars, Greek wars, Roman wars, hideous drenchings of the earth with blood; and we saw the treacheries of the Romans toward the Carthaginians, and the sickening spectacle of the massacre of those brave people. Also we saw Cæsar invade Britain—"not that those barbarians had done him any harm, but because he wanted their land, and desired to confer the blessings of civilization upon their widows and orphans," as Satan explained.

Next, Christianity was born. Then ages of Europe passed in review before us, and we saw Christianity and Civilization march hand in hand through those ages, "leaving famine and death and desolation in their wake, and other signs of the progress of the human race," as Satan observed.

And always we had wars, and more wars, and still other wars—all over Europe, all over the world. "Sometimes in the private interest of royal families," Satan said, "sometimes to crush a weak nation; but never a war started by the aggressor for any clean purpose—there is no such war in the history of the race."

"Now," said Satan, "you have seen your progress down to the present, and you must confess that it is wonderful—in its way. We must now exhibit the future."

He showed us slaughters more terrible in their destruction of life, more devastating in their engines of war, than any we had seen.[15]

"You perceive," he said, "that you have made continual progress. Cain did his murder with a club; the Hebrews did their murders with javelins and swords; the Greeks and Romans added protective armor and the fine arts of military organization and generalship; the Christian has added guns and gunpowder; a few centuries from now he will have so greatly improved the deadly effectiveness of his weapons of slaughter that all men will confess that without Christian civilization war must have remained a poor and trifling thing to the end of time."

Then he began to laugh in the most unfeeling way, and make fun of the human race, although he knew that what he had been saying shamed us and wounded us. No one but an angel could have acted so; but suffering is nothing to them; they do not know what it is, except by hearsay.

More than once Seppi and I had tried in a humble and diffident way to convert him, and as he had remained silent we had taken his silence as a sort of encouragement; necessarily, then, this talk of his was a disappointment to us, for it showed that we had made no deep impression upon him. The thought made us sad, and we knew then how the missionary must feel when he has been cherishing a glad hope and has seen it blighted. We kept our grief to ourselves, knowing that this was not the time to continue our work.

Satan laughed his unkind laugh to a finish; then he said: "It is a remarkable progress. In five or six thousand years five or six high civilizations have risen, flourished, commanded the wonder of the world, then faded out and disappeared; and not one of them except the latest ever invented any sweeping and adequate way to kill people. They all did their best—to kill being the chiefest ambition of the human race and the earliest incident in its history—but only the Christian civilization has scored a triumph to be proud of. Two or three cen-

[15] Paine and Duneka deleted a part of Satan's history pageant that included references to the Boer War, to Jameson's Raid, and to the Boxer Rebellion and the occupation of China.

turies from now it will be recognized that all the competent killers are Christians; then the pagan world will go to school to the Christian—not to acquire his religion, but his guns. The Turk and the Chinaman will buy those to kill missionaries and converts with."

By this time his theater was at work again, and before our eyes nation after nation drifted by, during two or three centuries, a mighty procession, an endless procession, raging, struggling, wallowing through seas of blood, smothered in battle-smoke through which the flags glinted and the red jets from the cannon darted; and always we heard the thunder of the guns and the cries of the dying.

["And what does it amount to?" said Satan, with his evil chuckle. "Nothing at all. You gain nothing; you always come out where you went in. For a million years the race has gone on monotonously propagating itself and monotonously reperforming this dull nonsense—to what end? No wisdom can guess! Who gets a profit out of it? Nobody but a parcel of usurping little monarchs and nobilities who despise you; would feel defiled if you touched them; would shut the door in your face if you proposed to call; whom you slave for, fight for, die for, and are not ashamed of it, but proud; whose existence is a perpetual insult to you and you are afraid to resent it; who are mendicants supported by your alms, yet assume toward you the airs of benefactor toward beggar; who address you in the language of master to slave, and are answered in the language of slave and master; who are worshiped by you with your mouth, while in your heart—if you have one—you despise yourselves for it. The first man was a hypocrite and a coward, qualities which have not yet failed in his line; it is the foundation upon which all civilizations have been built. Drink to their perpetuation! Drink to their augmentation! Drink to—" Then he saw by our faces how much we were hurt, and he cut his sentence short and stopped chuckling, and his manner changed. He said, gently: "No, we will drink one another's health, and let civilization go. The wine which has flown to our hands out of space by desire is earthly, and good enough for that other toast; but throw away the glasses; we will drink this one in wine which has not visited this world before."]

We obeyed, and reached up and received the new cups as they descended. They were shapely and beautiful goblets, but they were not made of any material that we were acquainted with. They seemed to be in motion, they seemed to be alive; and certainly the colors in them were in motion. They were very brilliant and sparkling, and of every tint, and they were never still, but flowed to and fro in rich tides which met and broke and flashed out dainty explosions of enchanting color. I think it was most like opals washing about in waves and flashing out their splendid fires. But there is nothing to compare the wine with. We drank it, and felt a strange and witching ecstasy as of heaven go stealing through us, and Seppi's eyes filled and he said, worshipingly:

"We shall be there some day, and then—"

He glanced furtively at Satan, and I think he hoped Satan would say, "Yes, you will be there some day," but Satan seemed to be thinking about something else, and said nothing. This made me feel ghastly, for I knew he had heard; nothing, spoken or unspoken, ever escaped him. Poor Seppi looked distressed, and did not finish his remark. The goblets rose and clove their way into the sky, a triplet of radiant sundogs, and disappeared. Why didn't they stay? It seemed a bad sign, and depressed me. Should I ever see mine again? Would Seppi ever see his?[16]

Chapter IX

It was wonderful, the mastery Satan had over time and distance. For him they did not exist. He called them human inventions, and said they were artificialities. We often went to the most distant parts of the globe with him, and stayed weeks and months, and yet were gone only a fraction of a second, as a rule. You could prove it by the clock. One day when our people were in such awful distress because the witch commission were afraid to proceed against the astrologer and Father Peter's household, or against any, indeed, but the poor and the friendless, they lost patience and took to witch-hunting on their own score, and began to chase a born lady who was known to have the habit of curing people by devilish arts, such as bathing them, washing them, and nourishing them instead of bleeding them and purging them through the ministrations of a barber-surgeon in the proper way. She came flying down, with the howling and cursing mob after her, and tried to take refuge in houses, but the doors were shut in her face. They chased her more than half an hour, we following to see it, and at last she was exhausted and fell, and they caught her. They dragged her to a tree and threw a rope over the limb, and began to make a noose of it, some holding her, meantime, and she crying and begging, and her young daughter looking on and weeping, but afraid to say or do anything.

They hanged the lady, and I threw a stone at her, although in my heart I was sorry for her; but all were throwing stones and each was watching his neighbor, and if I had not done as the others did

[16] Following this paragraph Paine and Duneka omitted from the manuscript about four thousand words concerning Satan's love of animals, his foreknowledge, and his turning a bully into a statue. A fly that is on the bully's face at the time is also turned to stone; a lengthy dispute concerns the question of whether or not it was just to punish the innocent fly as well as the guilty man.

it would have been noticed and spoken of. Satan burst out laughing.

All that were near by turned upon him, astonished and not pleased. It was an ill time to laugh, for his free and scoffing ways and his supernatural music had brought him under suspicion all over the town and turned many privately against him. The big blacksmith called attention to him now, raising his voice so that all should hear, and said:

"What are you laughing at? Answer! Moreover, please explain to the company why you threw no stone."

"Are you sure I did not throw a stone?"

"Yes. You needn't try to get out of it; I had my eye on you."

"And I—I noticed you!" shouted two others.

"Three witnesses," said Satan: "Mueller, the blacksmith; Klein, the butcher's man; Pfeiffer, the weaver's journeyman. Three very ordinary liars. Are there any more?"

"Never mind whether there are others or not, and never mind about what you consider us—three's enough to settle your matter for you. You'll prove that you threw a stone, or it shall go hard with you."

"That's so!" shouted the crowd, and surged up as closely as they could to the center of interest.

"And first you will answer that other question," cried the blacksmith, pleased with himself for being mouthpiece to the public and hero of the occasion. "What are you laughing at?"

Satan smiled and answered, pleasantly: "To see three cowards stoning a dying lady when they were so near death themselves."

You could see the superstitious crowd shrink and catch their breath, under the sudden shock. The blacksmith, with a show of bravado, said:

"Pooh! What do you know about it?"

"I? Everything. By profession I am a fortuneteller, and I read the hands of you three—and some others—when you lifted them to stone the woman. One of you will die to-morrow week; another of you will die to-night; the third has but five minutes to live—and yonder is the clock!"

It made a sensation. The faces of the crowd blanched, and turned mechanically toward the clock. The butcher and the weaver seemed smitten with an illness, but the blacksmith braced up and said, with spirit:

"It is not long to wait for prediction number one. If it fails, young master, you will not live a whole minute after, I promise you that."

No one said anything; all watched the clock in a deep stillness which was impressive. When four and a half minutes were gone the blacksmith gave a sudden gasp and clapped his hands upon his heart, saying, "Give me breath! Give me room!" and began to sink down. The crowd surged back, no one offering to support him, and he fell lumbering to the ground and was dead. The people stared at him, then

t Satan, then at one another; and their lips moved, but no words
ame. Then Satan said:

"Three saw that I threw no stone. Perhaps there are others; let
hem speak."

It struck a kind of panic into them, and, although no one answered
im, many began to violently accuse one another, saying, "You said
e didn't throw," and getting for reply, "It is a lie, and I will make you
at it!" And so in a moment they were in a raging and noisy turmoil,
nd beating and banging one another; and in the midst was the only
ndifferent one—the dead lady hanging from her rope, her troubles
orgotten, her spirit at peace.

So we walked away, and I was not at ease, but was saying to
nyself, "He told them he was laughing at them, but it was a lie—he
vas laughing at me."

That made him laugh again, and he said, "Yes, I was laughing at
ou, because, in fear of what others might report about you, you stoned
he woman when your heart revolted at the act—but I was laughing
t the others, too."

"Why?"

"Because their case was yours."

"How is that?"

"Well, there were sixty-eight people there, and sixty-two of them
ad no more desire to throw a stone than you had."

"Satan!"

"Oh, it's true. I know your race. It is made up of sheep. It is
overned by minorities, seldom or never by majorities. It suppresses
s feelings and its beliefs and follows the handful that makes the most
oise. Sometimes the noisy handful is right, sometimes wrong; but no
natter, the crowd follows it. The vast majority of the race, whether
avage or civilized, are secretly kindhearted and shrink from inflicting
ain, but in the presence of the aggressive and pitiless minority they
on't dare to assert themselves. Think of it! One kindhearted creature
oies upon another, and sees to it that he loyally helps in iniquities
hich revolt both of them. Speaking as an expert, I know that ninety-
ine out of a hundred of your race were strongly against the killing
f witches when that foolishness was first agitated by a handful of
ious lunatics in the long ago. And I know that even to-day, after ages
f transmitted prejudice and silly teaching, only one person in twenty
uts any real heart into the harrying of a witch. And yet apparently
verybody hates witches and wants them killed. Some day a handful
ill rise up on the other side and make the most noise—perhaps even a
ngle daring man with a big voice and a determined front will do it—
nd in a week all the sheep will wheel and follow him, and witch-
unting will come to a sudden end.

"Monarchies, aristocracies, and religions are all based upon that
rge defect in your race—the individual's distrust of his neighbor, and

his desire, for safety's or comfort's sake, to stand well in his neighbor's eye. These institutions will always remain, and always flourish, and always oppress you, affront you, and degrade you, because you will always be and remain slaves of minorities. There was never a country where the majority of the people were in their secret hearts loyal to any of these institutions."

I did not like to hear our race called sheep, and said I did not think they were.

"Still, it is true, lamb," said Satan. "Look at you in war—what mutton you are, and how ridiculous!"

"In war? How?"

"There has never been a just one, never an honorable one—on the part of the instigator of the war. I can see a million years ahead, and this rule will never change in so many as half a dozen instances. The loud little handful—as usual—will shout for the war. The pulpit will—warily and cautiously—object—at first; the great, big, dull bulk of the nation will rub its sleepy eyes and try to make out why there should be a war, and will say, earnestly and indignantly, 'It is unjust and dishonorable, and there is no necessity for it.' Then the handful will shout louder. A few fair men on the other side will argue and reason against the war with speech and pen, and at first will have a hearing and be applauded; but it will not last long; those others will outshout them, and presently the anti-war audiences will thin out and lose popularity. Before long you will see this curious thing: the speakers stoned from the platform, and free speech strangled by hordes of furious men who in their secret hearts are still at one with those stoned speakers—as earlier—but do not dare to say so. And now the whole nation—pulpit and all—will take up the war-cry, and shout itself hoarse, and mob any honest man who ventures to open his mouth; and presently such mouths will cease to open. Next the statesmen will invent cheap lies, putting the blame upon the nation that is attacked, and every man will be glad of those conscience-soothing falsities, and will diligently study them, and refuse to examine any refutations of them; and thus he will by and by convince himself that the war is just, and will thank God for the better sleep he enjoys after this process of grotesque self-deception."[17]

Chapter X

Days and days went by now, and no Satan. It was dull without him. But the astrologer, who had returned from his excursion to the moon, went about the village, braving public opinion, and getting a

---

[17] About three hundred words which followed here were omitted by Paine and Duneka. The passage contains further satire on the land-stealing tactics of the great powers.

stone in the middle of his back now and then when some witch-hater got a safe chance to throw it and dodge out of sight. Meantime two influences had been working well for Marget. That Satan, who was quite indifferent to her, had stopped going to her house after a visit or two had hurt her pride, and she had set herself the task of banishing him from her heart. Reports of Wilhelm Meidling's dissipation brought to her from time to time by old Ursula had touched her with remorse, jealousy of Satan being the cause of it; and so now, these two matters working upon her together, she was getting a good profit out of the combination—her interest in Satan was steadily cooling, her interest in Wilhelm was steadily warming. All that was needed to complete her conversion was that Wilhelm should brace up and do something that should cause favorable talk and incline the public toward him again.

The opportunity came now. Marget sent and asked him to defend her uncle in the approaching trial, and he was greatly pleased, and stopped drinking and began his preparations with diligence. With more diligence than hope, in fact, for it was not a promising case. He had many interviews in his office with Seppi and me, and threshed out our testimony pretty thoroughly, thinking to find some valuable grains among the chaff, but the harvest was poor, of course.

If Satan would only come! That was my constant thought. He could invent some way to win the case; for he had said it would be won, so he necessarily knew how it could be done. But the days dragged on, and still he did not come. Of course I did not doubt that it would win, and that Father Peter would be happy for the rest of his life, since Satan had said so; yet I knew I should be much more comfortable if he would come and tell us how to manage it. It was getting high time for Father Peter to have a saving change toward happiness, for by general report he was worn out with his imprisonment and the ignominy that was burdening him, and was like to die of his miseries unless he got relief soon.

At last the trial came on, and the people gathered from all around to witness it; among them many strangers from considerable distances. Yes, everybody was there except the accused. He was too feeble in body for the strain. But Marget was present, and keeping up her hope and her spirit the best she could. The money was present, too. It was emptied on the table, and was handled and caressed and examined by such as were privileged.

The astrologer was put in the witness box. He had on his best hat and robe for the occasion.[18]

Question. You claim that this money is yours?

Answer. I do.

Q. How did you come by it?

<hr>

[18] Paine and Duneka supplied this sentence and substituted "the astrologer" for "Father Adolf" in the preceding sentence.

A. I found the bag in the road when I was returning from a journey.

Q. When?

A. More than two years ago.

Q. What did you do with it?

A. I brought it home and hid it in a secret place in my observatory, intending to find the owner if I could.

Q. You endeavored to find him?

A. I made diligent inquiry during several months, but nothing came of it.

Q. And then?

A. I thought it not worth while to look further, and was minded to use the money in finishing the wing of the foundling-asylum connected with the priory and nunnery. So I took it out of its hiding-place and counted it to see if any of it was missing. And then—

Q. Why do you stop? Proceed.

A. I am sorry to have to say this, but just as I had finished and was restoring the bag to its place, I looked up and there stood Father Peter behind me.

Several murmured, "That looks bad," but others answered, "Ah, but he is such a liar!"

Q. That made you uneasy?

A. No; I thought nothing of it at the time, for Father Peter often came to me unannounced to ask for a little help in his need.

Marget blushed crimson at hearing her uncle falsely and impudently charged with begging, especially from one he had always denounced as a fraud, and was going to speak, but remembered herself in time and held her peace.

Q. Proceed.

A. In the end I was afraid to contribute the money to the foundling-asylum, but elected to wait yet another year and continue my inquiries. When I heard of Father Peter's find I was glad, and no suspicion entered my mind; when I came home a day or two later and discovered that my own money was gone I still did not suspect until three circumstances connected with Father Peter's good fortune struck me as being singular coincidences.

Q. Pray name them.

A. Father Peter had found his money in a path—I had found mine in a road. Father Peter's find consisted exclusively of gold ducats—mine also. Father Peter found eleven hundred and seven ducats—I exactly the same.

This closed his evidence, and certainly it made a strong impression on the house; one could see that.[19]

---

[19] Mark Twain wrote the trial scene that follows as a part of an initial spurt of work upon the "Eseldorf" version, either late in 1897 or in the early part of January 1898 (see note 9).

Wilhelm Meidling asked him some questions, then called us boys, and we told our tale. It made the people laugh, and we were ashamed. We were feeling pretty badly, anyhow, because Wilhelm was hopeless, and showed it. He was doing as well as he could, poor young fellow, but nothing was in his favor, and such sympathy as there was there was now plainly not with his client. It might be difficult for court and people to believe the astrologer's story, considering his character, but it was almost impossible to believe Father Peter's. We were already feeling badly enough, but when the astrologer's lawyer said he believed he would not ask us any questions—for our story was a little delicate and it would be cruel for him to put any strain upon it—everybody tittered, and it was almost more than we could bear. Then he made a sarcastic little speech, and got so much fun out of our tale, and it seemed so ridiculous and childish and every way impossible and foolish, that it made everybody laugh till the tears came; and at last Marget could not keep up her courage any longer, but broke down and cried, and I was so sorry for her.

Now I noticed something that braced me up. It was Satan standing alongside of Wilhelm! And there was such a contrast!—Satan looked so confident, had such a spirit in his eyes and face, and Wilhelm looked so depressed and despondent. We two were comfortable now, and judged that he would testify and persuade the bench and the people that black was white and white black, or any other color he wanted it. We glanced around to see what the strangers in the house thought of him, for he was beautiful, you know—stunning, in fact—but no one was noticing him; so we knew by that that he was invisible.

The lawyer was saying his last words; and while he was saying them Satan began to melt into Wilhelm. He melted into him and disappeared; and then there was a change, when his spirit began to look out of Wilhelm's eyes.

That lawyer finished quite seriously, and with dignity. He pointed to the money, and said:

"The love of it is the root of all evil. There it lies, the ancient tempter, newly red with the shame of its latest victory—the dishonor of a priest of God and his two poor juvenile helpers in crime. If it could but speak, let us hope that it would be constrained to confess that of all its conquests this was the basest and the most pathetic."

He sat down. Wilhelm rose and said:

"From the testimony of the accuser I gather that he found this money in a road more than two years ago. Correct me, sir, if I misunderstood you."

The astrologer said his understanding of it was correct.

"And the money so found was never out of his hands thenceforth up to a certain definite date—the last day of last year. Correct me, sir, if I am wrong."

The astrologer nodded his head. Wilhelm turned to the bench and said:

"If I prove that this money here was not that money, then it is not his?"

"Certainly not; but this is irregular. If you had such a witness it was your duty to give proper notice of it and have him here to—" He broke off and began to consult with the other judges. Meantime that other lawyer got up excited and began to protest against allowing new witnesses to be brought into the case at this late stage.

The judges decided that his contention was just and must be allowed.

"But this is not a new witness," said Wilhelm. "It has already been partly examined. I speak of the coin."

"The coin? What can the coin say?"

"It can say it is not the coin that the astrologer once possessed. It can say it was not in existence last December. By its date it can say this."

And it was so! There was the greatest excitement in the court while that lawyer and the judges were reaching for coins and examining them and exclaiming. And everybody was full of admiration of Wilhelm's brightness in happening to think of that neat idea. At last order was called and the court said:

"All of the coins but four are of the date of the present year. The court tenders its sincere sympathy to the accused, and its deep regret that he, an innocent man, through an unfortunate mistake, has suffered the undeserved humiliation of imprisonment and trial. The case is dismissed."

So the money could speak, after all, though that lawyer thought it couldn't. The court rose, and almost everybody came forward to shake hands with Marget and congratulate her, and then to shake with Wilhelm and praise him; and Satan had stepped out of Wilhelm and was standing around looking on full of interest, and people walking through him every which way, not knowing he was there. And Wilhelm could not explain why he only thought of the date on the coins at the last moment, instead of earlier; he said it just occurred to him, all of a sudden, like an inspiration, and he brought it right out without any hesitation, for, although he didn't examine the coins, he seemed, somehow, to know it was true. That was honest of him, and like him; another would have pretended he had thought of it earlier, and was keeping it back for a surprise.

He had dulled down a little now; not much, but still you could notice that he hadn't that luminous look in his eyes that he had while Satan was in him. He nearly got it back, though, for a moment when Marget came and praised him and thanked him and couldn't keep him from seeing how proud she was of him. The astrologer went off dissatisfied and cursing, and Solomon Isaacs gathered up the money and carried it away.[20] It was Father Peter's for good and all, now.

Satan was gone. I judged that he had spirited himself away to the jail to tell the prisoner the news; and in this I was right. Marget and the rest of us hurried thither at our best speed, in a great state of rejoicing.

Well, what Satan had done was this: he had appeared before that poor prisoner, exclaiming, "The trial is over, and you stand forever disgraced as a thief—by verdict of the court!"

The shock unseated the old man's reason. When we arrived, ten minutes later, he was parading pompously up and down and delivering commands to this and that and the other constable or jailer, and calling them Grand Chamberlain, and Prince This and Prince That, and Admiral of the Fleet, Field Marshal in Command, and all such fustian, and was as happy as a bird. He thought he was Emperor!

Marget flung herself on his breast and cried, and indeed everybody was moved almost to heartbreak. He recognized Marget, but could not understand why she should cry. He patted her on the shoulder and said:

"Don't do it, dear; remember, there are witnesses, and it is not becoming in the Crown Princess. Tell me your trouble—it shall be mended; there is nothing the Emperor cannot do." Then he looked around and saw old Ursula with her apron to her eyes. He was puzzled at that, and said, "And what is the matter with you?"

Through her sobs she got out words explaining that she was distressed to see him—"so." He reflected over that a moment, then muttered, as if to himself: "A singular old thing, the Dowager Duchess—means well, but is always snuffling and never able to tell what it is about. It is because she doesn't know." His eye fell on Wilhelm. "Prince of India," he said, "I divine that it is you that the Crown Princess is concerned about. Her tears shall be dried; I will no longer stand between you; she shall share your throne; and between you you shall inherit mine. There little lady, have I done well? You can smile now—isn't it so?"

He petted Marget and kissed her, and was so contented with himself and with everybody that he could not do enough for us all, but began to give away kingdoms and such things right and left, and the least that any of us got was a principality. And so at last, being persuaded to go home, he marched in imposing state; and when the

[20] Following this sentence, on page 386 of the holograph, the writing is in the gray ink that Mark Twain used in the later-written parts of the "Eseldorf" version, instead of the black ink that he used in the parts written near the end of 1897. It was here that Mark Twain, after inserting the denouement that he had written about two and one-half years earlier, continued his work upon the story in the summer of 1900.

crowds along the way saw how it gratified him to be hurrahed at, they humored him to the top of his desire, and he responded with condescending bows and gracious smiles, and often stretched out a hand and said, "Bless you, my people!"

As pitiful a sight as ever I saw. And Marget, and old Ursula crying all the way.

On my road home I came upon Satan, and reproached him with deceiving me with that lie. He was not embarrassed, but said, quite simply and composedly:

"Ah, you mistake; it was the truth. I said he would be happy the rest of his days, and he will, for he will always think he is the Emperor, and his pride in it and his joy in it will endure to the end. He is now, and will remain, the one utterly happy person in this empire."

"But the method of it, Satan, the method! Couldn't you have done it without depriving him of his reason?"

It was difficult to irritate Satan, but that accomplished it.

"What an ass you are!" he said. "Are you so unobservant as not to have found out that sanity and happiness are an impossible combination? No sane man can be happy, for to him life is real, and he sees what a fearful thing it is. Only the mad can be happy, and not many of those. The few that imagine themselves kings or gods are happy, the rest are no happier than the sane. Of course, no man is entirely in his right mind at any time, but I have been referring to the extreme cases. I have taken from this man that trumpery thing which the race regards as a Mind; I have replaced his tin life with a silver-gilt fiction; you see the result—and you criticize! I said I would make him permanently happy, and I have done it. I have made him happy by the only means possible to his race—and you are not satisfied!" He heaved a discouraged sigh, and said, "It seems to me that this race is hard to please."

There it was, you see. He didn't seem to know any way to do a person a favor except by killing him or making a lunatic out of him. I apologized, as well as I could; but privately I did not think much of his processes—at that time.[21]

Satan was accustomed to say that our race lived a life of continuous and uninterrupted self-deception. It duped itself from cradle

[21] Mark Twain changed to a different paper at this point. He used both the paper of the preceding part and the one of the following part for other manuscripts that he wrote in the summer of 1900 while in residence at Dollis Hill, London; however, the change may be one indication that he laid the "Eseldorf" manuscript aside for at least a short time at this point before continuing it. In a following, editorially deleted, part of this chapter, there are direct references to the death of King Humbert of Italy, which occurred on July 29, 1900, and to related events of the three weeks following that date (discussed in *Mark Twain and Little Satan* in the section of this book devoted to criticism). In all probability, Mark Twain wrote the remaining few pages of the "Eseldorf" version in August 1900, while these events were fresh in his mind (see note 22).

to grave with shams and delusions which it mistook for realities, and this made its entire life a sham. Of the score of fine qualities which it imagined it had and was vain of, it really possessed hardly one. It regarded itself as gold, and was only brass. One day when he was in this vein he mentioned a detail—the sense of humor. I cheered up then, and took issue. I said we possessed it.

"There spoke the race!" he said; "always ready to claim what it hasn't got, and mistake its ounce of brass filings for a ton of gold-dust. You have a mongrel perception of humor, nothing more; a multitude of you possess that. This multitude see the comic side of a thousand low-grade and trivial things—broad incongruities, mainly; grotesqueries, absurdities, evokers of the horselaugh. The ten thousand high-grade comicalities which exist in the world are sealed from their dull vision.[22] Will a day come when the race will detect the funniness of these juvenilities and laugh at them—and by laughing at them destroy them? For your race, in its poverty, has unquestionably one really effective weapon—laughter. Power, money, persuasion, supplication, persecution—these can lift at a colossal humbug—push it a little—weaken it a little, century by century; but only laughter can blow it to rags and atoms at a blast. Against the assault of laughter nothing can stand. You are always fussing and fighting with your other weapons. Do you ever use that one? No; you leave it lying rusting. As a race, do you ever use it at all? No; you lack sense and the courage."[23]

We were traveling at the time and stopped at a little city in India and looked on while a juggler did his tricks before a group of natives. They were wonderful, but I knew Satan could beat that game, and I begged him to show off a little, and he said he would. He changed himself into a native in turban and breech-cloth, and very considerately conferred on me a temporary knowledge of the language.

The juggler exhibited a seed, covered it with earth in a small flower-pot, then put a rag over the pot; after a minute the rag began to rise; in ten minutes it had risen a foot; then the rag was removed and a little tree was exposed, with leaves upon it and ripe fruit. We ate the fruit, and it was good. But Satan said:

"Why do you cover the pot? Can't you grow the tree in the sunlight?"

[22] The particular example of "high-grade comicality" that Mark Twain here cited concerns an action of the Pope, who first sanctioned and then condemned a prayer composed by Queen Margherita for her excommunicated husband, King Humbert, after his death. In a passage deleted by Paine and Duneka, Mark Twain considers this instance of papal vacillation in relation to the doctrine of infallibility.

[23] Mark Twain here observed that Robert Burns had used the power of laughter to free Scotland of the domination of the Presbyterian Church. Paine and Duneka deleted this observation too.

"No," said the juggler; "no one can do that."

"You are only an apprentice; you don't know your trade. Give me the seed. I will show you." He took the seed and said, "What shall I raise from it?"

"It is a cherry seed; of course you will raise a cherry."

"Oh no; that is a trifle; any novice can do that. Shall I raise an orange-tree from it?"

"Oh yes!" and the juggler laughed.

"And shall I make it bear other fruits as well as oranges?"

"If God wills!" and they all laughed.

Satan put the seed in the ground, put a handful of dust on it, and said, "Rise!"

A tiny stem shot up and began to grow, and grew so fast that in five minutes it was a great tree, and we were sitting in the shade of it. There was a murmur of wonder, then all looked up and saw a strange and pretty sight, for the branches were heavy with fruits of many kinds and colors—oranges, grapes, bananas, peaches, cherries, apricots, and so on. Baskets were brought, and the unlading of the tree began; and the people crowded around Satan and kissed his hand, and praised him, calling him the prince of jugglers. The news went about the town, and everybody came running to see the wonder—and they remembered to bring baskets, too. But the tree was equal to the occasion; it put out new fruits as fast as any were removed; baskets were filled by the score and by the hundred, but always the supply remained undiminished. At last a foreigner in white linen and sun-helmet arrived, and exclaimed angrily:

"Away from here! Clear out, you dogs; the tree is on my lands and is my property."

The natives put down their baskets and made humble obeisance. Satan made humble obeisance, too, with his fingers to his forehead, in the native way, and said:

"Please let them have their pleasure for an hour, sir—only that, and no longer. Afterward you may forbid them; and you will still have more fruit than you and the state together can consume in a year."

This made the foreigner very angry, and he cried out, "Who are you, you vagabond, to tell your betters what they may do and what they mayn't!" and he struck Satan with his cane and followed this error with a kick.

The fruits rotted on the branches, and the leaves withered and fell. The foreigner gazed at the bare limbs with the look of one who is surprised, and not gratified. Satan said:

"Take good care of the tree, for its health and yours are bound together. It will never bear again, but if you tend it well it will live long. Water its roots once in each hour every night—and do it yourself; it must not be done by proxy, and to do it in daylight will not answer.

If you fail only once in any night, the tree will die, and you likewise. Do not go home to your own country any more—you would not reach there; make no business or pleasure engagements which require you to go outside your gate at night—you cannot afford the risk; do not rent or sell this place—it would be injudicious."

The foreigner was proud and wouldn't beg, but I thought he looked as if he would like to. While he stood gazing at Satan we vanished away and landed in Ceylon.

I was sorry for that man; sorry Satan hadn't been his customary self and killed him or made him a lunatic.[24] It would have been a mercy. Satan overheard the thought, and said:

"I would have done it but for his wife, who has not offended me. She is coming to him presently from their native land, Portugal. She is well, but has not long to live, and has been yearning to see him and persuade him to go back with her next year. She will die without knowing he can't leave that place."

"He won't tell her?"

"He? He will not trust that secret with anyone; he will reflect that it could be revealed in sleep, in the hearing of some Portuguese guest's servant some time or other."

"Did none of those natives understand what you said to him?"

"None of them understood, but he will always be afraid that some of them did. That fear will be torture to him, for he has been a harsh master to them. In his dreams he will imagine them chopping his tree down. That will make his days uncomfortable—I have already arranged for his nights."

It grieved me, though not sharply, to see him take such a malicious satisfaction in his plans for this foreigner.

"Does he believe what you told him, Satan?"

"He thought he didn't, but our vanishing helped. The tree, where there had been no tree before—that helped. The insane and uncanny variety of fruits—the sudden withering—all these things are helps. Let him think as he may, reason as he may, one thing is certain, he will water the tree. But between this and night he will begin his changed career with a very natural precaution—for him."

"What is that?"

"He will fetch a priest to cast out the tree's devil. You are such a humorous race—and don't suspect it."

"Will he tell the priest?"

"No. He will say a juggler from Bombay created it, and that he wants the juggler's devil driven out of it, so that it will thrive and be fruitful again. The priest's incantations will fail; then the Portuguese will give up that scheme and get his watering-pot ready."

[24] This sentence is not in the holograph; Mark Twain added it in ink to the typescript.

"But the priest will burn the tree. I know it; he will not allow it to remain."

"Yes, and anywhere in Europe he would burn the man, too. But in India the people are civilized, and these things will not happen. The man will drive the priest away and take care of the tree."

I reflected a little, then said, "Satan, you have given him a hard life, I think."

"Comparatively. It must not be mistaken for a holiday."[25]

We flitted from place to place around the world as we had done before, Satan showing me a hundred wonders, most of them reflecting in some way the weakness and triviality of our race. He did this now every few days—not out of malice—I am sure of that—it only seemed to amuse and interest him, just as a naturalist might be amused and interested by a collection of ants.[26]

Chapter XI

For as much as a year Satan continued these visits, but at last he came less often, and then for a long time he did not come at all. This always made me lonely and melancholy. I felt that he was losing interest in our tiny world and might at any time abandon his visits entirely. When one day he finally came to me I was overjoyed, but only for a little while. He had come to say good-by, he told me, and for the last time. He had investigations and undertakings in other corners of the universe, he said, that would keep him busy for a longer period than I could wait for his return.[27]

"And you are going away, and will not come back any more?"

"Yes," he said. "We have comraded long together, and it has been pleasant—pleasant for both; but I must go now, and we shall not see each other any more."

"In this life, Satan,[28] but in another? We shall meet in another, surely?"

---

[25] Following this sentence, a passage deleted by Paine and Duneka describes the further sufferings of the Portuguese who has been condemned to water the tree and also tells of further feats of magic by Satan, who easily outdoes a rival conjurer.

[26] This paragraph is in neither the holograph nor the typescript and apparently was added by the editors, as transitional matter, when *The Mysterious Stranger* was in press.

[27] This paragraph, like the last paragraph of Chapter 10, was added by Paine and Duneka. The remaining part of Chapter 11—all of it that Mark Twain wrote—was not a part of the "Eseldorf" manuscript. Mark Twain wrote it in 1904 as the conclusion of the "Print Shop" version (DV 328, MTP), a later and quite different form of the story.

[28] Here in place of "Satan" the holograph (there is no typescript of this fragmentary chapter in MTP) reads "44," the number-name of the mysterious stranger in the "Print Shop" version. Paine and Duneka crossed out this name and inserted "Satan" to make this part fit the "Eseldorf" version.

Then, all tranquilly and soberly, he made the strange answer, "There is no other."

A subtle influence blew upon my spirit from his, bringing with it a vague, dim, but blessed and hopeful feeling that the incredible words might be true—even *must* be true.

"Have you never suspected this, Theodor?"[29]

"No. How could I? But if it can only be true—"

"It is true."

A gust of thankfulness rose in my breast, but a doubt checked it before it could issue in words, and I said, "But—but—we have seen that future life—seen it in its actuality, and so—"

"It was a vision—it had no existence."

I could hardly breathe for the great hope that was struggling in me. "A vision?—a vi—"

"Life itself is only a vision, a dream."

It was electrical. By God! I had had that very thought a thousand times in my musings!

"*Nothing* exists; all is a dream. God—man—the world—the sun, the moon, the wilderness of stars—a dream, all a dream; they have no existence. *Nothing exists save empty space—and you!*"

"I!"

"And you are not you—you have no body, no blood, no bones, you are but a *thought*. I myself have no existence; I am but a dream—your dream, creature of your imagination. In a moment you will have realized this, then you will banish me from your visions and I shall dissolve into the nothingness out of which you made me. . . .

"I am perishing already—I am failing—I am passing away. In a little while you will be alone in shoreless space, to wander its limitless solitudes without friend or comrade forever—for you will remain a *thought,* the only existent thought, and by your nature inextinguishable, indestructible. But I, your poor servant, have revealed you to yourself and set you free. Dream other dreams, and better!

"Strange! that you should not have suspected years ago—centuries, ages, eons ago!—for you have existed, companionless, through all the eternities. Strange, indeed, that you should not have suspected that your universe and its contents were only dreams, visions, fiction! Strange, because they are so frankly and hysterically insane—like all dreams: a God who could make good children as easily as bad, yet preferred to make bad ones; who could have made every one of them happy, yet never made a single happy one; who made them prize their bitter life, yet stingily cut it short; who gave his angels eternal happiness unearned, yet required his other children to earn it; who

---

[29] The holograph here reads "August," the name of the narrator in the "Print Shop" version. Paine and Duneka changed this name to that used in the "Eseldorf" version.

gave his angels painless lives, yet cursed his other children with biting miseries and maladies of mind and body; who mouths justice and invented hell—mouths mercy and invented hell—mouths Golden Rules, and forgiveness multiplied by seventy times seven, and invented hell; who mouths morals to other people and has none himself; who frowns upon crimes, yet commits them all; who created man without invitation, then tries to shuffle the responsibility for man's acts upon man, instead of honorably placing it where it belongs, upon himself; and finally, with altogether divine obtuseness, invites this poor, abused slave to worship him! . . .

"You perceive, *now*, that these things are all impossible except in a dream. You perceive that they are pure and puerile insanities, the silly creations of an imagination that is not conscious of its freaks—in a word, that they are a dream, and you the maker of it. The dream-marks are all present; you should have recognized them earlier.

"It is true, that which I have revealed to you; there is no God, no universe, no human race, no earthly life, no heaven, no hell. It is all a dream—a grotesque and foolish dream. Nothing exists but you. And you are but a *thought*—a vagrant thought, a useless thought, a homeless thought, wandering forlorn among the empty eternities!"

He vanished, and left me appalled; for I knew, and realized, that all he had said was true.

PART TWO/TEXT AND STRUCTURE

The Structural Problem of
The Mysterious Stranger

EDWIN S. FUSSELL

UNFORTUNATELY, MOST OF THE ATTENTION THAT HAS BEEN DIRECTED TO
Mark Twain's "sulphurous little fairy tale," *The Mysterious Stranger*,
has been oriented primarily toward biographical inquiry and conjecture, or toward observation of the book's obvious and superficial
relations with other of Twain's works; unfortunately, for the information that this tale offers in the study of Twain as a personality can only
be understood in the light of the curious structural stresses and strains
of the work itself, and because, finally, thematic comparisons are valid
only if we consider *realized* themes, which have achieved existence
through the formalizing processes of art. *The Mysterious Stranger* is
Twain's most audacious fictional venture, and an analysis of its workings ought to tell us something about Twain as an artist, and, finally
and peripherally, something about Twain as a man.

Twain struggled inordinately with this story; it was the last of
several abortive attempts to get his late philosophic obsessions into
fictional form,[1] and even *The Mysterious Stranger*, in which Twain
appeared at first to have solved his artistic problem, was started and
laid aside several times before it was finally abandoned. What is undoubtedly the final chapter was found in Twain's papers by Albert B.
Paine, and attached to the uncompleted story when it was posthumously published in 1916. Because the tale was never formally
completed, one cannot properly speak of Twain's formal achievement;
but the very fact that Twain, even though he left the story unfinished,
was able to construct the conclusion corroborates our impression that
The Mysterious Stranger is somewhat unique in Twain's writings in
its degree of coherence of theme and in its adjustment of technique to
the realization of that theme. Twain, briefly, must have had rather

---

Edwin S. Fussell, "The Structural Problem of *The Mysterious Stranger*,"
Studies in Philology, XLIX (January 1952), 95–104. Reprinted by permission of
the University of North Carolina Press.

[1] These are discussed and analyzed in Bernard DeVoto, *Mark Twain at Work*
(Cambridge, Mass., 1942), pp. 121–130.

definite objectives clearly in mind as he wrote; what these goals were is revealed in the final chapter, and supported by evidence in the rest of the book. There is no doubt of the passion with which Twain threw himself into the work of composition; in 1899, he wrote Howells:[95]

> For several years I have been intending to stop writing for print as soon as I could afford it. At last I can afford it, and have put the potboiler pen away. What I have been wanting is a chance to write a book without reserves—a book which should take account of no one's feelings, and no one's prejudices, opinions, beliefs, hopes, illusions, delusions; a book which should say my say, right out of my heart, in the plainest language and without a limitation of any sort. I judged that that would be an unimaginable luxury, heaven on earth.
>
> It is under way, now, and it *is* a luxury! an intellectual drunk. Twice I didn't start it right; and got pretty far in, both times, before I found it out. But I am sure it is started right this time. It is in tale-form. I believe I can make it tell what I think of Man, and how he is constructed, and what a shabby poor ridiculous thing he is, and how mistaken he is in his estimate of his character and powers and qualities and his place among the animals. . . .
>
> I hope it will take me a year or two to write it, and that it will turn out to be the right vessel to contain all the abuse I am planning to dump into it.[2]

Twain's philosophic position during his late years can be described as a grotesque medley of fatalism, misanthropy, and cynicism. In general, he reflects the post-Darwinian pessimism of the late nineteenth century; the use of an inverted "Great Chain of Being" concept, his attacks on the "Moral Sense," and his contempt for human reason and dignity might all be considered part of Twain's undifferentiated response to the impact of evolutionary ideas. Twain seems to have been, temperamentally, both romantic and idealistic, and it is not surprising, then, that as he was increasingly tortured by his ideas, he should finally have toyed with the possibilities of solipsism, the last refuge of the romantic subjectivist. The final chapter of *The Mysterious Stranger* outlines a general theory of solipsism, and if this is accepted as the ultimate framework of the story, meaningful analysis becomes possible.

The solipsistic position is expounded with force and some lucidity by Twain, and there is little reason to refuse him serious audience. His interests in mental telepathy, spiritualism and dreams indicate that he had been moving toward such a position for several years. The notebooks and manuscripts of these years are crowded with references to dream and the nature of reality; the apparent reality and duration of the dream state is a topic that constantly recurs.[96] The solipsistic conclusion towards which Twain was apparently working is a theme

---

[2] Albert B. Paine, ed., *Mark Twain's Letters* (2 vols.; New York, 1917), II, 681.

imbedded in the whole story, and Twain has liberally posted signs to indicate its presence.

In order to render his solipsism in narrative form, Twain fell back on the time-honored dream-vision structure. This framework is obvious only in the light of Twain's final intentions, but there are enough hints along the way to prepare us for the final revelation. The second sentence of the story reads: "Austria was far away from the world and asleep." If the reader misses this suggestion, he is reminded again in the next paragraph:

Yes, Austria was far from the world, and asleep, and our village was in the middle of that sleep, being in the middle of Austria. It drowsed in peace in the deep privacy of a hilly and woodsy solitude where news from the world hardly ever came to disturb its dreams, and was infinitely content.[3]

The dream of peace will become a racking nightmare, but a feeling of unreality has been established, and Twain continues to supply details to reaffirm this basic condition. When Satan chooses a name to use among the villagers it is Philip Traum. The boys are frequently reported as feeling that the action of the tale is either too wonderful or too painful possibly to be true. When Satan has vanished for the first time, one of them remarks: "I suppose none of it has happened" (p. 29). Relating this first meeting with Satan, the narrator observes: "It seemed almost too good to be true, that we were actually seeing these romantic and wonderful things, and that it was not a dream" (p. 25).

The Mysterious Stranger is full of such preliminary notations which Twain intended to catch up at the end in Satan's assertion that life is nothing but dream stuff, and in his wonder that, with so much evidence, man seems unable to draw such a simple inference (the movement of the story, then, follows in fictional form the intellectual process of a man thinking his way through to the final solution of a baffling problem—here is the first suggestion of Twain's underlying anagogical meaning):

"Strange! that you should not have suspected years ago . . . Strange, indeed, that you should not have suspected that your universe and its contents were only dreams, visions, fiction! Strange, because they are so frankly and hysterically insane—like all dreams." (p. 150[97])

And after a brief but painful atheistic outburst, he concludes:

"You perceive, *now*, that these things are all impossible except in a dream. You perceive that they are pure and puerile insanities, the silly creations of an imagination that is not conscious of its freaks—in a word, that they are a dream, and you the maker of it. The dream-marks are all present; you should have recognized them earlier.

[3] *The Mysterious Stranger* (New York, 1916), p. 1. All subsequent citations in the present essay are to this volume.

"It is true, that which I have revealed to you; there is no God, no universe, no human race, no earthly life, no heaven, no hell. It is all a dream—a grotesque and foolish dream. Nothing exists but you. And you are but a *thought*—a thought, wandering forlorn among the empty eternities!" (p. 151)

The narrator accepts this total destruction of objective validity, and the story is over, the framework established. That Twain has committed intellectual suicide must have no weight in our acceptance of this structure, for by appreciating the framework he intended, much that is initially confusing in *The Mysterious Stranger* can be clarified, though many peripheral ambiguities will defy explanation.

A first reading of *The Mysterious Stranger* is likely to give an impression of meaningless disorder and frustrated purpose. The existence of allegory and symbolism is indisputable, but it is extraordinarily difficult to relate the action and the extra-literal significances in any very satisfactory manner. In various places, the story operates on several levels, either consecutively or simultaneously, and there often appears to be insufficient cohesion among these levels. The values of objects, characters, and events are constantly shifting: now the significances are sharply focussed, easily read, while a few pages later they will blur and then fade from sight. It may be taken for granted that Twain's architectonic powers were not of the first order in the full-length novel, but this is a short piece, and one might expect a more unified impression from a work on which so much devotion and care were lavished. Twain has open to him, of course, an aesthetic rationale for this apparent lack of integration, for logical patterns and clear vision are hardly to be demanded from a world that is "a grotesque and foolish dream"; the "imitation," as well as the thing imitated, may have been deliberately given "dream-marks."

But the basic confusion in *The Mysterious Stranger* arises from the nature of the peculiar philosophy which Twain tried to load onto "this vessel of abuse." The fictional problem approaches the threshold of desperation with the assumption that objective reality[98] is totally non-existent. To meet this challenge, Twain is compelled to accept certain phenomenal levels as real in order to get on with the story, though he eventually will destroy the whole fabric. And this compromise indicates a tortured conflict in Twain's soul between the philosophy he believed he had worked out so carefully on the ratiocinative level, and his total reaction to experience which denied the truth of this philosophy and continually rejected it as it came into perspective during composition. It is the perennial conflict between "thought" and "emotion," the perpetual agony of the faulty hypothesis: failure satisfactorily to arbitrate the claims of objective and subjective phenomena ultimately explains the basic confusion in *The Mysterious Stranger*.

In order to illustrate the fluidity of Twain's method, one might consider briefly the shifting symbolic values attributable to Satan. He is first presented on the literal level as an unexceptionable and ordinarily attractive young man; his initial impression on Twain's boys is simply that of a pleasant stranger. Through his performance of a series of suggestive tricks, he is gradually given more extensive significance, though most of his legerdemain seems to have no further function than the establishment of his supernatural status.[4] A characteristically Twain detail, and one that sends us back into biography, is Satan's capacity in mental telegraphy.

Suddenly Satan assumes additional stature, as he commences the creation of microcosmic units for the pleasure and edification of his young friends (and the reader). Although he announces himself as an angel he is, at this point, a symbol of deity, and his actions imitate in little the creation of the world.[5] With this technique, Twain is enabled to hold forth simultaneously on the paltry and debased nature of man and the indifference or malignity of the[99] deity—two chief items in the "abuse" he was most anxious to load onto this fictional vehicle. The microcosm is, of course, the type of the macrocosm, and the boys, curiously detached from normal involvement by what can only be called "internal philosophic distance," are enabled to comprehend in one vision both Creator and Creation. Meanwhile, action on the superficial level continues: the Lilliputian inhabitants of the tiny world fall to blows and Satan indifferently snuffs them out. This action, of course, arouses, as Twain was determined that it should, the boys' "moral" and "Humanitarian" feelings, feelings which Twain was eager to discredit. Satan now assumes more explicitly his role of "angel," as he tries to explain how angels differ from men on these matters. This whole scene is realized with a surprising degree of imaginative integrity somewhat reminiscent of Voltaire; the use of suggestive detail is delicate, charming, and mordant, and the little world has all the appearance of reality. Both spectators and reader know otherwise, and this gives Twain an early opportunity to question the nature of reality; it also gives the skillful artist a complex ironic situation, obviously dependent upon different planes of experience and divergent points of view. And by a nearly inevitable logical extension, the empty and meaningless illusion of Satan's creation is transferred

---

[4] One exception might be taken: the boys have forgotten materials for lighting their pipes; Satan lights them by blowing on them. This may possibly be read as a back-handed slap at the *Genesis* account of man's creation, but this detail is not clarified in the context and remains nebulous. In "Sold to Satan," a brief sketch collected in *Europe and Elsewhere,* there is a somewhat similar incident, and the conclusion of the sketch also bears a vague resemblance to the end of *The Mysterious Stranger;* the analogous incidents are, however, so sharply different in tone and intention, that one can hardly bring evidence from the sketch for elucidation of the tale.

[5] Twain's "philosophy," at such a point, bears a curious resemblance to that of his near-contemporary, Thomas Hardy.

to the universe at large. In one sense, we are already arrived at the solipsistic conclusion, though epistemological difficulties remain. How, in other words, given Twain's general framework, can this episode (and others) be assumed to confer valid information? There is only one possible reconciliation, shoddy as it is, and it is in fact the one that seems to be imbedded in the structure of *The Mysterious Stranger:* for just as the microcosm is unreal, so is the whole event, Satan and all, equally unreal; what Twain has presented is not final truth, but simply preliminary approximation. Through a series of such apparent but only proximate truths, Satan conducts the narrator, as Twain conducts the reader, to the final revelation. In the last view, deity can hardly be either malignant or indifferent, for it is totally non-existent; nonetheless, the view of deity as evil is, one is supposed to believe, more consonant with the phenomena which the "thought" (or individual) is able to apprehend than are traditional theological notions of God's attributes, and this level of illumination may then be taken as a partial "enlightenment," a limited intellectual progress.[100]

Satan functions in a variety of ways in the implementation of Twain's theories. He is a detached satiric observer, a good mouthpiece for Twain's misanthropy; additionally, his supra-human status renders somewhat more palatable Twain's tortured assault on the rational and ethical pretensions of the "damned human race." But this role is more expository than functional, and of less importance than his utility as an artificer and explicator of mechanisms illustrative of Twain's sophomoric fatalism. Here Satan, omniscient and presumably omnipotent as well, demonstrates the excessive concentration on causation (without any very clear comprehension of the problems involved) that so overwhelmed Twain, simply by altering apparently insignificant links in the lives of the villagers, and thereby sending them to unsuspected disasters (according to human terms). Initially, this action is hardly motivated at all, and philosophically considered it is absurd, but once in operation and purely on the level of fantasy, it is surprisingly convincing, one of Twain's most aesthetically satisfying performances. One might notice, finally, Satan's intoxicating effect on the villagers, an effect which might be characterized as that of a low-voltage mystic experience. In his presence, feelings of ecstasy and enchantment gradually operate to overcome preconceptions and to pave the way for acceptance of startling new orientations. Considering Twain's views about the determinism of ideas, it would hardly have done for the narrator to accept at once the full implications of his world-view (nor could there have been any story, in such a case); his mind had to be prepared step by step, since the mind can only accept that for which it is prepared by previous experience. And in this progressive illumination resides, one finally sees, both the content and the form of *The Mysterious Stranger*. Abstracted, ideational determinism is plot; extended, it is also Twain's content, subject, and material.

Through an examination of these various roles emerges one constant factor. Satan is at all times the instructor, and every speech and action finally tends towards the communication of knowledge and "truth." Very little that Satan reveals (and this is the bulk of the tale) is ultimately true, yet he continually provides partial illumination, relative to the particular plateau of enlightenment that has been reached at that juncture in the story. And when he finally leads the narrator to the concluding vision, he says of himself:[101]

"I myself have no existence; I am but a dream—your dream, creature of your imagination. In a moment you will have realized this, then you will banish me from your visions and I shall dissolve into the nothingness out of which you made me . . .

"I am perishing already—I am failing—I am passing away. . . . But I, your poor servant, have revealed you to your self and set you free." (pp. 149–150)

Perhaps one ought not to press the issue, but in general function, if not in every detail, Satan has represented intuition all along. Gradually he has suggested the truth to the narrator, through a long series of lessons he has prepared the will for acceptance; one overpowering flash of insight, represented dramatically by Satan's last speech, is terminal:

He vanished, and left me appalled; for I knew, and realized, that all he had said was true. (p. 151)

By putting his figures through these various progressive phases from unreality (literal materiality) to reality (solipsistic ideality), Twain has forced a certain degree of unity on his episodic structure; by treating each phase provisionally as if it were the only reality, he has eaten his cake all along and still has it at the end. He has denounced with abandon and with gusto, passed moral sentence on man's activities, and he concludes by wildly controverting all injustice, pain, and evil whatsoever. Philosophically, *The Mysterious Stranger* is bunkum, but through the technique of gradual revelation, Twain has laid out his basic conceptions in an artistic pattern that demonstrates a surprising direction and continuity.[6]

And yet striking contradictions remain, despite Twain's potential achievement of a certain degree of formal unity, and they cannot easily be dismissed. The presence of a strong satiric intention, for[102]

---

[6] One very serious flaw in the general pattern of functional development ought to be noticed: Twain occasionally allows Satan to become a purely humorous character, temporarily obscuring his organic utility. At one point, for instance, the mysterious stranger is said to be the nephew of the more conventional Satan, the original fallen angel. The temptation to employ this uncle-nephew relationship for comic irony was apparently irresistible, and Twain was never one to pass up a good thing. But the comedy has no integral relation with the narrative progress, and is surely inconsistent with the larger effect. Such a lapse of decorum suggests a certain lack of control and vagueness of aim, and it points, once again, to the serious indecision underlying the whole work.

example, demands some examination. One of Satan's most significant speeches concerns the social efficacy of laughter, perhaps the most eloquent statement on the function of satire that Twain ever made. The speech in question is preceded by a bitter attempt to strip man of his illusory virtues; Satan proceeds to make a single concession to human dignity:

"You have a mongrel perception of humor, nothing more; a multitude of you possess that. This multitude see the comic side of a thousand low-grade and trivial things—broad incongruities, mainly; grotesqueries, absurdities, evokers of the horse-laugh. The ten thousand high-grade comicalities which exist in the world are sealed from their dull vision. Will a day come when the race will detect the funniness of these juvenilities and laugh at them—and by laughing at them destroy them? For your race, in its poverty, has unquestionably one really effective weapon—laughter. Power, money, persuasion, supplication, persecution—these can lift at a colossal humbug—push it a little—weaken it a little, century by century; but only laughter can blow it to rags and atoms at a blast. Against the assault of laughter nothing can stand. You are always fussing and fighting with your other weapons. Do you ever use that one? No; you leave it lying rusting. As a race, do you ever use it at all? No; you lack sense and the courage." (pp. 141–142)

Twain is here considering satire as a positive social force, not as the cynical and futile railing one might expect from a mechanistic and misanthropic philosopher in a "closed" universe. Correlated either with Twain's solipsism or with his fatalism, this satiric weapon could have no possible meaning. A satisfactory resolution of this confusion is manifestly impossible, but one may return to one of the structural qualities of *The Mysterious Stranger*, apply it here as a tentative hypothesis, and carry deep into the heart of the peculiar tensions of this tale. Twain was apparently compelled (and here the personal motivation reinforces the artistic), as he explored his fictive problem, to accept "reality" as a relative term, fashioning his attack to the level of reality then under consideration. Although the ultimate truth may be quite otherwise, the apparent reality (and here one is carried back to biography again, into the notebook entries on dream) is sufficiently vivid to force certain limited values. For, in spite of his more volatile outbursts, Twain's cynicism and misanthropy were sorrowfully inexpressive of his total orientation to life. Constantly, in reading *The Mysterious Stranger*, one observes Twain's emotional reactions in serious conflict with his theoretical formulations. His sympathies are deeply[103] involved in the human predicament, his heart continues to ache, as it always had, over injustice, misery, oppression, or sorrow. Life in the abstract may be paltry, meaningless, finally unreal; but in direct experience, in passion and suffering, certain values and a limited dignity emerge. In one suggestive passage, Twain illustrates what is happening:

He [Satan] had never felt a pain or a sorrow, and did not know what they were, in any really informing way. He had no knowledge of them except theoretically—that is to say, intellectually. And of course that is no good. One can never get any but a loose and ignorant notion of such things except by experience. (p. 112)

And with this statement, one must juxtapose another, chronologically the latest comment in the tale. The narrator is now an old man, recapturing in memory the essence of the past; he has long since accepted the belief that he is only a random thought, fictitiously creating and peopling a mechanistic and meaningless dream-universe, a world whose unreality is proved by its evil and insanity. Yet in recollection, reality and virtue furtively take on significance:

It was an awful eleven days; and yet, with a lifetime stretching back between to-day and then, they are still a grateful memory to me, and beautiful. In effect, they were days of companionship with one's sacred dead, and I have known no comradeship that was so close or so precious. (p. 101)

This is probably the final tension that Twain could never organize. Form, to a certain extent, he might have achieved, and in the face of such obstacles, his very attempt seems heroic. But Twain's failure as artist meant a partial personal salvation, for a total artistic integration could only have been purchased by a total destruction of the artist's humanity.[104]

An Auspicious Beginning, a Disjointed Middle, and a Great Final Chapter

EDMUND REISS

TWAIN OVERHAULED THE WORK [THE MYSTERIOUS STRANGER] AT LEAST twice; but even at the time of his death, he had not attached the ending. The great final chapter was "found" by Albert Bigelow Paine, Twain's literary executor, in a heap of fragmentary papers, selected as the intended ending, and attached to the work, which was first printed

From Edmund Reiss, Foreword to Mark Twain, "*The Mysterious Stranger*" *and Other Stories* (New York: New American Library of World Literature, 1962), pp. xiii–xv. Reprinted by permission of the publisher.

posthumously in 1916. Whether or not Paine's discovery represents the ending Twain intended for the piece, it nevertheless brings the work together and gives it direction.

Although beginning auspiciously, the novelette tends to become disjointed. The questions of the worth of man, of the ambiguity of good and evil, of free will, of the Moral Sense, begin to fade into the background as Twain emphasizes the adventurous part of the story. The wonderful irony of the boy-angel, Satan, in the earthly paradise, Eseldorf (Jackassville), of his being both the creator and destroyer of life, fades as Twain makes his narrator, Theodor Fischer, the center of his attention. Father Peter's freedom becomes a dominant issue, and we see Theodor almost become the boy-hero-rescuer—the Tom Sawyer freeing Jim from the bedpost—who is a stock character in a stock scene in Twain's fiction. Incidents that are interesting but distracting begin to appear. In not contributing much to the whole work, many of[xiii] Theodor's adventures, which may have been designed earlier as part of an initiation of sorts, are comparable to those of Faustus and Mephistophilis in the middle scenes of Marlowe's play— satirical, curious, but yet, as they stand, not really necessary. It is with the final chapter that *The Mysterious Stranger* regains the intensity of its opening episodes.

One must note, however, that Twain's works are rarely tied up neatly in packages of the right shape and the proper color; and usually the string around them is somewhat loose. The works rarely achieve the organized direction and unity found in *Huckleberry Finn,* but at the same time they also rarely achieve the intensity of language and general effect seen in *The Mysterious Stranger.* Moreover, while Twain had a tendency to concentrate on matters of momentary relevance at the expense of basic philosophical problems, he has here written a work unhurt by topical allegory or by matters belonging on the editorial page of a newspaper.

Still, one might question the effectiveness of the overt didacticism throughout and at the end of *The Mysterious Stranger.* Although the work is effective because of its philosophizing, it falls short of the artistic achievement of "The Man That Corrupted Hadleyburg." There Twain does not have to intrude into the story to announce his theme. Everything from the beginning of the story leads to the end, and the reader is swept along and made to see the theme and feel the author's attitude without the author's having to throw away his narrative garb and come out in front of the footlights to address him. "Hadleyburg," even with all is narrative art, is, however, tame and undramatic beside *The Mysterious Stranger,* especially beside its memorable and really tormenting conclusion. "Hadleyburg" is like the first two books of *Gulliver's Travels*—controlled and well organized—and Twain is like the Swift of these books—calm, detached, and objective. But *The Mysterious Stranger* suggests the account of Gulliver's fourth voyage, the voyage to Houyhnhnmland, with its bitter invective against mankind. Twain begins in full control but ends with a violent burst[xiv] suggestive of the savage frenzy of Swift in this section of the *Travels*.

The *Mysterious Stranger,* along with the other late writings of Twain, is not the work of an author sitting back in a comfortable easy chair dispassionately viewing life. It is rather the struggle of a man in the midst of life trying desperately to understand what he is and what he is a part of, what life is and why it is so bad. Twain is more than a *fin de siècle* writer fashionably mourning his fate; his cry is similar to that of all who have ever questioned and not been answered.[xv]

The Mysterious Stranger:
Mark Twain's Texts and the
Paine-Duneka Edition

JOHN S. TUCKEY

LEFT AMONG MARK TWAIN'S PAPERS AT THE TIME OF HIS DEATH WERE three versions of a story of a mysterious stranger, a character of superhuman powers. They are, as named and catalogued by Bernard DeVoto, the "Hannibal" manuscript of about fifteen thousand words; the "Eseldorf," of about fifty-five thousand words; and the "Print Shop," of some sixty-five thousand words. All are in Mark Twain's own handwriting. There are also in existence typescripts of the "Eseldorf" and of the "Print Shop" manuscript, as prepared under Mark Twain's direction and revised by him. These manuscripts and typescripts are among the Mark Twain Papers at the General Library of the University of California at Berkeley. They are the same materials that were available to Albert Bigelow Paine, Mark Twain's official biographer and literary executor, and to Frederick A. Duneka, then general manager of Harper & Brothers, when they edited what was posthumously published in 1916 as *The Mysterious Stranger*.[1] What these editors did in preparing the story for publication is itself a remarkable story.

Some idea of their massive editorial revisions can at once be suggested by saying that from the "Eseldorf" manuscript, used for all but the final brief chapter of *The Mysterious Stranger*, fully one-fourth of Mark Twain's wordage was deleted. One of Mark Twain's characters, Father Adolf, was partly edited out of the story, and another character, the astrologer, *whom Mark Twain did not have in his story at all*, was written in and made to perform most of the evil deeds that Mark Twain had attributed to Father Adolf, his intended villain.

The three versions are not so much different drafts of one story as three different stories. Each has for the most part different characters, situations, and actions. Even the mysterious strangers are differently characterized in each manuscript. Paine believed (and probably not mistakenly) that "Eseldorf" was the best of the versions. But the manuscript must have seemed to him quite unpublishable as it stood. The first chapter was largely devoted to a hostile characterization of the "dissolute and profane and malicious" priest[2]—and Paine and Duneka were probably hoping to provide a new Mark Twain story that would be suitable for the Christmas trade! Furthermore, "Eseldorf" had no well-sustained plot; the tale became by turns a satire on religious hypocrisy, an allegory of human life as seen in miniature, a sermon on the moral sense and its degrading effect upon the species, a story of youthful romance and love rivalry, an exemplum of deterministic doctrines, a burlesqued philosophical dispute, and a long, long diatribe on the corruption of *fin de siècle* civilization—to mention only some of the more lengthy sections. Insofar as there was a basic plot, it concerned the finding of the gold coins by the good priest Father Peter; his arrest for a theft charged against him by the bad priest; his imprisonment and trial; his finding happiness at last in insanity. But there were some almost unrelated episodes. Modes and moods were as variable: the story was satiric, comic, sentimental, farcical, didactic. Clearly, it needed integration. Paine and Duneka were not overly concerned with such matters as preserving the purity— what there was of it—of their author's text. Mark Twain's adverse representations of Father Adolf were either toned down or taken out entirely; the astrologer was introduced as a more acceptable villain. Also almost entirely deleted was a long passage in which the young Satan vied with youths of the village of Eseldorf for the regard of Lilly and Marget, using his powers to outdo his rivals. Only one

[1] *The Mysterious Stranger* was first published serially in *Harper's Magazine*, beginning with the issue of May 1916.

[2] See John S. Tuckey, *Mark Twain and Little Satan: The Writing of "The Mysterious Stranger"* (Lafayette, Ind.: Purdue University Studies, 1963), pp. 17–21.

paragraph of this passage survives in *The Mysterious Stranger*.[3] Like some other sections that were cut out, this one was very much aside from the main plot; moreover, much of it was not in the sombre mood that Paine and Duneka tended to emphasize by deleting other kinds of material.

Although Paine and Duneka allowed a considerable part of Mark Twain's satire to remain in *The Mysterious Stranger*, they also deleted much of it. For example, they struck from the typescript of "Eseldorf" that was used as the printer's copy for the published story more than forty pages of satiric commentary on civilization in the late nineteenth century. Moreover, they blunted or obscured much of the satire that was retained by omitting the specific objects of Mark Twain's attack. Explicit references to the Boer War, the actions of the Allied Powers in China, and the Spanish-American War were all carefully omitted. Printing the author's fulminations against wartime hypocrisies and atrocities without letting him say just what had provoked them tended to make Mark Twain appear bitter without sufficient grounds for bitterness, more despairing than there was any evident reason for being; in a word, pessimistic.

The "Eseldorf" manuscript also lacked an ending. But Paine had found a manuscript fragment that he believed to be Mark Twain's intended conclusion for *The Mysterious Stranger*. In his introduction to the story in the Definitive Edition, Paine related that one day at Stormfield (Mark Twain's home at Redding from June 1908 until his death) the author had said to him, "I always had a good deal of fancy for that story of mine, 'The Mysterious Stranger.' I could finish it, I suppose, any time, and I should like it some day to be published."[4] Paine also recalled, "A considerable time after his death—after the publication of my biography of him . . . I found among a confusion of papers that tremendous final chapter, which must have been written about the time of our conversation. It may even have been written prior to that time, laid aside and forgotten, for his memory was very treacherous during those later days." He added, "Happily, it was the ending of the story in its first form."[5]

Actually, as I have attempted to demonstrate in another context, there is strong evidence that Mark Twain wrote "that tremendous final chaper" in 1904, while he was living at Florence during Olivia's last illness. There is also positive evidence that he wrote it as a conclusion for the "Print Shop" version. The characters named in it, August and "44," are respectively the narrator and the mysterious

---

[3] In Chapter 7, where it is related that Satan charmed Marget by reciting poetry and that Wilhelm Meidling became jealous.

[4] Albert Bigelow Paine, introd., *The Mysterious Stranger and Other Stories*, in *The Writings of Mark Twain* (New York: Gabriel Wells, 1922–1925), XXVII, ix.

[5] *Ibid.*, x.

stranger of "Print Shop." These names were struck out and the names "Theodor" and "Satan" were inserted—in what appears to be Paine's handwriting.[6] Paine allowed himself to speak somewhat loosely in saying that the ending was that "of the story in its first form," since he believed (and rightly) that "Eseldorf" was the earliest version, and since he knew that the characters in Mark Twain's conclusion were not those of "Eseldorf." But if he had attempted to say anything at all about textual alterations, he might have had to say a great deal. And it must be remembered that Mark Twain had not yet become very much the concern of the scholarly; Paine would hardly have thought it needful to give an account that would interest textual critics.

Some further tinkering was needed to make the "Print Shop" ending fit the "Eseldorf" manuscript. Two transitional paragraphs were added—apparently while *The Mysterious Stranger* was in proof. The last paragraph of Chapter 10 and the first paragraph of Chapter 11 cannot be found in either the "Eseldorf" holograph or in the typescript that went to the printer. In all probability it was Paine who composed the transitional paragraphs, and one can admire his deftness if not his presumption. What he wrote is sufficiently in keeping with Mark Twain's own habits of thought and expression. Indeed, one writer has partly based a critical point regarding Mark Twain's pessimism on that editorially supplied last paragraph of Chapter 10. He ventures to find, in the comparison of Satan's attitude toward human beings to a naturalist's interest in a collection of ants, an indication that Mark Twain was drawing upon his reading of John Lubbock's *Ants, Bees, and Wasps* and Charles Darwin's *The Descent of Man*.[7] His point may still hold well enough, for the paragraph is quite passably, though not actually, Twainian. It should nevertheless be noted that the Paine-Duneka edition does have its pitfalls for literary critics.

Such traps are always likely to exist when a text deviates from the author's intended forms and usages. And it is perhaps only a mild exaggeration to say that the Paine-Duneka edition is about as far from Mark Twain's own latest intended form of *The Mysterious Stranger* as it would, on any ordinary working day, be possible to get. Paine, it has been seen, used what he believed (correctly) to be the *earliest* version—and gave the impression that even the concluding "Print Shop" chapter was written for that version. He explained that the other, *later* forms of the story were "lacking in interest, being mainly wanderings in those fantastic fields into which Mark Twain was prone to be tempted."[8] Although he underrated the interest of these other versions, Paine was probably right about the superior literary quality of the manuscripts he and Duneka used. In good

[6] See *Mark Twain and Little Satan,* p. 61.

[7] Edward Stone, *Voices of Despair: Four Motifs in American Literature* (Athens: Ohio University Press, 1966), pp. 64–65.

[8] *The Writings of Mark Twain,* XXVII, x.

time the world will be able to judge, for the three versions as Mark Twain wrote them will presently be available in a volume of the Mark Twain Papers series as prepared for publication by Professor William M. Gibson. That volume will be of great value for biographical and critical study, for it will reveal much about Mark Twain's processes of literary creation; it will also invite, indeed demand, comparison with the Paine-Duneka edition. But in any case *The Mysterious Stranger* not only does not represent Mark Twain's own intended form of the manuscripts on which it was based; it also does not represent Mark Twain's latest intended version of his story of a mysterious stranger. Moreover, the only version that Mark Twain himself seems ever to have *called* "The Mysterious Stranger" is the "Print Shop" manuscript. His title for the "Eseldorf" version had been "The Chronicle of Young Satan"; and he had designated the "Hannibal" version as the "Story of little Satan Jr. who came to Hannibal." When he took the initial chapter from the "Eseldorf" manuscript (after abandoning work on that version) and used it in beginning "Print Shop," he crossed out his original title and wrote "The Mysterious Stranger" as the name of his latest version.

It was the "Print Shop" version that Mark Twain was writing when he referred to his work on "The Mysterious Stranger" in letters and memoranda of the summer and fall of 1905. And it was that version that he would have had in mind in his dictation of August 30, 1906, when, after speaking of some of his half-finished books, he said, "There is yet another—*The Mysterious Stranger*. It is more than half finished. I would dearly like to finish it, and it causes me a real pang to reflect that it is not to be." He was, he said, "tired of the pen."[9]

That Paine and Duneka did not publish Mark Twain's own intended form of *The Mysterious Stranger* was not made evident by Bernard DeVoto's interpretations as put forward in his generally perceptive psychological study "The Symbols of Despair."[10] Although he acknowledged that he had not been able to date many of Mark Twain's later manuscripts and that he could not be sure of their chronology, DeVoto did perforce assume a chronology. But he believed that the "Eseldorf" version was the *latest* form of *The Mysterious Stranger* and that it had been written about 1905, marking the restoration of Mark Twain's literary talent after seven or eight barren years. There is evidence, however, that "Eseldorf" was indeed the earliest version, as Paine had thought, and that Mark Twain began it late in 1897 and at that time carried the tale well into the fifth chapter. He then wrote the brief "Hannibal" version in November 1898, between spurts of work on "Eseldorf." He worked again upon the "Eseldorf"

[9] *Mark Twain in Eruption,* ed. Bernard DeVoto (New York: Grosset & Dunlap, 1940), pp. 198–199.

[10] Bernard DeVoto, *Mark Twain at Work* (Cambridge, Mass.: Harvard University Press, 1942), pp. 105–130. (Reprinted in Part 3.)

manuscript in the fall of 1899 and again in the summer of 1900, and then abandoned it (references to contemporary events make firm datings possible). During several working periods between the fall of 1902 and the summer of 1905, he wrote the "Print Shop" version. He composed the greater part in 1904, and wrote the seven-hundred-word "Print Shop" ending, proclaiming life to be *only a vision, a dream,* in the spring or summer of that year. Thus *The Mysterious Stranger* as published was, except for the last few hundred words, written not about 1905 but between 1897 and 1900, or during what DeVoto believed had been the lowest ebb of Mark Twain's literary ability.[11] It was exactly during this supposed time of impotence and failure that Mark Twain composed all but one brief fragment of what DeVoto called "an almost perfect book—perfect in expression of his final drive, in imaginative projection of himself, in tone and tune, in final judgment"[12]—*The Mysterious Stranger.*

DeVoto was nearly silent regarding the gross revisions of Paine and Duneka. He wrote as if *The Mysterious Stranger* had been published just as Mark Twain had written it—except for the addition of the brief final chapter, which he regarded as Paine's greatest service to Mark Twain. Presumably he had examined "Eseldorf" closely enough to realize how very much it differed from the Paine-Duneka edition; yet it seems curious that he did not credit those collaborators, or coauthors, for a more considerable part of the supposed perfection of the story as published. His reticences, following those of Paine, have allowed an extraordinary textual problem to remain, for half a century, almost unrecognized.

The Paine-Duneka edition is really so different from the manuscripts upon which it was based that it is in some measure a fourth version, a collaborative creation. Despite its imperfections, it is also the only existing form of the story that has the coherence and completeness of a realized literary work ("Print Shop" has an ending— the only ending—but is lacking in integration; "Hannibal" is hardly more than a beginning). Corrupt as it is, the Paine-Duneka edition has held a place in our literature for more than half a century. Generally regarded as the most important work of Mark Twain's later years, it has received and is receiving much critical attention. Here, then, is the problem: to what extent must the merit and validity of such a literary creation depend upon its textual authority? *The Odyssey* is still *The Odyssey* no matter how many Homers it took to create it. To be sure, *The Mysterious Stranger* is no *Odyssey,* and Paine and Duneka are less than Homeric. But does the Paine-Duneka edition, under the existing circumstances, deserve to perish, to endure, or to prevail?

[11] See *Mark Twain and Little Satan,* pp. 16–78.
[12] *The Portable Mark Twain* (New York: The Viking Press, Inc., 1958), p. 25.

PART THREE/BACKGROUNDS

The Ordeal of Mark Twain

VAN WYCK BROOKS

IN 1899, WE FIND HIM [MARK TWAIN] WRITING AS FOLLOWS TO HOWELLS: "For several years I have been intending to stop writing for print as soon as I could afford it. At last I can afford it, and have put the potboiler pen away. What I have been wanting is a chance to write a book without reserves—a book which should take account of no one's feelings, and no one's prejudices, opinions,[240] beliefs, hopes, illusions, delusions: a book which should say my say, right out of my heart, in the plainest language and without a limitation of any sort. I judged that that would be an unimaginable luxury, heaven on earth. It is under way, now, and it *is* a luxury! an intellectual drunk." The book was *The Mysterious Stranger*. While he was under the spell of composing it, that sulphurous little fairy-tale seemed to him the fruition of his desire. But he was inhibited from publishing it, and this only poured oil upon the passion that possessed him. At once the craving reasserted itself with tenfold intensity. He tinkered incessantly at *What Is Man?* He wrote it and rewrote it, he read it to his visitors, he told his friends about it. Eventually he published this, but the fact that he felt he was obliged to do so anonymously fanned his insatiable desire still more. Something more personal he must write now! He fixed his mind on this with a consuming intensity. To express himself was no longer a mere artistic impulse; it had become a categorical imperative, a path out of what was for him a life of sin. . . .[241]

Was it not all, in that sound and healthy frame, the index of a soul that was mortally sick? Mark Twain's attack upon the failure of human life was merely a rationalization of the failure in himself.

And this failure was the failure of the artist in him.[248]

From Van Wyck Brooks, *The Ordeal of Mark Twain,* Revised Edition (New York: E. P. Dutton & Co., Inc., 1933), pp. 240–241, 248, by permission of the publisher. First published in 1920.

The Symbols of Despair

BERNARD DEVOTO

THIS ESSAY IS A CHAPTER, HITHERTO UNWRITTEN, IN THE BIOGRAPHY OF Mark Twain. Mr. Paine's *Mark Twain: a Biography* lists some of the manuscripts dealt with here and even devotes a few sentences of description to a few of them. But it is clear that Mr. Paine did not understand their significance and, if he had understood them, I think he would have regarded it as his duty to say nothing about them. Certainly as one reads his *Biography* one gets no proper sense of the effect on Mark Twain of the disasters which these manuscripts deal with.

Those disasters are agonizing as personal history. Our interest, however, is in the manuscripts which came out of them—we are concerned with them as a series of literary episodes. Those episodes occur in the life of a literary genius and by chance, a fortunate chance for criticism, they partly open up an area of literature which is usually closed. They make it possible to document, and so in some small degree to analyze, certain processes of creation. Criticism is usually altogether unable to say how a writer's experience is transformed into works of art. In these manuscripts we can actually see that transformation while it is occurring. We are able to watch Mark Twain while he repeatedly tries and repeatedly fails to make something of experiences that were vitally important to him—and finally we are able to see him fuse and transform them in a work of art. We are able to see the yeasts and ferments actually at work. In the end they do not justify us in saying much about how creative processes may work in other writers. But I think that even a single exposition of how they once worked in one writer is worth making.[105]

One caution. Both psychology and literary criticism are highly speculative fields. This inquiry is more speculative still, in that it is carried on in the no man's land between them. The findings I bring in here are essentially speculative: I cannot prove them. That being said, I may also say that throughout the essay my reference is to

"The Symbols of Despair," from Bernard DeVoto, *Mark Twain at Work* (Cambridge, Mass.: Harvard University Press, 1942), pp. 105–130. Copyright 1942 by the President and Fellows of Harvard College and the Belknap Press of Harvard University Press. Reprinted by permission of the publisher.

demonstrable fact wherever possible. The facts that support my findings are far more numerous, and my argument has a much more solid base, and much stronger links, than there is room even to suggest in the course of a single essay.

A Connecticut Yankee in King Arthur's Court was published in December, 1889. It is the last of Mark Twain's books which we can call certainly of the first rank, and its publication furnishes a convenient date. He was then the most widely known and admired writer in America, and very likely in the world. He was at the summit of his personal happiness. His books had won him not only world-wide fame but a fortune as well. He was the husband of a greatly loved wife, the father of three delightful children, the master of a house famous for the warmth of its hospitality, the center of a small cosmos of beloved friends, an intimate of the famous men and women of his time, courted, praised, sought after, universally loved. His life had a splendor that marked him as the darling of the gods, and that and the splendor of his imagination made more than one person think of him as a mysterious sojourner from somewhere outside the orbit of this earth. The backwoods boy, the tramp printer, the Mississippi pilot, the silver miner, the San Francisco bohemian had become one of the great men of the earth, the hero of a story more romantic than any of Tom Sawyer's dreams.

Our first concern is the series of catastrophes that came in the 1890's. Some years before, he had established his own publishing firm, to publish his books. He had expanded it in order to publish the memoirs of General Grant, and the over-extended business required better management[106] than Mark could give it, better management than anyone could give it whom he hired. The firm faltered, the going got worse, and finally, as a result of the freezing of credit in the panic of 1893, it had to go into receivership. It could have been saved—except that a greater loss had drained Mark's fortune and his wife's as well. Always a speculator, a Colonel Sellers who dreamed of millions but was a predestinate sucker for all salesmen of gold bricks, he had poured nearly a quarter of a million dollars into the development of an invention that was going to make him many times a millionaire. This was the Paige typesetting machine, and his grandiose dream was not absurd, considering the millions which the Mergenthaler Linotype has made. But the Mergenthaler machine succeeded, whereas the Paige machine failed altogether and carried Mark Twain down with it, just at the time when his publishing firm went bankrupt. Furthermore, these same years saw a mysterious alteration in the personality of his youngest daughter, Jean, and finally the terrible mystery was cleared up by the discovery of the still more terrible truth, that she was an epileptic. During these years also his capricious but usually exuberant health failed. He was racked by the bronchitis which he was never again to lose, by the rheumatism which was the inheritance of his frontier youth, and by other ailments which were the result of the enormous strain he was under.

So, in 1895, a bankrupt, little better than an invalid, four months short of sixty years old, Mark Twain started on a lecturing tour which was to take him round the world and pay off his creditors dollar for dollar. His wife and one of his daughters went with him, but they left behind them in America their youngest daughter and their oldest one, Susy, the one who Mark felt was nearest him in mind and spirit. Just a year later, the exhausting trip ended in London, and the children were to join them there. They did not. Across the Atlantic from her parents, Susy died of[107] meningitis. And in the months following, Mark's wife began to decline into the invalidism that was to last through the remaining eight years of her life.

The gods had turned against their darling. Such a sequence of calamities might well drive a man mad; there would be little to wonder at if Mark Twain had broken under them. And the truth is that for a time he lived perilously close to the indefinable line between sanity and madness. Passages of his private anguish in the unpublished papers show to what a tautness the membrane of the mind was stretched, and come near breaking the reader's heart. But we are concerned, not with the man's grief but rather with the use the artist made of it.

For, of course, it is obvious that such events as these cannot occur to the man without happening to the artist as well. The rich man had been bankrupted, and the threatened poverty had imperilled his wife and children. The man of great fame had, or so to the tortured ego it must seem, been somehow toppled from his high place, and always thereafter Mark Twain must carry in his heart some remnant feeling of disgrace. Necessarily, his image of himself had been impaired. These blows which had fallen on him, which had been struck at him, had made him something other than he had been—or at least something other than he had believed and seemed. A man's position in the world, his various successes, his public reputation are interstitial with his ego; an injury to any one injures all and so injures his secret image of himself. But also interstitial with that image is a writer's talent. In the deepest psychological sense, even in a biological sense, a man's work is his life. That is to say, the sources of his talent are inseparably a part of his feeling of wholeness, of his identity, and even, quite nakedly, of his power. An injury to the man must necessarily be an injury on this deep level of personal power—a blow at his virility. And equally, an injury to the inner picture of the man by which[108] life is sustained, must be an injury working outward to impair his work as well. In the dark areas where the roots of life go down, the threatened soul cannot easily distinguish among the parts and organs of personality, and if one of them is endangered then the dim mind knows that all have come in peril.

All this is the merest commonplace of experience. Remembering it, we should expect the series of disasters to have a powerful effect on Mark Twain's writing. And also, remembering that it is the nature of writers to forge their art out of the materials of their lives, we should expect to find in his writing some effort to grapple with the disasters. Art is the terms of an armistice signed with fate. Or, if you like the words better, art is experience appraised, completed, neutralized, or overcome. . . . So let us see.

It was July, 1896, when the lecture tour ended in London. The lectures had made almost enough money to clear Mark's debts but not quite, and there remained to write the book about his trip, *Following the Equator*, which was to complete his task. It was in August, 1896, that Susy died. He began the book in October. And he wrote to his friend Twichell:

> I am working, but it is for the sake of the work—the "surcease of sorrow" that is found there. I work all the days, and trouble vanishes away when I use that magic. This book will not long stand between it and me, now; but that is no matter, I have many unwritten books to fly to for my preservation; the interval between the finishing of this one and the beginning of the next will not be more than an hour.[1]

Observe that he was relying on work, on writing, to hold his grief at arm's length, the grief of Susy's death. But, besides that pitiful purpose, are we not already entitled to see something else? There seems to me already a hint of what was soon to be plainer, that part of his necessity[109] to write was to vindicate himself as a writer, to restore the image that had been impaired. He had to write: he was compelled to.

Following the Equator is the dullest of his books, and writing it was a laborious and sometimes agonizing task. He rebelled at writing it for money. He rebelled at the meanginglessness of the pursuit, which was part of the meaninglessness of life. For, with Susy dead, life seemed to have no meaning except loss and cruelty. But he kept at work and on April 13, 1897, a notebook entry says, "I finished my book today." But it needed revising and on May 18, the notebook says, "Finished the book again." Several pages of notes follow, some of them for a story I shall be describing in a moment, and then on May 23, five days after the end of the book, the notebook says, "Wrote first chapter of above story today." The interval had been a little longer than the hour he predicted to Twichell, but not much.

With that first chapter, Mark had begun the series of experiments and failures that are our central interest. And also he began other experiments and other failures not closely related to them. What the next months show is a man writing in the grip of a compulsion, driven to write, flogged and scourged to write by the fierce drive within

[1] Letter of Jan. 19, 1897.

him—a man under compulsion to write for "surcease of sorrow," but still more to reintegrate a blasted talent, and most of all to restore his image of himself after the intolerable impairment it had suffered. But also this compulsive need to write is constantly blocked, displaced, and distorted. It is so frenzied that it seems aimless—and also it is perpetually frustrated. "I couldn't get along without work now," he wrote to Howells. "I bury myself in it up to the ears. Long hours—8 and 9 at a stretch, sometimes."[2] That shows the compulsiveness, and we get a glimpse of the frustration when he writes to Howells in[110] August, 1898, fifteen months after that confident notebook entry, "Last summer I started 16 things wrong—3 books and 13 mag. articles—and could only make 2 little wee things, 1500 words altogether, succeed—only that out of piles and stacks of diligently-wrought MS., the labor of 6 weeks' unremitting effort." But the truth was more startling and more serious than this glimpse shows, for the inability to make more than on an average two little wee things come out of sixteen starts was to last longer than he thought. It was to last through 1898 and on to 1899, to 1900, to 1904—and in fact the jobs that he completed from 1897 on through the rest of his life represent only a small fraction of the jobs he began. From 1897 on there are scores of manuscripts in the Mark Twain Papers which begin bravely enough and then peter out, some of them after only a few pages, some of them only after many hundred pages of stubborn and obviously heart-wrenching work. Now it is certain that, as Mark grew older, he did not intend to finish some of them—that he began them merely to amuse himself or to jot down a passing observation or perception, or to find release from some mood in the only remedy he was able to depend on. But other manuscripts, especially those we are to deal with, he meant and desperately wanted to complete. He was impelled to come back to them time after time, take them up again, try some other beginning or some other set of characters, impose some other form on them or some new outcome or some other meaning or some other moral—but get on with them, sweat them through, mould them to an end. So time after time he came back to them. And time after time he failed. He could not finish them.

Such a frustration is a striking thing. There must be a significant reason for the repeated failure of a practiced literary artist, a man who had been writing all his life with marked success. True, Mark Twain had always been[111] subject to enthusiasms and his enthusiasms were short-lived, so that normally he began a good many manuscripts which he never bothered to finish after the going got hard. But this is something else, a repeated and habitual failure, and he did try to finish them—he tried repeatedly, under the compulsion that had enslaved him. He kept coming back to them—and always he failed. This is no

---

[2] Letter of Jan. 22, 1898.

casual or meaningless failure; it is obviously closely interwrought with the fundamental energies of his personality.

The end of our search will come in 1905, but we are most concerned with the two and a half years following that notebook entry of May 18, 1897. During that period he wrote so much that, turning the manuscripts over in my hands and trying to make out their relationships, I have frequently told myself that some of them could not possibly belong to these years, that no man could write so much. But there they are, manuscript after manuscript, a staggering number of them, a still more staggering grand total of words. He actually wrote them during these years. During the same years of course, he also wrote other essays, sketches, reminiscences, newspaper articles, which he succeeded in completing and which were published. But here is a many times greater number of manuscripts which he could not finish.

The force that was impelling him to write was, clearly, both desperate and remorseless. Only a man who was hellridden could write so much. Think of the inner desperation this indicates—and think how that desperation must have grown and spread when time after time he was forced to realize that he could not finish what he had begun. His invention ran out, he could not solve the ordinary problems of structure and technique, he could not overcome the ordinary difficulties of his own intentions, he could not push the thing through to an end. Apart from the manuscripts themselves there is little record of his distress, but surely it was a long agony. Secretly, in the [112] hours of black brooding which had become habitual since Susy died, he must have been forever grappling with the most terrible fear that any artist can feel: the fear that his talent has been drained away, that his spark has been quenched, that his achievement is over forever. It is a poison which acts two ways, spreading back to reinforce the poison that begot it. For the failure of the artist must strike close to the deepest identity and potency of the man—and that identity and potency had already been challenged and grievously impaired by the catastrophes we have glanced at. Of course, it must have proceeded out of those catastrophes, or at least been set in motion by them, and few would doubt that his new impotence was related to the impairment he had suffered or that these literary failures issued from the complex sense of failure that had been created in him.

Much of this heap of manuscript is at random. I disregard that part and consider now only what seems significant in the end. And the first support of what I have just said about impairment comes from Mark's attempts to make use once more of the immortal boys who had conferred immortality on his two finest books—and whom he had called upon again, during the anxieties of the early '90's, for those two lesser stories, *Tom Sawyer Abroad* and *Tom Sawyer Detective*. So now he put them to work again, involving them in a long conspiracy of

Tom's invention more preposterous and much drearier than the one that turns the last part of *Huckleberry Finn* into burlesque. It is a maze of romance and rank improvisation that is trivial to begin with and speedily becomes disheartening. It is wholly without structure and moves without plan by dint of a feverish extemporization which gets more mechanical and improbable as it goes on. It is dull, humorless, without the enchantment of the great originals. Mark's[113] touch is altogether gone from it and, what points most vividly to the truth, even the prose is dead.

It is pitiful to see a great writer turning back, in such a desperate mood, to the works of his greatness. And this effort to repeat what he had done at the height of his power, summoning ghosts from his earlier books, shows the strength of his fear that power had departed from him. It is the more pitiful that the effort to save himself does not save him: the book is a merciless parody of the great books it turns back to. He must have realized the true nature of the effort he was making, and certainly its failure could not be hidden from him. Few more bitter experiences can happen to an artist. Nor is this manuscript the only one in which he tried to use the two boys, as we shall see, nor are *Huckleberry Finn* and *Tom Sawyer* the only earlier books he called on in his need. Through much of the unfinished work of this period runs a diluted strain of other books, *Pudd'nhead Wilson* in particular, and of ideas, devices, stock themes and treatments which he had found effective in his great days but which were not effective now when he needed them most.

It was at this time, also, that Mark began to think seriously about his autobiography. He had written fragments of it before, notably the account of his publication of Grant's memoirs contained in the first volume of the published portions. But now he wrote a number of more or less systematic sketches and planned to buckle down and write the book. He made many pages of notes for it—lists of people, character sketches, memoranda of exciting or important or amusing events. These jottings run through all the notebooks he kept during this period, a long sequence of them in one book shows a comprehensive plan for the book, and there is a forty-page catalogue of Hannibal people which is well along toward actual biography.[3]

Of all this autobiographical material, by far the largest[114] part concerns two periods of his life. Scattering memoranda cover many years, but most of them deal either with the dead child Susy or with the Hannibal of his boyhood. One long section of a notebook describes the agonizing details of Susy's illness and death, and yearns over the little, trivial, pitiful incidents of her childhood, the promise of her life, the loss and stunning cruelty of her death. These notes he actually worked up into a biographical sketch of Susy; but he could not finish

3 "Villagers of 1840–43."

it. He was to come back to it some years later, and to work much of it into the *Autobiography*. But there is even more about Hannibal, and the friends and neighbors of the Clemenses, than there is about Susy.

What is the importance of these facts for our inquiry? Well, it is significant that, in this time of impotence and failure, his mind was constantly turning over not only his memories of his dead daughter, but also his memories of his boyhood. For we know from his books that boyhood was his golden time and that Hannibal was his lost, immortal idyl, not of boyhood only but of home as well. It meant whatever home means of peace, happiness, fulfillment, and especially of security. In the time of desolation whose symbol he was not yet able to forge, he turned back to the years and the place that meant safety. Presently we shall understand why.

Finally, it was at this time that he began to write what he called his Gospel. Twenty years ago or more he had read a paper on philosophical determinism to a club in Hartford, and from time to time thereafter he had shown that the idea was working in him. Now suddenly it began to demand expression—and it was to go on demanding it until he died. A large part of the Mark Twain Papers consists of argumentative or analytical chapters, dialogues, letters, some of them finished, more abandoned, which develop and embroider the twinned themes: man's complete helplessness in the grip of the inexorable forces of the[115] universe, and man's essential cowardice, pettiness, and evil. He went on writing them until within a few months of his death, but actually he began to write them, and wrote the most consecutive of them, in the period we are dealing with. Probably the greater part of those which he privately printed in 1904 as *What Is Man?* were written during these years.

The importance of *What Is Man?* to our inquiry is that it provides the first dependable indication, very possibly the earliest one, of what was going on in the ferments that were at work. We have asked what was the result on the artist of the calamities that had all but broken the man, and with this book we may make a start toward an answer. For *What Is Man?* is not only a treatise on man's instability, weakness, cowardice, cruelty, and degradation. It is not only an assault on the illusions of free will, integrity, decency, and virtue with which mankind makes tolerable its estate. It is not only an assertion of the familiar logic of determinism, the fixed universe, the infrangible sequence of cause and effect from the beginning of time, holding man helpless, and unalterable by will or wish or effort. If that were all there were to it, surely there would be significance in its getting itself written at this particular period. But it is much more than that. For clearly *What Is Man?* is also a plea for pardon. In describing man's helplessness, it pleads that man cannot be blamed. In asserting man's cowardice, it asserts also that man is not responsible. In painting man as enslaved and dominated by inexorable circumstance, it argues that the omnipotence of circumstance must answer for what Mark is inwardly afraid he is being held to answer for. If man is weak, cowardly, and sentenced to defeat, then one who feels himself weak, cowardly, and defeated cannot be to blame. If man is not responsible, then no man can be held responsible. No one, I think, can read this wearisomely repeated argument without feeling the terrible force of an inner cry: Do not blame me, for it was not my fault.[116]

That theme, which is to be repeated in many forms, is struck clearly in *What Is Man?* So we may now move on to the three groups of manuscripts from whose chaos was to be resolved the answer to that troubled cry. I cannot be sure that my arrangement is chronological—I cannot date all of them in relation to one another. But that does not matter much, for they are variations on themes common to them all, the themes come together in the end, and I can date most of the significant steps in the evolution that is really a debate.

We will follow them rather by idea than by manuscript. A number of ideas are repeated over and over in the various manuscripts, modulated, changed, adapted, blended, and in the end, harmonized.

One of these ideas, and probably the earliest, is that of the great stretch of time which may seem to elapse in a dream whose actual duration, in waking time, is only a few minutes or perhaps a few seconds. And mingled with this idea is another one, which holds the germ of the eventual conclusion, the idea of confusing dream with reality. The notebook entry I have quoted, which says that Mark began the "above story" on a certain day, proposes a story in which a man is to nod for a moment over a cigarette, dream a sequence of events which he thinks has lasted for seventeen years, and on waking from his momentary sleep, so have confused the dream with the reality that he cannot recognize his wife. Accompanying this entry is a list of characters for the story which identifies many of them as actual persons from Mark Twain's past. The significance of this is made greater by the fact that, as I have said, Mark was making plans for his autobiography at exactly the same time.

But the story which he actually began to write, though it preserves the framework of the dream, mostly disregards it in favor of another idea, a different theme, whose significance is apparent at sight and which was to arouse, following this story, his most persistent effort. It is the story[117] of a world-famous personage who is cast down from his high estate. The time is shortly after the Mexican War of 1846, and the hero is the youngest major-general in the American army, whose heroism and gallantry have made him a world figure and destined him for the Presidency as soon as he shall be old enough to hold that office. He is not only world famous but very rich as well, fortunate and happy, married to a beautiful woman whom he worships, the father of two small girls whom he adores, one of whom is talented and promising. He falls asleep over his cigarette and in his dream the family's magnificent house is burned down and, following that, a greater catastrophe swiftly engulfs them. A trusted relative of the general's wife, who has been trusted with the management of their fortune, proves not only to have dissipated the fortune but to have become involved in widespread chicanery and fraud as well. The general's reputation is blackened, he and his beloved family are plunged not only into abject poverty but into overwhelming disgrace as well, and in all ways he and they are ruined. He sinks into unconsciousness, wakes from that a year and a half later, finds himself and his family living in a squalid log cabin in California, learns the bitter struggle his wife has made to support them—and here the manuscript breaks off. It had broken off before this and been resumed, but this time the break was final. Mark Twain could go no farther.

Already my point must be clear; it hardly needs my assurance that the story is crowded with undisguised autobiographical material—lifelong friends of Mark Twain, members of his family, enemies, incidents that had happened to him, scenes and speeches straight from his life. Notice the starkness of the theme: a great and fine personage of unimpeachable integrity is struck down by catastrophe and disgraced in the eyes of all the world. Notice also how it is made clear that the personage was innocently betrayed, that the catastrophe was not his fault.[118]

Following this story, Mark separated out the dream idea and confined it to a sequence which I will describe in a moment, while proceeding to carry the theme of the virtuous man cast down from his high estate into a series of manuscripts which together represent the strongest and most persistent effort in our whole cycle. He kept coming back to this story not only during 1898 and 1899 but as late as 1904. How many different essays he made I cannot say, I can only say that he made them repeatedly. The thing obsessed him and he must get it out. But time after time he found himself blocked and had to quit.

It is much too long a story and, as his efforts crisscrossed and failed, much too complex a story for me to tell here. It concerns the leading citizen of a town which hardly differs from the St. Petersburg of *Tom Sawyer* and the Hannibal of the *Autobiography,* and not only the squire but another citizen, formerly wealthy, who had suffered the loss of his fortune and is now reduced to poverty but everywhere respected for his virtue and integrity. Through an intricate series of circumstances the virtuous man is led by his own weakness to commit murder, and other intricately wrought circumstances throw suspicion on the squire. The theme is frequently lost sight of in the melodramatic incidents that Mark frantically invented to get it told somehow, or anyhow, and in a flood of other themes from all the other ventures of this period. But the theme is the moral cowardice and hypocrisy of mankind, the liability of everyone, even the most virtuous, to yield to his secret weakness, provided only he is tempted, or there is some seeming necessity, or mere chance comes his way. Back and forth across this theme play related themes from *What Is Man?*

Now see what has happened. The theme of catastrophe has been modulated. The protagonist has been split in two. The victim of catastrophe is no longer innocent, as in the major-general's story, he is guilty and knows he is[119] guilty, and a large part of the story is his effort to appease and justify himself. But, though he is guilty, the plea is made for him that he cannot be blamed. In different attempts different reasons are given but they all come to the same thing in the end—that circumstance is omnipotent and what happens must happen, alike to all men. If all men would sin in the given circumstance, then none can be blamed for sinning—the responsibility must be turned back to impersonal fate or to the malevolent God who designed it. But notice that there is here a psychic admission, or an accusation, which the earlier story did not contain. The major-general was betrayed by one he had trusted, but the virtuous man of this cycle, though the plea is made that he was not responsible, is cast down by his own act.

This cycle too is crowded with unmistakable portraits and events from the actual world of Mark's own experience. A greater effort is made to transform and adapt them, but they are there. And it should be clear that they are there by the same compulsion that put the admission or accusation there.

Bear in mind that none of the expedients, new starts, or changed devices had worked: Mark had proved unable to bring any version of his story to fruition. Not even when he went back and borrowed from its predecessor. He tried, that is, telling the same story of the virtuous man made murderer and coward and hypocrite by calamity, as something that happened in a dream—in a dream, furthermore, that was to last for a few minutes only, though it seemed to consume many years. So what began as an independent story became essentially the same story, though with the modulation I have pointed out. And that modulation, I think, discloses the secret self-accusation as it is met by a counter assertion that all men are guilty as circumstances compel them to be.

We have now got far along in our period and must go[120] back, to where the idea of the dream began a different evolution. A number of apparently aimless sketches which have no surface relationship to our inquiry had dealt with sailors or other people marooned in the vast Antarctic waste of ice and darkness. In one of these there had been introduced a legend of an enchanted sea wilderness in the midst of this eternal winter where ships were caught in a central place of calm, circumscribed by the ice and snow, and held drifting forever there with the dead bodies of their crews and passengers preserved by the unearthly cold. Various components of this idea run back farther in Mark's thinking than I can trace them here, but now they have come together in a striking and terrible symbol of desolation.

Mark had not been able to complete any of these casual sketches, but, whether consciously or not, they led to a re-entry and flashed across his mind the bright hope that he had found a variation of the story that tormented him which, this time, he would be able to complete. Again we have the happily married man who is the father of two delightful daughters and again he falls asleep and is to waken after a few minutes, believing that years have passed. But this time, before he falls asleep he looks through a microscope at a drop of water—and that item changes and immensely deepens the story. For in his dream, he and his family are on a mysterious ship sailing they know not where in a perpetual darkness filled with storms of snow and ice. This proves to be an Antarctic waste in the drop of water which he had looked at in the microscope, and in that tortured dream the voyage progresses in mystery and terror—and also in what I feel to be significance. No one knows where they are, no one knows where they are going or for what purpose or under whose command, but they are in the Great Dark at the edge of the microscope's field, a place of unimaginable desolation, and somewhere far off is the horror of the Great White Glare, which is[121] really the beam cast through the microscope's field by the reflector.

Moreover, on this ship there is some recollection of waking life—the world of reality outside both the microscope and the dream. But this fades, and one comes to doubt it, one comes in the end to believe that the reality one remembers was a dream after all, and that the dream one lives in is the reality. Furthermore, there is a supernatural being on board the ship, the Superintendent of Dreams, who has power over both the ship and the minds of its passengers, who steadily, vindictively, cultivates in their minds the doubt of reality which becomes the belief in dream.[4] And in the terrible darkness, monsters roam the freezing ocean, threatening to snatch victims from the ship and devour them. And finally, there is mutiny and betrayal on this ship, trusted officers who will be untrue and produce catastrophe.

This story also Mark could not finish. He came back to it several times, trying to find an effective outcome for it, trying to give it this slant or that, trying to crystallize round these symbols a coherent expression of the dread they had for him. The frustration still held and he could not do it, but what he did write is markedly superior to anything I have previously mentioned. It is a strange, powerful, and moving story, this uncompleted fragment, which holds you fascinated despite some crudities of construction. There is significance for us in

[4] I need not point out that the Superintendent of Dreams exactly corresponds to God in *What Is Man?* Watch him become Satan.

the fact that he was able to make it better literature. And there is more significance in the notes that show how he wanted to finish it. For as the voyage went on, still greater afflictions were to visit the ship. It was to meet other ships caught in the same terrible enchantment. One of them was to contain a fabulous treasure in gold, and this was to madden certain of the already mutinous crew. The baby who had[122] been born to our married couple was to be carried off on another ship, the search for the child was to mingle with the crew's mad lust for the treasure, the wife's heart was to break, her hair was to turn white, and she was finally to go mad with grief, during the ten fruitless years while they tried to find the child. They were to catch up with the other ship at last—but in the Great White Glare, where the child and all the crew and passengers of the second ship were to be killed by the merciless heat. And the Glare was to further madden the gold-maddened mutineers and to dry up the sea, the monsters were to gather, and in a final, apocalyptic phantasy of destruction, the two beloved daughters were to be killed, the grief-crazed wife was to die, all remaining survivors of the first ship were to die also, leaving only the helpless narrator and the loyal Negro who was his servant.

Once more, a great part of the detail of this story was from Mark's experience. Most of the characters are identifiable from his life, or correspond to characters elsewhere in our material who are identifiable. The children's parties, the servants, the arguments can be annotated. The girl who is so loved and who is killed with such cruelty dies in exactly the delirium that the faithful notebooks record of Susy Clemens' fatal illness. And so on.

The pattern had now been repeated many times. We have seen Mark's compulsion to write it and the inhibition that withheld him from working it out to an end. So now, I think, we may make some judgments. We have seen in fiction the shape of the imprint left on Mark Twain's mind and heart by the series of catastrophes I began by describing. For essentially they are the catastrophes that obsess him in these uncompleted stories, nor can there be any doubt what great personage is cast down from his high place, what beloved wife is maddened by despair, what beloved daughter dies in agony. But if we recognize all that, then we must also recognize the terrible accusation that[123] had risen in his heart. I said, far back, that he walked the narrow edge between sanity and madness. How close he came to madness may be understood in this cry, "It must have been my fault!"

We need neither the anthropology of primitive religions nor the psychology of the unconscious mind to understand, for in all of us a similar fear and accusation hover about the margin of the mind, to come forward a little and lose some of their vagueness in moments when discouragement is on us or when the menace of living has suddenly sharpened. That primal guilt is of one tissue with our primal despair, but happily those are brief moments when we are in health.

Yet we all know, of our own experience or experience near to us, that the shocks of life may sometimes prolong those moments, bring the accusation into the center of the mind, delay the healthy reaction from it—and then we have at best despair and at worst insanity. This close had Mark Twain come: that there had been set up in him a contention, an accusation he could not bear, a repudiation he could not make. In the yeasty darkness at the mind's base, he had, of his own fault, brought on himself this disgrace and degradation and humiliation. In the phantasy that underlay both his grief and his rebellion, he was the author of his own fall, and the author also of his wife's and daughters' illness, of his daughter's death, of the unabated agony that had come upon his family.

So now he had found the symbols of despair. Through stormy darkness and hemmed in by ice, directed by some unknown and malevolent will, a ship sails a terrible sea where no chart can be had and where monsters lurk that may strike and destroy at any moment. The ship sails there forever, there is no plan or sense to its voyage and no hope that the agony will end, and the helpless passengers are menaced not only by the Great Dark without but by mutiny and greed and maniac revenge within. And quite surely there will come to them bereavement, the death of[124] their loved ones, the triumph of an idle and unmitigated malevolence whose terrible decoys are love and hope and human warmth, to lure humanity to destruction.

The artist is driven to make what he can of experience, and art is the terms of an armistice made with fate. Yet the compulsiveness he shows and above all his frustration make clear that here we are dealing with more than the comparatively simple way of art. The impact of calamity had been too great, he had taken one step too near the edge, and there is evident a struggle not only to make terms with his experience but also to vindicate himself. And not only to vindicate himself but, quite literally, by that vindication to integrate a mind that had been blasted and restore a talent that had been blown asunder.

We have seen his first attempt to still that accusation: the "It was not my fault" of the story where the major-general is betrayed by a trusted relative. That would not suffice: the excuse was too transparent. There followed the assertion in *What Is Man?* that no one can be blamed since the chain of circumstance holds him fast in a plan determined by a vindictive God. That would not move the judge's heart, nor could the voice be stilled by the argument of the cycle to which he returned so often (in the stories of the virtuous man turned murderer) that all men are weak and all men fall when tempted.

But important modulations had been made in the dream story. And let me add that at one time, as his notes show, he contemplated going back to the disgraced major-general and setting him out also on the dreambound ship in the eternal ice, together with a company of fellow-victims living out their diverse fates in the same predestined anguish and despair. He did not write it. If he had begun it, he would not have finished it. For though this addition to the idea had hope in it, he had not yet found the reconciliation.

But he had come close to it. There was a grotesque[125] hope, or at least an alleviation, in the position he had now reached. For this dream idea has two parts, one that dreams are brief though their agony may seem to last forever, and the deeper one that the reality may fade into the dream, that one may not be sure, that as one wakes from dream so perhaps one may wake from a lesser to a greater dream. Here the perturbed spirit finds comfort, though not quite enough, in the simple thought, so direct and inevitable, so characteristic of the helplessness of our deepest selves: "It may not be true after all. It may be a dream. Maybe I have dreamed the whole agony. Maybe loss and suffering and despair are false, are only a dream."

Remember that this compulsive writing had produced other manuscripts, apparently at random and without relation to this bitter debate. Among them was a story about Tom Sawyer and Huck Finn, which I briefly described. But that story could not have been altogether aimless and at random. It was, in a way, a premonition. For in his winnowing of his own books and his lost years, he happened upon a mysterious stranger in the town of Hannibal. I do not know much about this man, for he takes various forms, but the important thing is his secret, the fact that there is noble or perhaps royal blood in his veins. This made him kin to Mark Twain, in whose veins ran the blood of an English earldom as well as that of a regicide. And was not Mark, besides, that most mysterious of strangers on this earth, a genius, a man born unlike other men, to a strange destiny? Somehow the image of this unrecognized nobleman blends with another image that has fascinated Mark all his life long, the figure of Satan. And this was a fruitful time to remember Satan, for Satan is an angel and angels are exempt from loss and pain and all mortal suffering, they are exempt from guilt and conscience and self-condemnation also, and temptation has no meaning for them and they have no moral sense, and neither humiliation nor death nor the suffering of anyone affects them in[126] the least. Moreover, of the angels who were all that Mark needed most to be, he felt nearest to Satan, the one who had revolted against the inexorable laws of the universe stated in *What Is Man?* and the one whose insatiable curiosity about the ways of man kept him going up and down on the earth and to and fro therein.

So it is not surprising when, presently, young Satan, a son of the fallen angel, comes to Hannibal and falls in with Tom Sawyer and Huck Finn. This first manuscript is not remarkable, being little more than a succession of marvelous works done by the young angel for the admiration and stupefaction of the village. It was fumbling and tentative and it frayed out. But in it and in the notes made for carrying it on Mark found the vital clues, the seeds that were to bear fruit at last.

At first young Satan was no more than a vehicle for Mark's derision of the God whose vengefulness creates human pain and for his scorn of the ant-like race pain is inflicted on, and an identification, infantile at base, with a supernatural being who can perform wonders that make him distinguished and envied, a being also of irresistible strength. But he became more than that, and the way out of the basic frustration was his miracles. So another manuscript begins with Tom and Huck and young Satan in Hannibal, but this soon breaks off and a longer, better, and more deeply wrought one begins. The same story has been transferred to Eseldorf, in Austria, centuries ago—but if we needed any clue by now, note that this story includes a printshop such as young Sam Clemens worked in when he was the age of these boys. I will say nothing of this manuscript except that it led directly to the one that came through to triumph at last, the book which, after it had been painfully written over and changed and adjusted and transformed, was to achieve the completion denied its many predecessors, the book which we know as *The Mysterious Stranger*.

In those tortured revisions and adjustments, which are[127] part of the same desperate effort to make the story go somehow that I have traced in other sequences, we see the thing finding expression at last. Or, if I may so phrase it, we see the psychic block removed, the dilemma solved, the inhibition broken, the accusation stilled, and Mark Twain's mind given peace at last and his talent restored. The miracles, which at first are just an idle game for the amusement of the boys and the astonishment of the villagers, become finally a spectacle of human life in miniature, with the suffering diminished to the vanishing point since these are just puppets, unreal creatures moving in a shadow-play, and they are seen with the detachment of an immortal spirit, passionless and untouched. And so from a spectacle they become a dream—the symbolic dream of human experience that Mark had been trying to write in such travail for so many years.

So an unrecognized purpose had dominated the chaos of those efforts, after all, and out of it had come *The Mysterious Stranger*, a minor masterpiece, with its clear, subdued colors, its autumnal pity and compassion, its fine, silvery echo of mortality and of hope destroyed and of man's pettiness somehow given the nobility of suffering, the thread of pain binding all living things together. But what is it? Eseldorf—Assville—is just Hannibal, seen far away, softened by the mist of centuries. The boys who are eager and cowardly, aspiring and cruel, are just Tom and Huck once more, which is to say they are what Mark had found best in himself and his long phantasies. The villagers, the human race in little, are just his friends and neighbors, his detractors and enemies and those who had undone him. The deaths died, the injuries suffered and agonies endured—we do not need to inquire what they are, after the innumerable times he had tried to give them meaning in art. Nor can there be any doubt who the immortal Antagonist is, the enemy of God, which is to say the rebel against law—and so against responsibility. Here[128] the dreadful things alleged against mankind, and so made as a confession, in *What Is Man?* are said again, but now they are tolerable, conformable, acceptable, for they have been removed far away, over them broods the peace of distant dream. And now we know that the dream had closed the arc and permitted him to say what he must say and enabled him at last to live at peace with himself.

You perceive, *now* [Satan says, just before he vanishes and the book ends] that these things are all impossible except in a dream. You perceive that they are pure and puerile insanities, the silly creations of an imagination that is not conscious of its freaks—in a word, that they are a dream, and you the maker of it. . . .

It is true, that which I have revealed to you; there is no God, no universe, no human race, no earthly life, no heaven, no hell. It is all a dream—a grotesque and foolish dream. Nothing exists but you. And you are but a *thought,*—a vagrant thought, a useless thought, a homeless thought, wandering forlorn among the empty eternities!

The dream, that is, was the answer and the proof. He had tried to say: it was not my fault, I was betrayed. But the accusation could not be stayed so easily. He had tried to say: it was not my fault, for the fixed universe of inescapable law intended from the beginning that this should happen. But that was too easily exposed as subterfuge. He had tried to say: it was not my fault, for anyone would have done the same, but the remorseless feet that follow, follow after had driven him from that refuge. He had tried to say: it is just a delusion, a dream I will wake from—and that had almost served, but not quite. Susy's delirium was not his delusion and there could be no waking from it—and if that was so, then the terrible accusation still held.

But there was still an answer. If nothing existed but a homeless thought wandering forlorn among the empty eternities, then his smaller agony and his personal guilt[129] were also a dream. If everything was dream, then clearly the accused prisoner might be discharged. The accusation begotten by his experience could be stilled by destroying all experience. It was possible to uproot terror and guilt and responsibility from his little world, by detonating the universe. He could end his contention with the vengeful God and put away remorse forever by reducing all contention, vengeance, pain, degradation, guilt, sin, and panic to a lonely dream.

That was the price he paid for peace. It seems a high price. But art is the terms of an armistice signed with fate, and the terms one makes are the terms one can make. At this cost the fallen angel of our literature, the mysterious stranger who seemed only a sojourner in the cramped spaces of our mortal world, saved himself in the end, and came back from the edge of insanity, and found as much peace as any man may find in his last years, and brought his talent into fruition and made it whole again.[130]

The Background of
The Mysterious Stranger

COLEMAN O. PARSONS

IN THE MYSTERIOUS STRANGER, MARK TWAIN STARTS WITH THE PROBLEM and assumptions of "Ode on a Distant Prospect of Eton College," only to part company with the gentle Gray in his solution. After imagining from a distance "the little victims" at play, oblivious to the sorrow and degeneration awaiting them through passions, misfortune, and death, the eighteenth-century spectator refrains from approaching to warn them of their fate: "Thought would destroy their paradise." Resenting the same bliss of ignorance, Twain through Satan enters the dreaming boys' world of Eseldorf (Ass Village) and enlightens the narrator, Theodor Fischer, cruelly searing away every illusion, even that of an external guide.

The task of making the blind see proved so difficult that Twain composed four different versions of his novel between 1898 and 1906. How much he put into the work of his own reading and experience will never be fully known, but I shall mention sources already known, suggest a few more sources, and discuss analogues which show that Twain did not travel alone, even though he may not have been acquainted with his fellow travelers. These background materials will be grouped under five headings: Title, Setting, Characters, Plot, and Ideas.

I. Title

Carroll D. Laverty believes that "The Genesis of *The Mysterious Stranger*" was Jane Taylor's brief moral tale, "The Mysterious Stranger," reprinted in McGuffey's *Rhetorical Guide and Fifth Reader* and in the *New Sixth Eclectic Reader*. It concerns a striking, dignified, intelligent stranger from "yon silvery star" who thinks mankind trivial and death fortunate.[1] Even if Twain forgot school reading matter, he could have encountered the title in other works: Amelia Opie's *The Mysterious*

Coleman O. Parsons, "The Background of *The Mysterious Stranger*," *American Literature*, XXXII (March 1960), 55–74. Reprinted by permission of the author and of Duke University Press.

[1] *Mark Twain Quarterly*, VIII, 15–19 (Spring–Summer, 1947). Twain's novel is like "a satirical expansion" of Taylor's fable.

Stranger, and Other Tales, 1870;[55] *Mysterious Stranger,* an "Ethiopian Drama" published in New York about 1874; and *The Mysterious Stranger,* Charles Selby's adaptation (1844) of a play which was published in Boston as *Satan in Paris; or, The Mysterious Stranger* in 1855 and was acted in New York and other American cities until 1890.[2] The play will be discussed in the section on ideas.

II. Setting

Eseldorf and its surroundings have been thought of as Hannibal and its environs.[3] For several weeks in 1898, the Clemenses lived in the summer resort of Kaltenleutgeben, a village ten miles southwest of Vienna. Mark describes Eseldorf as drowsing "in peace in the deep privacy of a hilly and woodsy solitude," and Baedeker presents Kaltenleutgeben as "charmingly situated in the valley of the *Dürre Liesing,*" an hour's hike from the Höllenstein (Hell Stone) and the Föhrenberg (Pine Hill), whose moderate elevations afford beautiful views.[4] In shifting the scene from Hannibal to Eseldorf in the final draft of *The Mysterious Stranger,* Twain may have begun to create in terms of an Austrian setting.

III. Characters

Characters who depend in part on originals are Nikolaus Bauman, Theodor Fischer, the good and the bad priest, and Satan. A description of boys' life in Missouri towns intended for his *Autobiography* was transferred by Mark Twain to pages of *The Mysterious Stranger.*[5] More specifically, drowning as an alternative to a worse fate enabled him to imbed a little of his boyhood friend, Tom Nash, in Nikolaus Bauman. De Lancey Ferguson notes this connection in writing of Clemens's two friends who were drowned in the Mississippi and of Tom Nash, who got drenched in perspiration when skating with Sam on the frozen river at midnight—"without permission"—and fell into the water. He suffered weakening diseases, climaxed by scarlet fever, and emerged from his torment stone-deaf[56] and impaired in speech.[6] Satan explains the alternative to Nikolaus's drowning:

2 Alternate titles were *Satan* and *The Devil in Paris.*

3 Van Wyck Brooks, *The Ordeal of Mark Twain* (New York, 1922), p. 8; Edward Wagenknecht, *Mark Twain: The Man and His Work* (New Haven, Conn., 1935), p. 60; and Bernard DeVoto, *Mark Twain at Work* (Cambridge, Mass., 1942), p. 128.

4 Karl Baedeker, *Austria,* 12th rev. ed. (Leipzig, 1929), p. 144.

5 *Mark Twain: An Exhibition . . . in the Huntington Library* (San Marino, Calif., 1947), pp. 9, 23.

6 Ferguson, *Mark Twain: Man and Legend* (Indianapolis and New York, 1943), p. 24.

"If I had not done this, Nikolaus would save Lisa, then he would catch cold from his drenching; one of your race's fantastic and desolating scarlet fevers would follow, with pathetic after-effects; for forty-six years he would lie in his bed a paralytic log, deaf, dumb, blind, and praying night and day for the blessed relief of death."

The protracted death escaped by Nikolaus combines, I believe, two instances or versions of the "hard and fast" laws which, in lieu of "sentimental justice," control life. After all, Tom Nash came out of his scrape impaired but ambulant and cheerful, not so Twain's fictional character or a certain student about whom the novelist made this entry in his Notebook at Kaltenleutgeben on May 27, 1898:

I knew a man who when in his second year in college jumped into an ice-cold stream when he was overheated and rescued a priest of God from drowning; suffered partial paralysis, lay in his bed 38 years, unable to speak, unable to feed himself, unable to write; not even the small charity of quenching his mind was doled out to him—he lay and thought and brooded and mourned and begged for death 38 years.[7]

Informed by Satan that Nikolaus will drown in twelve days, Theodor Fischer becomes sentimentally mindful of their "good days" together, winter skating and sliding when their parents thought they were in school. Then Theodor's "heart was wrung with remorse" for wrongs done Nikolaus: cheating him in a trade, making him the scapegoat in a school whipping, and jeeringly eating an apple intended for Nikolaus's convalescent sister. "There was a wounded look in his face as he turned away toward his home which rose before me many times in after years, in the night, and reproached me and made me ashamed again."

Samuel Clemens, like Theodor, had been strangely apprised of a playmate's approaching death. In 1858, he circumstantially dreamed of his brother Henry's end. When the event matched the warning,[57] unavailing regrets intertwined with the survivor's memories. In "The Facts Concerning the Recent Carnival of Crime in Connecticut" (1876), the spiteful dwarf, Conscience, reminds Clemens of his younger brother's doglike, loving trust, despite heartless treachery on the part of the elder.

". . . The latest picture you have of him in health and strength must be such a comfort to you! You pledged your honor that if he would let you blindfold him no harm should come to him; and then, giggling and choking over the rare fun of the joke, you led him to a brook thinly glazed with ice, and pushed him in; and how you did laugh! Man, you will never forget the

[7] Mark Twain's Notebook, ed. A. B. Paine (New York and London, 1935), p. 363. This almost lifelong obsession appears with grisly humor in the prayer to visit a rival's household with "scarlet fever . . . to result in deafness and imbecility." See Twain's "Letter from the Recording Angel" (1888), MS published by Bernard DeVoto in Harper's Magazine, CXCII, 106–109 (Feb., 1946).

gentle, reproachful look he gave you as he struggled shivering out, if you live a thousand years! Oho! you see it now, you see it *now!*"

"Beast, I have seen it a million times, and shall see it a million more!"[8]

In one aspect of his life, Father Peter is like a San Francisco eccentric known to Mark Twain, Emperor Norton, who was free from all sorrow in his triumphant insanity.[9] When lyingly informed by Satan that he has been found guilty of stealing the ducats which he actually discovered in a purse, the good priest goes insane and is completely happy.

I believe that the bad priest also had an original, a more three-dimensional one than Father Peter's. This was Martin Luther, to whom Twain attributes an "asbestos" temperament in "The Turning-Point of My Life" (1910). Father Adolf frightens Eseldorfers by the "something supernatural" which makes him scoff at, namecall, and generally defy the Evil One. Indeed, on one occasion, "he quarreled with the enemy and intrepidly threw his bottle at him, and there, upon the wall of his study, was the ruddy sploch where it struck and broke." Luther's enemies declared him to be devil-contracted, devil-possessed, and devil-begotten. His friends listened with awe to his anecdotes of numerous encounters with Satan, in some of which he obscenely mocked his adversary. Legend, variously attaching itself to stains on a wall of the Wartburg Castle (1521–1522), a Wittenberg room, and the Coburg Fortress, has vividly sketched the scene of Luther's disputation with the devil, at whom[58] he hurled his inkpot.[10] It remained for Mark Twain to insinuate that the contents of the bottle were vinous.

Mark Twain's Satan, unostracized nephew of the Old Serpent, has points of similarity with several personages. The black-robed, white-faced Pausanias (Deliverer from Pain) in Adolf Wilbrandt's *Der Meister von Palmyra* (1889), as an infernal-celestial visitor to earth, is both "comforter" and destroyer, Death.[11] Twain praises the

---

[8] The episode of Sam Clemens's goading Henry to jump over a splintery stump, then laughing at the "cotton-tail rabbit's" ruined cotton velvet breeches and his retreat home in tears, is in the same tone of juvenile cruelty.

[9] Laverty, pp. 16–17.

[10] Twain's readiest source for Luther lore may have been W. E. H. Lecky's *History of the Rise and Influence of the Spirit of Rationalism in Europe* (1865). See New Impression (London, 1904), I, 8, 59–62; *Autobiography . . . of Moncure Daniel Conway* (Boston and New York, 1904), II, 306; and *Materials toward a History of Witchcraft*, collected by H. C. Lea, ed. A. C. Howland (New York and London, 1957), I, 417–423.

[11] Friedrich Schönemann, "Mark Twain and Adolf Wilbrandt," *Modern Language Notes*, XXXIV, 372–374 (1919); Max Lederer, "Einige Bemerkungen zu Adolf Wilbrandts *Der Meister von Palmyra*," *Modern Language Notes*, LXI, 551–555 (1946); Théodore Henckel's edition of the play (New York, 1900); and Harriott S. Olive's translation in *Poet-Lore*, XIII, 161–248 (1901). One ignored fact should be added: Apelles, the disillusioned victim of earthly immortality, is called the mysterious stranger ("wunderlicher Fremdling").

metaphysical dramatic poem in an essay "About Play-Acting" (published October, 1898), interpreting it as "just one long, soulful, sardonic laugh at human life" and revealing himself more than Wilbrandt in his comment that the presence of death makes "the fussy human pack seem infinitely pitiful and shabby."

Although Frederick Cowper concludes that "the Faust influence is only pictorial," Goethe's Mephistopheles is temperamentally akin to Satan in his cynicism and his contempt for men, with their absurd aspirations and petty deeds. Contact with a mocking spirit matures both Faust and Theodor Fischer. Although he overstresses the source value of Faust, Cowper is judicious and convincing in his discussion of *Zadig*. Voltaire's celestial fatalist is a radiant, youthful angel, Jesrad, appearing on earth as a hermit who teaches lessons in humility and hospitality by a theft and a gift, sets fire to a house in order to do good, and drowns an accomplished youth to avoid evil. Alternate patterns of existence would turn out badly, too. Thus, like Satan, Jesrad nonchalantly instructs a mortal in determinism (Providence in *Zadig*) and man's insignificance.[12][59]

Satan was given even more than his due in the nineteenth century, and Clemens, the defender of underdogs who remembered his mother's speaking indulgently of the devil, was not the least charitable: "I have always felt friendly toward Satan."[13] The work of sentimental rehabilitation by scholars and skeptics was going on all around him. His "warm personal friend," Robert G. Ingersoll, whose writings he *devoured*,[14] is a serviceable *advocatus diaboli* in *The Gods* (1872): "In nearly all the theologies, mythologies and religions, the devils have been much more humane and merciful than the gods."[15] Another friend of Twain's, Moncure D. Conway, devotes a chapter to "Le Bon Diable" in *Demonology and Devil-Lore* (1878).[16]

Twain cites Jules Michelet's *Jeanne d'Arc* as one of the "authorities examined in verification of the truthfulness" of *Personal Recollections of Joan of Arc* (1896). His study of that "witch" and "child

---

[12] Cowper, "The Hermit Story, as Used by Voltaire and Mark Twain," *In Honor of . . . Charles Frederick Johnson* (Hartford, Conn., 1928), pp. 313–337. Cowper adds that the second part of *Faust* contains good material for Twain in the character of the astrologer; however, Merlin in *A Connecticut Yankee in King Arthur's Court* offers better material. Twain owned translations of *Faust* by T. J. Arnold and Bayard Taylor, as well as the Moritz Retzsch illustrations. See Anderson Auction Company, *Catalogue of the Library and Manuscripts of Samuel L. Clemens*, Part I (New York, 1911), pp. 28, 31.

[13] *The Autobiography of Mark Twain*, ed. Charles Neider (New York, 1959), p. 16.

[14] *Mark Twain's Letters*, ed. A. B. Paine (New York and London, 1917), I, 371, 373–374; II, 682.

[15] *The Works of Robert G. Ingersoll*, New Dresden Ed. (New York, 1900), I, 17.

[16] See 3rd ed. rev. (New York, 1889), II, 381–400.

of Satan" may have been supplemented by Michelet's *La Sorcière* (1862), translated the following year by L. J. Trotter as *La Sorcière: the Witch of the Middle Ages*. In "a cruel, cruel time" which transfixes the rehabilitater of Satan with "pity and indignation" and which strikes Mark Twain as "the brutalest, the wickedest, the rottenest in history since the dark ages," Michelet finds the Prince of this World an amusing fellow, a consoler and healer displaying compassion, curiosity, and reason in an irrational creation. "Unjustly driven out of Heaven," pale and majestic Satan became not only "the witch's dream" but also the great civilizer and educator, an embodiment of life, liberty, and charity. "If Satan does this, we are bound to pay him homage, to admit he may well be after all one of the aspects of God."[17]

Mark Twain's Satan, compounded just as strangely, baffles Eseldorfers. Urged by necessities beyond lowly comprehension and unfettered by earthdwellers' Moral Sense, he acts and thinks like both god and devil. This double personality, I believe, derives in part[60] from Jesus in the *Apocryphal New Testament*, "A Curious Book" which Twain discussed in a letter of June 2, 1867, to the San Francisco *Alta California*. The boy Savior cures the dumb and the leprous, turns a bewitched youth from mule to man, creates living animals out of clay, throws dyed garments into the fire for miraculous ends, widens or contracts objects botched by his father, and quickens a dead boy to vindicatory speech. He also "causes blindness to fall upon his accusers," withers the hand of his teacher before occasioning his death, and makes three boys die for such offenses as breaking his fish-ponds and jostling him. No wonder parents take Jesus for a sorcerer and order their children "to seek better company." After all, "his society was pleasant, but attended by serious drawbacks."[18]

The character Twain needed as a mouthpiece must combine just such moral ambivalence (i.e., freedom) with lancet-sharp criticism. The latter quality was a specialty of Voltaire's, exploited in *Zadig* and in a satirical little tale, *Micromegas*, which reduces mankind and the earth to minuscule importance in the eyes of an inquisitive inhabitant of Sirius who is millennia-old and endowed with sidereal perspective and a thousand senses. Like Satan, who is 16,000 years old (and not full grown yet), he visits our little ball and reflects on the pettiness of humanity.

Twain's Satan is complexly compounded. He is the remote traveler of fiction and drama, as well as a god; he is Mark Twain returning to

---

[17] Michelet, *La Sorcière*, trans. by A. R. Allinson as *Satanism and Witchcraft* (New York, 1939 and 1946), pp. xvii, 19, 46, 66, 103, 308–309, 326, 331. For dream interpretation, see pp. 21, 27, 65, 68, 76, and 326.

[18] *Mark Twain's Travels with Mr. Brown*, ed. Franklin Walker and G. Ezra Dane (New York, 1940), pp. 251–254, part of Letter xxiv from New York.

Hannibal-Eseldorf, where he sees the deeds and motives of men and boys stripped of their nostalgic glamor; he may also be reminiscent of an actual mysterious stranger who came to Hannibal and aroused juvenile conjecture; and yet he remains a supernatural visitant with a ruthless wisdom, a strange innocence, and a detachment which are beyond mortal compass.

IV. Plot

The plot of *The Mysterious Stranger* is as episodic as that of a picaresque novel. Its substance, however, is not the activity of a rogue, despite traits of the *picaro* or antihero in Satan, but the production of a wise youth. The chief characters, like Mark Hopkins and James Garfield on a "log hut ... bench," are the celestial impresario[61] or educational P. T. Barnum, Satan, and his star pupil, Theodor Fischer, in whom he finally submerges himself. The principal events are supernaturally manipulated experience, demonstrations in Satan's pedagogical workshop.

Correspondences between Twain's novel and Goethe's masterpiece have been listed by Frederick Cowper. "In *Faust*, Mephistopheles takes Faust to the Brocken on Walpurgis Night and shows him a witches' sabbath. In *The Mysterious Stranger*, Young Satan takes one of the boys traveling and shows him a pageant of the history of the world." *Faust* has the miraculous supplying of drinks in the first part and of money in the second, as well as discourse on war.[19] To this analysis of Goethe's influence, Edgar Lee Masters adds that Satan's destruction of a miniature castle and its little workmen by fire and death "is much like the disaster that came to Philemon and Baucis in the Second Part of *Faust*." He suggests that the wonderworks of Satan, the flying birds made out of clay, for instance, are "reminiscent of certain apocryphal miracles of Jesus. Satan also makes wine."[20]

Mark Twain did not need to fly to Goethe's Brocken for Satan's visionary "history of the progress of the human race" from the clubbing of Abel to "slaughters more terrible" in a future "raging, struggling, wallowing through seas of blood." Closer to Twain, I believe, was the eleventh book of *Paradise Lost*, in which Michael shows Adam in a vision "The whole Earth fill'd with violence, and all flesh Corrupting" (ll. 888–889) from the primal murder to the Flood. Twain does not omit the Flood, but unlike Milton's archangel, who in the twelfth book

[19] Cowper, pp. 334–337. Laverty proposes Greek mythology, Swift's "Baucis and Philemon," or Hawthorne's "The Miraculous Pitcher" as source of the wonderful production of food and drink for humble people.

[20] Masters, *Mark Twain: A Portrait* (New York, 1938), p. 223. See *The Bible of the World*, ed. Robert O. Ballou (New York, 1939), p. 1256, for the child Jesus making sparrows of clay.

offers the hope of the Incarnation, he marshals his historical procession toward despair.[21]

Paradise Lost was favored reading of Clemens's young manhood, as was Voltaire. Twain's angry demonstration of the insanity of[62] "wars, murders, and massacres" approximates that of the French skeptic in tales like "The World Is Like That; or, The Vision of Babouc" and treatises like "On Tolerance," "We Must Take Sides" (Il faut choisir), and "Gods and Men," in which Christianity is held accountable for the deaths of at least 9,468,800 victims.[22] Satan is less the accountant than Voltaire in his sarcasm: "A few centuries from now . . . all men will confess that without Christian civilization war must have remained a poor and trifling thing to the end of time. . . . It will be recognized that all the competent killers are Christians." W. E. H. Lecky perhaps supplied ammunition for Mark Twain's war on war. In his *History of European Morals from Augustus to Charlemagne* (1869), of which Twain had a "much worn" copy, Lecky insists that Christian fanaticism "has caused the effusion of oceans of blood, and has been productive of incalculable misery to the world."[23]

Satan's dramatized review of history for the benefit of three Austrian boys occurs "in the woods" near Eseldorf (Cowper's account telescopes different events). Before that performance, he takes Theodor Fischer to China, and after it to India and other places "around the world . . . showing me a hundred wonders, most of them reflecting in some way the weakness and triviality of our race." Although these glimpses of the East should have sharpened the insight fomented by the bloodletting and futility of the West, Mark Twain did not know— and despise—Eastern man. The only despicable person encountered in the East is Occidental, a Portuguese.

The eastern travels may be a casual and partial return to a project abandoned much earlier than 1896, when Twain crossed India at ground level as a popular, though bankrupt, lecturer. In the summer of 1868, he thought up a story about a thirty-four-year-old French convict's escape by air: "Trip of a man in a balloon from Paris over India, China, Pacific Ocean, the plains to a prairie in Illinois." Finding that

---

[21] Comte de Volney's *The Ruins; or, A Survey of the Revolutions of Empires* (1791), long popular in America, ends on a note of secular hope. The "Genius of tombs and ruins" reviews the pessimistic past from the air for a "friend of truth" in order that experience may create an optimistic future. In *Paradise Regained*, Satan conjures up for Christ a mountain-top panorama of the kingdoms of the earth, but this is more static than Milton's earlier pageant.

[22] Also see Voltaire's "On Superstition" ("Every [Christian] dispute has caused torrents of blood to flow"); "On the Interpretation of the New Testament" ("Our theological quarrels . . . have flooded the earth with it [blood]"); and "The Sermon of the Fifty" ("The Christian religion . . . has caused so much blood to flow"), Voltaire, *Toleration and Other Essays,* trans. Joseph McCabe (New York and London, 1912), pp. 94, 124, 176.

[23] Lecky, *History of European Morals,* 3rd ed. rev. (New York, 1900), II, 255.

he had been anticipated by Jules Verne's *Cinq Semaines en Ballon* (1862; translation published in New York,[63] 1869), Twain gave up his plan.[24] In *Tom Sawyer Abroad* (1894), he increased his passengers from the original one to three and sent the fictional balloon over North Africa, thereby turning former chance similarities to Verne's aerial "voyages et découvertes en Afrique par trois Anglais" into real ones.

In flying "over India, China," part of the convict's terrain, Satan and Theodor Fischer are supernaturally airborne, without benefit of balloon. The same kind of travel is used in George MacDonald's *At the Back of the North Wind* (1871). His readings from "that beloved book" were so much appreciated by the Clemens girls that Mark "had to invent some more." Whether his oral sequels continued the boy Diamond's mystical flights in the arms of a beautiful lady, the North Wind, is not recorded. In 1899, when his favorite listener, Susy, was dead, what Twain chiefly remembered of the story was the peace and insight gained by Diamond, who is visited a final time by the North Wind in the guise of "kind, benignant" Death.[25]

Twain's two aeronauts descend on "a little city in India," where Satan transforms himself into a turbaned native and in five minutes makes a cherry stone grow into a great tree whose branches are heavy with ever-renewed "oranges, grapes, bananas, peaches, cherries, apricots, and so on." When a Portuguese claims the tree because it is on his property, Satan makes the fruits rot and the leaves wither and fall, and he ties the selfish owner's life to that of the tree. Jules Verne limits himself to describng African "fig-palms" with double fruit. Twain's episode belongs among the Indian, Amerindian, and Irish folk tales of multiple fruits and of magical growth and withering. "Every fruit... From east, from south, and from north... Used to come from the top of the one tree."[26] The parent[64] stock of many of

[24] *Mark Twain's Notebook*, pp. 118–122. See D. M. McKeithan, "Mark Twain's *Tom Sawyer Abroad* and Jules Verne's *Five Weeks in a Balloon*," *University of Texas Studies in English*, XXVIII, 257–270 (1949), and McKeithan, *Court Trials in Mark Twain and Other Essays* ('S-Gravenhage, 1958), pp. 156–168.

[25] Clara Clemens, *My Father Mark Twain* (New York and London, 1931), pp. 25, 242; A. B. Paine, *Mark Twain*, Stormfield Ed. (New York, 1929), XXXII, 1074. In Pedro Antonio de Alarcón's *The Strange Friend of Tito Gil*, translated by Mrs. Francis Darr in 1890, Tito has a happy dream between taking vitriol in 1724 and waking on Judgment Day in 2316. His friend Death conducts him on an international, aerial journey to a tomb.

[26] "Vision of Cathair Mor," *Journal of the Royal Historical and Archaeological Association of Ireland* (Dublin, 1874), 4th ser., II, 43. Twain used to tell stories in the manner of *The Arabian Nights*, but his tree is not among the marvelous trees of that collection. See *The Book of the Thousand Nights and a Night*, trans. Richard F. Burton (New York, 1934), III, 1840; J. Oestrups, *Studien über 1001 Nacht*, aus dem Dänischen übersetzt von O. Rescher (Stuttgart, 1925), pp. 113, 117, 134; and Nikita Elisséeff, *Thèmes et motifs des mille et une nuits* (Beyrouth, 1949), p. 173.

these wondrous trees is perhaps the Tree of Life in the New Jerusalem, "which bare twelve manner of fruits, and yielded her fruit every month" (Revelation, 22:2). A definite source of Twain's version probably exists, but I have not discovered it.

In the fruit tree episode, the punishment, despite its fairy tale severity, is justified by wickedness. In his Austrian miracles, Satan may be punitive or cruel to forestall greater cruelty, but he is also capricious and stonyhearted. Mark Twain could not clear his consciousness of the spectacle of the Creator's taking life as magnificently and unfeelingly as he bestows it. No illusion about the dignity or value of human life clouds the eyes of divinity; humanity is definitely expendable. Verne describes a sandstorm which overturns, breaks, and completely buries a caravan, while horses moan, men shriek, and the wind roars. His balloonists look down from the air grieved and helpless.[27] Twain parallels the destruction of the desert innocents in *Tom Sawyer Abroad.* The same mood and emotion reappear in the storm, earthquake, and lightning, resulting in fire, with which Satan wipes out his newly created castle and people, while the victims shriek, the wind howls, and the Eseldorf boys, like clumsy Gullivers, weep in futile pity.

Mark Twain was obsessed by fire, as in his memory of giving a drunken tramp lucifers with which he set fire to a calaboose and perished in it. He built up the danger of "three days of fire" which visited the Clemenses in Hartford the winter of 1880–1881.[28] In his copy of *Magnalia Christi Americana* (purchased November, 1881), he underlined three words in Cotton Mather's account of a man's house burning with "*his three children,* which were all he had, consum'd in it," and wrote in the margin, "The miserable injustice of it."[29] And one of his unfinished manuscripts contains a dream in which a home is burned, a fortune dissipated, and a family disgraced.[30]

His nerve ends exposed, Mark Twain no doubt reacted keenly[65] to the fires in *Zadig, Faust,* and *The Master of Palmyra.* But the fire in his own novel has an unusual combination of features: the relation of a ruthless creator (owner) to his creatures, an enhancement of pathos through scale, and juvenile spectators in whom emotion mounts painfully. The fire episode before *The Mysterious Stranger* which comes nearest to containing or suggesting these three features is in the eighth chapter of Louisa May Alcott's *Little Men* (1871). Mark's inclusion of this popular book in reading to his three daughters is purely conjectural.

The Plumfield youngsters are persuaded to sacrifice to an invisible

27 Verne, *Five Weeks in a Balloon,* trans. Arthur Chambers, Everyman's Library, No. 779 (London, n.d.), p. 158.

28 Paine, *Mark Twain,* Chap. xxx, 65, and Chap. xxxi, pp. 699–700.

29 *Catalogue of the Library of Samuel L. Clemens,* Part I, p. 49.

30 DeVoto, *Mark Twain at Work,* p. 118.

spirit. Because there are no "live creatures," dolls and leaden soldiers are put to the flames, then a new toy village:

> The children arranged the doomed village, laid a line of coals along the main street, and then sat down to watch the conflagration. . . . The wooden population . . . also caught and blazed away without a cry. It took some time to reduce the town to ashes, and the lookers-on enjoyed the spectacle immensely, cheering as each house fell, dancing like wild Indians when the steeple flamed aloft, and actually casting one wretched little churn-shaped lady, who had escaped to the suburbs, into the very heart of the fire.

In *The Mysterious Stranger*, when "the people came flying out, shrieking . . . Satan brushed them back, paying no attention to our begging and crying and imploring . . . not one of the five hundred poor creatures escaping. Our hearts were broken; we could not keep from crying." The demonic nature having been aroused in Miss Alcott's innocents, Teddy throws a pet lamb and Annabella into the holocaust. Then, as a victim seems to come to life, horror, pity, and fright awaken.

> Poor dear Annabella . . . expressed her anguish and resentment in a way that terrified her infant destroyer. Being covered with kid, she did not blaze, but did what was worse, she *squirmed*. First one leg curled up, then the other, in a very awful and lifelike manner; next she flung her arms over her head as if in great agony. . . . This unexpected demonstration startled every one and frightened Teddy half out of his little wits. He looked, then screamed and fled toward the house.

In *Personal Recollections of Joan of Arc,* fire is a symbol of man's utmost inhumanity to man. It is rekindled by Eseldorfers in 1590 during their worst witch-terror. "The more of them we burned the[66] more of the breed rose up in their places." In the trials a "witch commission" asks the questions "written down for the use of witch-commissioners two centuries before." Twain undoubtedly had in mind the first reduction of "the doctrine of witchcraft . . . to a regular system," the inquisitor Jacob Sprenger's Hammer of Witches, *Malleus Maleficarum* (1486). The manual is discussed in one of Twain's most read books, Andrew D. White's *A History of the Warfare of Science with Theology in Christendom* (1896), in Thomas Wright's *Narratives of Sorcery and Magic* (1851), of which Twain obtained the 1852 edition in 1885, and in Michelet's *La Sorcière*.[31]

---

[31] White, *History* (New York and London, 1896), I, 352 and n., 385; II, 118; Wright, *Narratives* (London, 1851), I, 153–159. Twain's misdating the treatise may be due to careless reading of Michelet, who begins an extended note on literature of sorcery and witchcraft about 1400 and discusses "the great Sprenger" without dating his work. In the text, while dating the "pocket manual of folly," Michelet refers to its predecessor, the *Directorium* for the inquisition of heresy, as being a hundred years behind the times in the fifteenth century.

The cruelty of Satan by means of fire prepares the reader for man's use of the same element. Ten school girls are "burned at the stake all together." Gottfried Narr's grandmother is burned "in our market-square." Frau Brandt is condemned as a witch, "blasphemer and heretic," excommunicated, chained, and consumed by fire. Before her words turn to shrieks of agony, she forgives her tormentors. Impatient at the commission's delays, a howling, cursing mob pursues "a born lady," who finds all doors of escape closed in her face; she is hanged and stoned. Frightened by public opinion, Theodor Fischer throws a stone, and the young daughter looks on and weeps, "afraid to say or do anything."[32] The astrologer is in danger, and so is Marget, but the boys are afraid to warn her.

In the pathetic incident of Grandmother Narr's death, Mark Twain seems to be indebted to Sir Walter Scott's account of the execution of two Scottish witches.

Parallel columns will best reveal the connection:

The Mysterious Stranger

Chapter VI

"I am old and very poor," she said, "and I work for my living. There was no way but to confess. If I hadn't they might have set me free. That would ruin me, for no one would forget that I had been suspected of being a witch, and so I would get no more work, and wherever I went they would set the dogs on me. In a little while I would starve. The fire is best; it is soon over." ... She snuggled closer to the fire, and put out her hands to warm them.

Letters on Demonology and Witchcraft

(1830)   Letter IX

"One of them, who was a silly creature, told me under secresie, that[67] she had not confest because she was guilty, but being a poor creature who wrought for her meat, and being defamed for a witch, she knew she would starve, for no person thereafter would either give her meat or lodging, and that all men would beat her and hound dogs at her, and that therefore she desired to be out of the world." ... The victim was an insane old woman ... who had so little idea of her situation as to rejoice at the sight of the fire which was destined to consume her.[33]

"It was bitter cold weather when Gottfried's grandmother was burned." The detail of a bewildered beldam's stretching her hands

---

[32] See W. E. H. Lecky, *A History of England in the Eighteenth Century*, New Impression (London, 1920), II, 331–333, for a general parallel to this witchcraft episode. Twain owned an 1887 edition of Lecky's *History*.

[33] In the quotation, Scott is using Sir George Mackenzie's *The Laws and Customes of Scotland, in Matters Criminal* (1678). In the other instance, he may be drawing on his friend, Charles Kirkpatrick Sharpe: "The grandmother was executed at Dornoch; and it is said, that ... the weather proving very severe, she sat composedly warming herself by the fire prepared to consume her, while the other instruments of death were making ready" (*A Historical Account of the Belief in Witchcraft in Scotland*, London, 1884, p. 200).

to the fire is found in the oral lore clinging to Sir Walter's second narrative, that of Janet Horne's execution in Sutherland in 1722 or 1727: "The lady well remembered the awe-struck yet excited crowd, the lighting of the fire, and the miserable appearance of the poor fatuous creature whom it was kindled to consume, and who seemed to be so little aware of her situation, that she held out her thin shrivelled hands to warm them at the blaze."[34]

V. Ideas

Mark Twain yearned for the good and compulsively gaped at the evil. Guilt, resentment, suffering imaginary and real built up in him an intolerable tension. For this tension there were safety valves: (1) exploding in humor, satire, or crusading fervor; (2) reasoning his way out of the moral issue by determinism; (3) evading all issues by losing himself in time, space, or dreams. Stripped of imagination, these transcendences would have been guffaw, sneer,[68] or curse; obvious rationalization; escapism or schizophrenia. Evidently, Twain was not a systematic or objective thinker. He tinkered with ideas, hoping to put together a combination which would make life bearable. His thought was not constructive but destructive, its end being exculpation and protection, its means negation of free will, conscience, and finally life itself.

A foundation tenet in Mark Twain's creed is that man is despicable. Minnie Brashear reminds readers that both Swift and Twain find the comparison of men and animals favorable to the latter. To the Swift of *Gulliver's Travels*, men are "curious little vermin," a "most pernicious race of little odious vermin," and to Twain, "shabby, poor worthless vermin."[35] The ghost of Twain's Cincinnati mentor, Macfarlane, has also been seen flitting through *The Mysterious Stranger*. About the time he began the novel, Twain was recalling the winter of 1856/57 and the Scotchman's abuse of vindictive, retrograde man, whose heart was the only bad one "in the animal kingdom" and whose atrocious intellect "degraded him to a rank far below the plane of the other animals."[36]

Another tenet is that man's actions are predetermined, as in Macfarlane's contention that everything traces back to the Creator's "few microscopic seed germs, or perhaps *one* microscopic seed germ." Why man should be despised for being what fate makes him is not explained.

[34] Hugh Miller, *An Autobiography* (Boston, 1858), p. 120.

[35] Minnie Brashear, *Mark Twain: Son of Missouri* (Chapel Hill, N.C., 1934), p. 240. Satan's description of ignorant, conceited, diseased mankind reads, "a shabby, poor, worthless lot all around." See *Mark Twain's Notebook*, p. 337, for a story project on "the little stinking human race … the vermin that infest" the living globe (perhaps *The Mysterious Stranger*). For Twain on Swift, see Coley B. Taylor, *Mark Twain's Margins on Thackeray's "Swift"* (New York, 1935), p. 55.

[36] *The Autobiography of Mark Twain*, p. 97.

Yet when Twain read in Jonathan Edwards's *Freedom of the Will* such assertions as "nothing ever comes to pass without a Cause" and "moral Necessity and Inability . . . [are] consistent with blameworthiness," he thought he was in the presence of "a drunken lunatic."[37]

In *Zadig*, chance does not exist, because immutable law governs our "little atom." Voltaire's philosopher reasons at times like the Old Man in *What Is Man?*, "Man can give himself neither ideas nor sensations" (H. I. Woolf's translation). In *The Mysterious Stranger*, man has no choice, but a supernatural being may start a[69] different chain of causation by means of a gift, false accusation of theft, fire, burning at the stake, or drowning in order to ameliorate man's sorry destiny. Although Carlyle's metaphysical thought has also been suggested as affecting Mark Twain's determinism,[38] a stronger influence, demonstrated by Albert Bigelow Paine and others, was that of Lecky's *History of European Morals*. Its greatest service, perhaps, was to clarify Twain's choice by reducing the opposed schools of morals to two: (1) the stoical, sentimental, intuitive, with a rational reference, and (2) the epicurean, selfish, inductive, with an experiential reference.[39]

A third tenet of Twain's is that the conscience is a morbid and deceitful growth. The first group of moralists discussed by Lecky assert the existence of a "natural Sense of Right and Wrong" (Shaftesbury, 1699), of a Moral Sense or "Faculty of perceiving moral excellence" (Francis Hutcheson, 1728). Satan's rebuttal in 1590 is over a century ahead of the joining of issue: "The Moral Sense degrades him to the bottom layer of animated beings and is a shameful possession." John Clarke and other "selfish moralists," Lecky's second group, deny the innate perception of moral values and define the inclusive virtue of benevolence as self-love in disguise.[40]

Whether Mark Twain read beyond Lecky on this subject, I do not know,[41] but he was obsessed by the Moral Sense, believing with Jeremy Bentham that its exponents were prigs who abetted hypocrisy, sin, and guilt by imposing a false interpretation on the realities of life.

[37] *The Works of President Edwards* (Worcester, Mass., 1808–1809), V, 54, 176; and E. Hudson Long, *Mark Twain Handbook* (New York, 1957), pp. 296–297.

[38] Edgar H. Hemminghaus, *Mark Twain in Germany* (New York, 1939), p. 110.

[39] Lecky, *History of European Morals*, I, 2 ff. See Wagenknecht, *Mark Twain*, p. 243: "The influence of Lecky is unquestionable." Twain first read Lecky about 1874.

[40] See Thomas Fowler, *Shaftesbury and Hutcheson* (New York, 1883), and William Robert Scott, *Francis Hutcheson* (Cambridge, 1900).

[41] Brashear's tentative extension of Twain's knowledge of rationalists like Hobbes, Locke, Newton, and Hume beyond Lecky is as shaky as my conjecture about his acquaintance with the moral-sense writers and the selfish moralists. But Thomas Paine is different; Twain read him in his youth.

He would have scoffed at Archbishop Richard Whately's pronouncement, "The Moral faculty...is one of which brutes are destitute" (1827),[42] much in Satan's fashion, "A bullock...is not besmirched with the Moral Sense, but is as the angels are, and knows no wrong, and never does it....There shouldn't be any wrong; and without the Moral Sense there couldn't be any." Twain[70] might damn the fraudulent Moral Sense and fall back on volitionless self-interest with La Rochefoucauld, but the emancipation he longed for was from his Presbyterian conditioning: "Mine was a trained Presbyterian conscience and knew but the one duty—to hunt and harry its slave upon all pretexts and on all occasions, particularly when there was no sense nor reason in it."[43]

The very vehemence with which Twain supported determinism and denied free will operating through conscience and the Moral Sense reveals unsureness. Further relief was found in the supposition that the ugly and incongruous reality of conscious, necessitarian life is after all a dreary nightmare. Satan's simple advice is, "Dream other dreams, and better." The "romantic solipsism" of *The Mysterious Stranger* has been traced to Carlyle, to William James's psychology, and for its most artistic interpretation to Emerson.[44] In Wilbrandt's play, the Master of Palmyra wonders about Phoebe's soul, "Is it, like life itself, only a dream?" The metempsychotic adventures of another character, Zenobia, gave Twain "the sense of the passage of a dimly connected procession of dream-pictures." Unfortunately, the somnolence of Palmyra, like that of Eseldorf, is agitated by intolerance and mob violence.

Solipsistic conjecture crosses many boundaries: Pascal's *Thoughts,* "It may well be that this life itself is but a dream"; Schopenhauer's *The World as Will and Idea,* "We have dreams; may not our whole life be a dream?"; Pater's *Studies in the History of the Renaissance,* "...each mind keeping as a solitary prisoner its own dream of a world." Mark Twain may not have read Calderon's *La Vida es Sueño* (*Life Is a Dream*) in Edward Fitzgerald's translation, *Such Stuff As Dreams Are Made Of* (1865), but acquaintance with *The Tempest* probably began in his piloting days. He quotes from Act IV, scene 1, in *Is Shakespeare Dead?*

> The cloud-cap'd towers, the gorgeous palaces,
> The solemn temples, the great globe itself,
> Yea, all which it inherit, shall dissolve,
> And, like an [this] insubstantial pageant faded,

---

[42] *New English Dictionary, s. v.* moral sense.

[43] *The Autobiography of Mark Twain,* p. 41.

[44] Hemminghaus, p. 107, n. 32, and p. 116. Hemminghaus is discussing Friedrich Schönemann's *Mark Twain als literarische Persönlichkeit* (Jena, 1925) and Walther Fischer's review (1926). Cf. Masters, *Mark Twain,* p. 231.

Leave not a rack behind. We are such stuff[71]
As dreams are made on, and our little life
Is rounded with a sleep.[45]

If there is one central source of Twain's dream musings, I suggest
that it is Prospero's haunting speech. To Twain (or Satan), the whole
bitter spectacle is a dream, and the dreamer is no more than "a useless
thought . . . wandering forlorn among the empty eternities!"

I have already mentioned Louis François Clairville's comédie-
vaudeville, *Satan; ou, Le Diable à Paris,* which combines Twain's title
(in the translation), Satan as pedagogue, and dream philosophy. In
this play, Fernand de Mauléon pledges his soul to Satan in exchange
for ten years of renewed fortune. Again and again Satan proves to
Fernand that his fiancée, his banker, and his protesting friends are
false. When Satan turns out to be the disguised daughter of a man he
once saved from bankruptcy, Fernand recaptures love in a comic
reversal of the Timon of Athens theme. Like the Satan of Mark Twain's
story, the mentor in Clairville and in his translator, Charles Selby, is
a gentleman who seems at times an evil spirit from hell, at others "the
heavenly spirit of my dream." His mission is to destroy all Fernand's
"beautiful dreams." The emphasis on life as a dream is persistent. "Do
I dream?" provokes this reply from Satan, "You were blind until now."
Selby's Fernand (rechristened Count Henry Beausoleil) exclaims, "I
wake as from a dream." Regretting his "bright and blessed delusion,"
he sings a melancholy song, "The Happy Dream." Later, he protests
in prose, "O! Heaven, in mercy, since to live is misery, take my life,
and give me back my dream." Even when the visitant transforms herself into an adorable maiden, he insists, "Our world is still a world of
dreams." The hero has learned the lesson that his values are *ignes
fatui;* though confused about dream and reality, he is closer to essential
truth.[46] His counterpart in *The Mysterious Stranger* is known to pur-
blind mortals as Philip Traum (Philip Dream).

If Twain saw this play, the dream interpretation and the presence
of a didactic mysterious stranger would have impressed him. The
resemblances to *The Mysterious Stranger* may well be coincidental,[72]
but they are nonetheless indicative of current speculations which
stimulated Mark Twain.

VI. Conclusion

Twain's sources were formative, corroborative, and illustrative.
They shaped his outlook, supported and clarified attitudes already

---

[45] *Is Shakespeare Dead?* (New York and London, 1909), p. 125.

[46] Clairville et Damartin, *Satan; ou, Le Diable à Paris* (Paris [1845?]), pp. 6,
12–13, 23, 26, 31–33; Selby, *The Mysterious Stranger* (London [1844]); Selby,
Satan in Paris; or, The Mysterious Stranger (Boston, 1855), pp. 50, 52–53, 61–62,
68–70.

formed, and afforded graphic instances of life as he understood it. The shaping influences on *The Mysterious Stranger* were probably (1) from life: Twain's Presbyterian upbringing, boyhood friendships and experience, horror of fire, remorse, conversations with Macfarlane, suffering and loss in maturity; (2) from literature: Voltaire's *Zadig*, the *Apocryphal New Testament, Paradise Lost, Gulliver's Travels*, Prospero's speech, and possibly Jane Taylor's "The Mysterious Stranger," as well as *Micromegas* and other works by Voltaire. Corroborative influences were Carlyle, Ingersoll, *Faust*, Wilbrandt's *Der Meister von Palmyra*, Lecky's *History of European Morals*, and possibly Michelet's *La Sorcière* and the Clairville-Selby play. Illustrative matter came from sources already mentioned, as well as from Emperor Norton's happy insanity, the life of Luther, MacDonald's *At the Back of the North Wind*, Scott's *Letters on Demonology and Witchcraft*, and possibly from Verne's *Cinq Semaines en Ballon* and Alcott's *Little Men*. The greatest influence was the heredity or experience which gave Samuel Clemens a sense of guilt and a desire to escape from it, and the next in potency was Voltaire.

In this summary, the Age of Reason is represented by Voltaire and Swift and interpreted by Macfarlane, Lecky, and that belated Tom Paine, Colonel Robert Ingersoll. Miss Brashear finds Twain relatively untouched by nineteenth-century speculation; instead, "Mark Twain's philosophy of life, one is forced to conclude, must have had its foundation in the more rigid eighteenth-century trends of thinking."[47] These trends of thinking had their appropriate literary media in the educational tale and the philosophical romance. Theodor Fischer's passivity makes him like the hero of many a "story of instruction and delight" whose mentor frees him from the misconceptions of his time. Although he is apparently unlike those heroes of philosophical romance who initiate their own search for truth, his mentor, Satan, is at last disclosed to be the active, critical part of his own consciousness. Despite that revelation, Theodor[73] is blood brother to Candide, the formation of his mind and character being outside his control in a fatalistic world. He is only a distant relative of later, *Bildungsroman* heroes like Wilhelm Meister, who exercise free will.

A novel should have careful motivation, character development, and tight narrative structure. A pedagogical-philosophical romance, if it is to be judged by the laws of its own nature, should achieve interest and significance through its type characters and episodic events. Judging *The Mysterious Stranger* as a novel, Edwin S. Fussell finds it structurally weak because of the "serious conflict" between "Twain's emotional reactions" and "his theoretical formulations"

[47] Brashear, *Mark Twain*, p. 242.

(humanity and world view),[48] but this tension or interplay creates the interest and reveals the significance of Twain's didactic romance. If the ideas are not taken at their face value and then rejected as "sophomoric fatalism" and "bunkum,"[49] they may be read as figures of speech expressing the despair of man's spirit in its growing awareness of life's sadness and inscrutability. Determinism and solipsism are autobiographical-experiential projections on a narrative canvas, human and emotional to their very roots, not intellectual. What saves the romance from the anticlimax of defeat is not the logic—for it has none—but the truth of feeling and beauty of phrasing of Satan's final speech:

".... There is no God, no universe, no human race, no earthly life, no heaven, no hell. It is all a dream—a grotesque and foolish dream. Nothing exists but you. And you are but a *thought*—a vagrant thought, a useless thought, a homeless thought, wandering forlorn among the empty eternities!"[74]

[48] Fussell, "The Structural Problem of *The Mysterious Stranger*," *Studies in Philology*, XLIX, 103 (1952). Cf. p. 101: "Abstracted, ideational determinism is plot; extended, it is also Twain's content, subject, and material."

[49] *Ibid.*, pp. 101–102. Granville Hicks calls Twain "the sophomoric philosopher" (*Mark Twain: Selected Criticism*, ed. Arthur L. Scott, Dallas, Texas, 1955, p. 221).

Mark Twain and Little Satan: The Writing of *The Mysterious Stranger*

JOHN S. TUCKEY

THE MYSTERIOUS STRANGER, AS PUBLISHED, BEGINS WITH A DESCRIPTION of the sleepy village of Eseldorf, "in the middle of Austria."[1] It is possible to show that Mark Twain began his story in Austria in fact as

From John S. Tuckey, *Mark Twain and Little Satan: The Writing of "The Mysterious Stranger"* (Lafayette, Indiana: Purdue University Studies, 1963). By permission of the Purdue Research Foundation.

[1] *Definitive Edition,* XXVII, p. 3. This edition, used for this and subsequent references to the published works unless otherwise noted, is *The Writings of Mark Twain* (New York: Gabriel Wells, 1922–1925), 37 vols., hereinafter cited as *Writings.*

well as in his fiction. There is evidence that he started writing it either late in 1897 or very early in 1898, and that "Eseldorf," which has been generally thought to have been written last, was begun before either "Hannibal" or "Print Shop."

After having spent the summer at Weggis, Lake Lucerne, Switzerland, Twain moved with his family to Vienna, where he took residence at the Hotel Metropole on September 28, 1897.[2] He was received with great acclaim, and his quarters at the Metropole soon resembled "a court, where with those of social rank assembled the foremost authors, journalists, diplomats, painters, philosophers, scientists, of Europe, and therefore of the world. A sister of the Emperor of Germany lived at the Metropole that winter and was especially cordial. Mark Twain's daily movements were chronicled as if he had been some visiting potentate."[3] During the early part of his stay, however, an illness kept him from taking an active part in the life of the Austrian capital. As Max Lederer has noted, Twain was suffering from what he described as a "toothache in the big toe"—presumably an attack of gout; he "received his guests in bed, clad in a white flannel jacket." At this time of sickness, he reportedly said that he was looking forward "with special joy" to gathering his impressions of Vienna: "I would stand at the street corner and let the stream of humanity rush past me, trying to grasp even the slightest difference between these people and those whom I have observed before."[4] It is clear that he had come to Vienna with the intention of making literary use of such impressions.[16] "Asked on his arrival, if he would work in Vienna, he answered: 'I am a diligent man, a year must be used.'" And upon then being asked if he expected to work on a Viennese topic, he replied, "Certainly, Vienna is such an interesting place that at any rate something—I cannot say yet what it may be—will force itself upon my mind and ask to be worked upon."[5]

It was an accurate prediction. Something in Vienna did soon capture his interest. Exciting political events were in progress, and he become intensely absorbed in following them. Lederer has recorded:

A short time after his arrival Mark Twain attended a session of the City Council of Vienna. He took a seat in the press gallery where he had a good view of the magnificent hall which he much admired. Dr. Karl Lueger, then Mayor of Vienna, was at the same time President of the City Council. He was the leader of the Anti-Semitic Christian Social Party, which had its

[2] See *Mark Twain's Notebook,* ed. Albert Bigelow Paine (New York: Harper Brothers, 1935), p. 339.

[3] Max Lederer, "Mark Twain in Vienna," *Mark Twain Quarterly,* VII (Summer–Fall 1945), p. 2. This useful article is mainly a digest of news items about Mark Twain as reported in the *Neue Freie Presse.*

[4] *Ibid.,* p. 2.

[5] *Ibid.,* p. 2.

supporters mainly among the lower middle classes, and had come to power after brutally smashing all resistance, even that of the Crown. He had to be elected three times by making use more of demagogic than of democratic methods before his election got the sanction of the monarch.

The fact that only the Mayor spoke during the proceedings struck him as odd, and he asked ironically if the councillors were not permitted to speak as well. . . . At the close, Mark Twain remarked with "a peculiar smile," that he had been much interested in the session.[6]

Twain had also the opportunity of observing Dr. Lueger in the sessions of the Reichsrath, or Imperial Parliament, of which this demagogic mayor was a member. The Reichsrath was having turbulent times as a result of a recent shift in the balance of power. He started covering its sessions as a kind of reporter-at-large for America.[7] Notebook entries that he made in November, 1897, include lengthy memoranda of proceedings, with the hour and minute noted in some instances.[8] On November 4, Twain was present at one of the more riotous sessions, during which Dr. Otto Lecher made a historic twelve-hour speech and Dr. Lueger also spoke. The *Neue Freie Presse* reported Twain's reactions, as here summarized by Lederer:

Mark Twain was all attention, watching the turbulent events with intense interest. He was shown those members of Parliament whose names were known to him through the newspapers. . . . At length Mark Twain drew out his notebook from his pocket and began to put down his . . . impressions of the uproar. An expression of greatest astonishment appeared on[17] his face when a chorus of yelling voices and hammering the wooden desks with bare fists and all kinds of instruments filled the noble ampitheatre. . . . He stared down into the hall as if something was happening there which he had believed impossible. . . . Mark Twain who had come before the session opened remained seated in his place taking notes as late as 11 p.m.[9]

It is evident that he believed he was seeing history made before his eyes, and that he missed little of the spectacle, of which he wrote in "Stirring Times in Austria," a masterful exposition of complex political events.[10] These happenings had an impact upon his composition of "Eseldorf." To begin with, it can be shown that three of his story characters were given names of actual persons who had played prominent roles in the Reichsrath meetings and had thus figured as important characters in the dramatic incidents that he described in "Stirring Times." One of these legislators was Deputy Wohlmeyer,

[6] *Ibid.*, p. 3.

[7] *Mark Twain: A Biography* (New York: Gabriel Wells, 1923), 4 vols., III, pp. 1050–1052.

[8] These memoranda are not in *Mark Twain's Notebook* but are available in the holographic notebooks and in full typescript copies in the Mark Twain Papers at the University of California, Berkeley. See Typescript 32b (II), pp. 44–48.

[9] "Mark Twain in Vienna," pp. 3–4.

[10] In *Literary Essays, Writings,* XXII, pp. 197–243.

whose name is found in "Eseldorf" (and in *The Mysterious Stranger*) as that of Theodor's comrade Seppi Wohlmeyer. Another was Vice President Fuchs, whose name occurs in the story as that of a wealthy young brewer, Joseph Fuchs. (The latter appears as a disappointed suitor in a long passage, deleted from the published tale, in which the young ladies of the village fall in love with young Satan, the mysterious stranger.) The third person, who was especially prominent in the events that led to the outbreak of rioting on the floor of the assembly, was Dr. Karl Lueger, leader of the anti-Jewish Christian Socialist Party and Burgomeister of Vienna.[11]

The manuscript shows that in beginning "Eseldorf," Twain at first called one of his characters "Father Lueger." He then began writing "Adolf" in place of "Lueger" a few pages before he reached the end of the first chapter; thereafter he went back and substituted the new name wherever he had already written "Lueger."[12]

There is reason to think that the impression he gained of Dr. Karl Lueger inspired his characterization of Father Lueger, as well as his initial choice of that name. What his appraisal of Dr. Lueger would have been may be readily inferred from the representation of him by the *Britannica* as the leader of "a clerico-anti-Semitic Tammany in Vienna."[13] It will be recalled that he soon thereafter championed the Jewish people in his essay "Concerning the Jews,"[14] and that some three years later he was to lead a vigorous attack upon New York's Tammany.[15] There can be little[18] doubt that he conceived a strong dislike for Dr. Lueger, regarding him as a conniving opportunist, a politico-religious power-seeker.[16] In his notebook he recorded his impression that "the clever Lueger is a graceful man & most persuasive *looking* speaker—and probably *is* a competently bitter one."[17] In the "Stirring Times" article he described Lueger as one who knew how to "trim his sails to any wind," and, sardonically,

[11] *Ibid.;* the name "Wohlmeyer" appears on p. 227 and p. 229, "Fuchs" appears on p. 240, and "Lueger" is mentioned fifteen times in pp. 224–233. The passage of "Eseldorf" in which a character named Fuchs is presented will be further discussed in the next chapter.

[12] Beginning on p. 17 of the 22-page chapter, "Adolf" appears in the holograph as originally written. "Lueger" was written initially on pp. 5, 7, 8, and 10 and then crossed out with wavy lines and replaced with "Adolf."

[13] Fourteenth ed., II, p. 77.

[14] *Writings*, XXII, pp. 263–287. On the first page of this article, he indicates that it was written in response to inquiries he had received concerning what he had said about the Jews in "Stirring Times in Austria."

[15] See *Mark Twain: A Biography*, III, pp. 1145–1148.

[16] *Britannica*, s. v. "Lueger, Karl," describes him as "zealous" in his religious duties, wishing to "capture the university" for his church.

[17] Typescript 32b (II), p. 46. This note bears comparison with "Eseldorf," p. 6, where Father Lueger is said to have "belonged to the village Council, & lorded it there, & played smart dodges that carried his projects through." Copyright 1963, Mark Twain Company.

as "that distinguished religious expert."[18] He also reported the remarks of those who styled Lueger as "the shifty trickster of Vienna"[19] and "Betrayer of the People."[20] It is therefore of particular significance that in the "Eseldorf" version the priest who was initially called "Father Lueger" is a thoroughly bad priest, a greedy, power-seeking hypocrite. Some of the bad priest's activities, as represented by Twain, probably had direct reference to events in which the actual Dr. Lueger had figured. Here is a likely example. The Austrian elections of 1895 had resulted in a sweeping victory for the anti-Jewish faction. In October of that year, the municipal council of Vienna had elected Dr. Lueger as mayor. He thereupon became the leader of his party, displacing the former leader Prince Liechtenstein, whose policies had been more acceptable to the emperor.[21] These events may be related to Twain's statement, which appears in "Eseldorf" and in *The Mysterious Stranger* near the end of Chapter I, that the good priest "Father Peter had been out a couple of years, and our other priest, Father Adolf [Twain first wrote Lueger] had his flock."[22] By the fall of 1897, it was literally true that the (good) Prince Liechtenstein had been out for some two years and that Dr. Lueger "had his flock." A further consideration is that Mark Twain was on visiting terms with the royal family and sympathetic to their side of the political contest in which Dr. Lueger was leading the opposition. A notebook entry of Sunday, October 10, 1897, reported that he had discussed with the princess the harm done by priests when they meddled in politics.[23] It is likely that their remarks included oblique, if not direct, references to Dr. Lueger.

It is necessary to explain that the bad priest has been edited almost entirely out of the published version. He was, as the manuscript clearly reveals, intended by Twain as the villain of the tale, the one who falsely accused Father Peter of stealing money from him, gave false testimony at the trial, and committed many other misdeeds. Whereas in the published story he is initially described merely as "a very zealous and strenuous priest, much considered,"[19] Twain actually described Father Lueger at this point as "a very loud and zealous and strenuous priest ... always working to get more reputation," and added, satirically, that "he was dissolute and profane and malicious but otherwise a good enough man, it was generally thought."[24] Furthermore, it appears that A. B. Paine and

18 *Writings*, XXII, p. 229.

19 *Ibid.*, p. 231.

20 *Ibid.*, p. 227.

21 *Britannica*, II, p. 77.

22 *Writings*, XXVII, p. 7.

23 *Mark Twain's Notebook*, p. 340.

24 "Eseldorf," p. 5. Copyright 1963, Mark Twain Company.

F. A. Duneka, who shared the work of editing the story for publication, actually invented another character, the astrologer, whom Twain did not have in the story, and attributed to him the villainies of the bad priest that could not be deleted without destroying the plot. In the original typescript that was prepared for use as the printer's copy, derogatory references to the bad priest have been systematically put upon the astrologer—ofter simply by substituting "the astrologer" for the other name. For example, in the published text Nikolaus observes, "Father Peter, with the exception of the astrologer you haven't a real enemy in the village."[25] However, the manuscript, as well as the typescript before editing, had read " . . . with the exception of Father Adolf."[26] When necessary, more extensive rewriting was done to effect the substitution. Once these matters are understood, the connection between Twain's adverse impression of Dr. Lueger and his strongly unfavorable characterization of Father Lueger (Adolf) becomes sufficiently evident. It may be considered that in writing "Stirring Times in Austria," a work of literary journalism, he had had to try to remain objective, or nearly so. He did, as has been shown, find opportunity to quote several disparaging remarks that had been directed at Dr. Lueger, and had in one or two places brought in his own satirical touches, as when in mock praise he had termed him "that distinguished religious expert." But these hits were surely mild and decorous in comparison to the manner in which he would have wished to vent his rage or scorn upon this leader of a "clerico-anti-Semitic Tammany." In a tale such as *The Mysterious Stranger,* he could fully let himself go in vituperative denunciation.

Some working notes that he made for the beginning of "Eseldorf" may indicate that a need to have his full say against Lueger furnished the impetus which carried him into composition. These notes, which are on a single sheet of paper matching that of the first part of the manuscript and which are especially relevant to the dating of Mark Twain's composition of it, are here presented. They were originally made in pencil; later, in black ink, most of the deletions (shown in brackets) and additions (shown in italics)[20] were made. It will be seen that he began with a hostile description of Lueger (his subsequent assigning of this name to a girl character will be explained later):

Plenty Jews

[Father] *Marie* Lueger, a drinking, spiteful, prying, over-godly, malicious priest. Supplanter of Kitchelt

Father Kitchelt (Block)
Margarethe (niece)

---

[25] *Writings,* XXVII, p. 30.
[26] "Eseldorf," p. 65. Copyright 1963, Mark Twain Company.

Nikolaus (Nick) Baumann [(Huck)] *Tom Sawyer [master miller's]*
                                                     son of judge
Seppi Wohlmeyer [(Pole)] *good but simple the innkeeper's*
Theodor Fischer [*Tom*] *Huck* (I.   *—sexton, organist, leader of*
   Son of Hans   *the village band, commune tax collector*
                                 & some other things.

Wilhelm Meidling (Tom Andrews)
The Bishop
              Philip Traum
Procession to quiet Satan (table rapping)
Bridge—Satan built it)
      B. Langenan's tale of the Virgin—
      Wayside shrines—crown & nails and paint
      Old women and dogs harnessed—and carrying bricks & mortar

The great noble Prince—owner of the estate. His hunting-stags destroy
crops. The forester (game-keeper)

Village [Hasenfeld] Eseldorf   Castle on heights—precipice—long
Castle park wide   winding road to it—it overlooks
Other sid [*Sic*] river in a rich plain, river—boats & rafts. With garden in
   monkery in a grove.   front on bank.

	New Jerusalem		Ghetto
			Jew
Stephan	Lehrer	I.	Goldschmid[t]
Edmund	Herold	I.	Nussbaum
	Bochner		Blumenduft[27]

Several things may be learned from these notes. First, it is evident that they were made after Mark Twain had been attending the
Reichsrath sessions, but while their events were still fresh in his mind.
Indeed, the characterization of Lueger as "drinking, spiteful, prying,
over-godly, malicious," which closely parallels that of him in the
story as "dissolute and profane and malicious," suggests that he both
made the notes and began composition while his adverse impression
of the actual Dr. Lueger was so strong and compelling that he had to
write about it. The name "Wohlmeyer"[21] which also appears here
as well as in the story, further shows that he was finding material
in his experience of the parliamentary meetings, in which a person so
named had figured. Also, the last items on the sheet, consisting of
listed names headed "New Jerusalem" placed opposite those headed
"Ghetto/Jew," are probably references to the anti-Semitism that had
been a prominent aspect of those proceedings. In a letter of October
23, 1897, to J. H. Twichell, he had reported that he found "much
politics agoing," and that it was "Christian and Jew by the horns."[28]

[27] Notes for *The Mysterious Stranger*, numbered DV 327bb in the Mark
Twain Papers. Copyright 1963, Mark Twain Company.

[28] *Mark Twain's Letters*, ed. Albert Bigelow Paine (New York: Gabriel
Wells, 1923), II, p. 647.

All of this evidence reinforces the consideration that he wrote these working notes and very likely began the story not long after his viewing of those historic sessions of the Austrian parliament, which continued until November 26, when an uprising caused the suspension of parliamentary government.[29]

Second, the notes contain other items which confirm that they were, in fact, made for and before the writing of the beginning of "Eseldorf." The setting that is briefly sketched—"Castle on heights—precipice—long winding road to it—it overlooks river—boats & rafts"—was used at the start of the story as that of the village of Eseldorf, with its "vast castle" that frowned from the top of a "lofty precipice," beyond which "flowed the tranquil river."[30] And it is noteworthy that alongside this setting he wrote "Village Hasenfeld" and then, in the same pencil-writing, struck out "Hasenfeld" and inserted "Eseldorf." That the change was made in pencil, not in ink as were other revisions, makes it seem likely that he changed the name almost immediately after putting down "Hasenfeld" (i.e., Rabbitfield). And, nominally speaking, when this change was made, the "Eseldorf" version as such was originated.

Third, most of the items that Twain added in black ink were apparently noted after he had written the first chapter but before he began the second. Several additions provided the backgrounds of the three principal boy-characters, who had not figured much in the initial, "Lueger-inspired" chapter. At the start of Chapter II, this material was used, with some elaboration. Nikolaus, designated in the notes as "son of judge," became "son of the principal judge of the local court"; Seppi, noted as "the innkeeper's [son]," became "son of the keeper of the principal inn." And in a similar fashion Twain followed his notes in describing Theodor as "son of the church organist, who was also leader of the village musicians,[22] teacher of the violin, composer, tax-collector of the commune, sexton."[31] Also added in black ink was "Philip Traum," the name that was to be assumed by the young Satan in Chapter II. And "Father" was deleted and "Marie" inserted before "Lueger." He had already changed the name of the bad priest to "Adolf" before he had finished writing the first chapter; while reviewing his notes he evidently shifted the original name to the girl-character who bears it in the published story as well as in the manuscript as the only surviving usage of "Lueger": at the end of Chapter IV, it is related that Father Peter's niece Marget was "at the spinnet teaching Marie Lueger."[32] Marie is described as an "influential" pupil, without any explanation of the source of her influ-

[29] See "Stirring Times in Austria," pp. 236–243.

[30] *Writings*, XXVII, p. 3.

[31] *Writings*, XXVII, p. 8.

[32] *Ibid.*, p. 34.

ence. Twain may at first have intended to present her as the niece of the powerful Father Lueger.

Fourth, the notes reveal that he was actually planning the story as an adaptation of a previously written draft, a few pages of which he was to include, with revisions, in "Eseldorf." By adding the names "Huck," "Pole," and "Tom Andrews," he was identifying several characters of the earlier draft with those he now planned to call by other names. There are nineteen pages of "Eseldorf" in which, as they were originally written, one of the boys was regularly called "Huck"; this name was later deleted and "Nikolaus" inserted. By similar changes "Pole" became "Seppi" and "Tom Andrews" became "Wilhelm Meidling" (the latter is Father Peter's lawyer and Marget's suitor). Likewise, the good preacher of the "pre-Eseldorf" draft, a "Mr. Block," became "Father Peter" by Twain's revision.[33]

Before such changes had been made, these pages had told of Mr. Block's finding of a fortune of "eleven hundred dollars-odd!" which a young Satan had made to appear in his path, and of his agreeing—after much persuasion by Huck and his comrades—to keep the money.[34] As the presence of Huck in the story suggests, this earlier draft had an American setting. It was probably written before Twain's creative imagination had been influenced by the Austrian events that, as has been shown, soon found their way into "Eseldorf." Inasmuch as the letter of October 23 which has already been quoted is mostly about Austrian politics, a likely conjecture is that he had already written, some time previously, the "pre-Eseldorf" pages. Just when he did write them is uncertain; however, the evidence of the materials indicates that he probably did not do so[23] until he had come to Vienna. These pages are on the same paper as that of the rest of the first eighty-five "Eseldorf" pages and of ten additional ones originally numbered 84–93 but later repaginated 377–386. The notes for the beginning of "Eseldorf" are, as has been mentioned, also on this paper. As it happens, this particular paper—of heavy, buff sheets, size 5¼″ by 8⅜″—seems to have been used only during the first few months of Twain's stay at Vienna; a systematic search of the manuscripts has revealed no use of it at other times. In particular, it is significant that none of it is to be found in the manuscripts he is known or believed to have written while at Weggis, where he stayed for more than two

[33] In his notes, Twain listed the new name for the good priest as "Father Kitchelt." This name does not appear in "Eseldorf," and it seems that before beginning that version he had decided to call him "Father Peter."

The "pre-Eseldorf" pages were originally numbered 12, 16–18, 20, 20–32 (two pages were numbered 20), and 34; in revision, these numbers in "Eseldorf" became, respectively, 53, 56–72, and 74.

[34] As incorporated in "Eseldorf" and in *The Mysterious Stranger*, with revisions, this material may be found in *Writings*, XXVII, p. 24 and pp. 27–34.

months before going to Austria.[35] It is likely, then, that he composed the [Hannibal-based] "pre-Eseldorf" draft some time within the first several weeks following his arrival in Vienna. If he did write it then, he would at the time of making notes for beginning "Eseldorf" have still had his first set of characters well in mind—as seems to have been the case.[24]. . .

One sees the creative momentum of the Hannibal-inspired effort suffering the counter-impact of the "strong impression" of Viennese events and losing its force. As Twain had foreseen, his new experiences soon became a compelling subject for literary work. It is evident that the impact of stirring times in Austria changed the course of his composition of *The Mysterious Stranger*. In the "Eseldorf" version, probably begun in November or December, he adapted the previous draft by introducing an Austrian setting and other Austrian material.

Perhaps his attendance of those historic meetings of the Reichsrath defined for him, more clearly than had any previous experience, the role of the detached, ironic observer looking down upon the follies and depravities of the human race and making his sardonic comments. It was a part that he was to continue playing. Within the next few years, as Paine has written, he came to be regarded not "merely as a humorist, but as a sort of Solon presiding over a court of final conclusions."[36] This role was, of course, also that of his mysterious stranger, who was a most appropriate persona for the later Mark Twain.

"Eseldorf," "Stirring Times in Austria," and "The Man That Corrupted Hadleyburg" all had a common origin in Twain's response to the events of his first two months in Vienna—particularly those that occurred on the floor of the Imperial Parliament. . . .[36]

The part of "Eseldorf" that he wrote at this time parallels "Hadleyburg" and "Stirring Times" in its initial emphasis upon the tranquillity of the scene that is thereafter to become one of violence and clamor when those who should represent the best of the human family dishonor themselves. Also, this part of the manuscript culminates in a courtroom scene, even as the principal action of "Hadleyburg" at the town hall assumes the aspect of a public trial and as an account of actions on the floor of the legislature constitutes the substance of "Stirring Times." Mark Twain was already presiding over his

---

[35] "Hellfire Hotchkiss," an incomplete, unpublished story, was written at Weggis; see *Mark Twain: A Biography*, III, p. 1045. Other manuscripts which may have been written there were searched for evidence of possible use of the buff paper of "Eseldorf." Most . . . include pages that are on a cross-barred paper which Twain used extensively at Weggis and perhaps there only. But no paper matching that of pp. 1–85 and 377–386 of "Eseldorf" was found.

He took residence at Weggis on July 18, 1897; see *Mark Twain's Notebook*, p. 331.

[36] *Writings*, XXIX, p. xxxv.

"court of final conclusions." Satan, of course, in a sense holds court throughout *The Mysterious Stranger,* as he examines, judges, and condemns the human race. In all three of these writings, humanity is confronted as it stands openly disgraced; the first reaction of those who look on is one of shock, and the one that soon follows manifests itself in cynical[37] snickers. And that is clearly the effect that Mark Twain intended.[37]

He was writing well. And it is noteworthy that Hannibal seems not to have been the imaginative base of much of this writing. He had found significant new material and an appropriate way of treating it. He had, moreover, developed a new persona—one representing his elder self; his sadder-and-wiser self; his *august* self (it will be seen later that he called his "Print Shop" narrator "August"). It may be granted that the role of a Solon or public conscience could hardly have been a congenial one for Mark Twain, as indeed it could not for anyone conceivably worthy of such an office. But it is evident that a new surge of creative power had been generated by the friction of momentous Austrian events that had charged his thoughts; his artistic potential or potency had seldom, since the 1880's, been greater. Probably it was not because of any marked decline in talent that he did not at this time write the rest of "Eseldorf" but discontinued work upon it after writing about ninety-five pages.

It is entirely certain that he did not write all of the 423-page "Eseldorf" version at this time; it will presently be shown that there are in the latter part of it unmistakable references to historical events of August, 1900. Thus, the problem is to determine how long he continued his initial spurt of work upon the tale and to what point he carried it. The available evidence weighs in favor of his having taken it through that part which is on the buff paper—pages 1–85 and 377–386 (originally 84–93). Inasmuch as he used this paper in two other manuscripts that may be dated as of late in 1897 or early in 1898,[38] but seems not to have used it at any later time, it is likely that

[37] In *The Mysterious Stranger,* Theodor, the naive boy-narrator, does not snicker; however, the reader, who also "looks on," is in effect invited to do so.

[38] These manuscripts in the Mark Twain Papers are "Lecture Times," DV 274 (6), and "Ralph Keeler," DV 274 (7), used in *Mark Twain's Autobiography* (New York: Gabriel Wells, 1924), I, pp. 147–153 and 154–164. Paine, who edited the *Autobiography,* tried to present the materials "in the order in which they were written" (Vol. I, ln); he placed these two selections consecutively just preceding an item—"Beauties of the German Language"—which bears Twain's internal dating of February 3, 1898. Moreover, Twain wrote in his notebook, some time between December 1 and 11, 1897, "Ralph Keeler, Gloverson and His Silent Partner; librarian had a copy" (Typescript 32b (II), p. 50), recalling incidents that figure in "Ralph Keeler." He would in all probability have written of these matters soon after thus gathering his recollections of them. It appears that he had and was using, near the end of 1897, the "rare" buff paper of "Eseldorf." Copyright 1963, Mark Twain Company.

he wrote at this time all of "Eseldorf" that is on these buff sheets.[39] That he wrote no more is suggested, though not proved, by the fact that the remaining part is not only on different paper but differs also in its inks and even in the handwriting (which changed markedly during Twain's later years).[40] Additional support for these views is to be found in the contents of pages 1–85 and 377–386, which in themselves present a story that has a unity and even a kind of completeness. In the first eighty-five pages, he brought the story through the beginning description of Eseldorf; the characterization of Father Lueger (Adolf); the presentation of the other principal characters, including the young Satan; the showing of the latter's wonderful[38] abilities and contempt for humanity; the finding of the gold coins by the needy good priest; the false accusation of Father Peter by the bad priest; and the extreme poverty suffered by Father Peter's household after his imprisonment. In the ten pages at first numbered 84–93, Twain carried the story at once into the trial scene, showing the bad priest's false testimony against his rival; the ineffectual defense attempted by Wilhelm Meidling; the subsequent discovery (prompted by Satan) that the coins had been minted too recently to have been in existence at the time of the supposed theft; the exoneration of the good priest; and, finally—as an ironic reversal—Satan's conferring insanity upon the latter as the only real and lasting happiness possible to a human being.[41] This portion of the manuscript might thus be considered a tale in itself. He had, it seems, written through to his denouement too quickly. He may have stopped work on the story at that time as a result of his not knowing just what else to do to keep his plot going.

He probably had laid the story aside before the middle of January, 1898. A notebook entry reads, "*Jan. 14, 1898*. Began to write comedy 'Is he Dead?' (Francois Millet.)"[42] And his letter of January 22, 1898, to William Dean Howells shows that he could very well have been working on *The Mysterious Stranger* just before beginning the play:

[39] More precisely, a change of inks on the last page of this sequence (p. 386, originally 93) indicates that he broke off in the middle of this page, then filled out the rest of it upon taking up the story later. Mark Twain had been leading up to the disclosure of Father Peter's "happy insanity"; it is with this disclosure that the later written part begins.

[40] The paper of pp. 86–376 and 387–392 is of a light-weight, cream-colored stock, 5″ by 8″, with vertical watermark lines spaced 1″ apart; that of pp. 393–423 is of stock of the same weight, ochre, 5″ by 7⅞″, with vertical watermark lines spaced 15/16″ apart. The ink on both papers is gray.

[41] The writing of pp. 1–85 brought the story to a point about one-third of the way through Chapter V (*Writings*, XXVII, pp. 3–40); pp. 377–386 (originally pp. 84–93) became part of Chapter X (*Ibid.*, pp. 124–128).

[42] Typescript 32b (II), p. 53. Copyright 1963, Mark Twain Company.

I couldn't get along without work now. I bury myself in it up to the ears. Long hours—8 & 9 on a stretch, sometimes. And all the days, Sundays included. It isn't all for print, by any means, for much of it fails to suit me; 50,000 words of it in the past year. It was because of the deadness which invaded me when Susy died. But I have made a change lately—into dramatic work. . . .[43]

His words indicate clearly enough that during the earlier part of January he had been deeply absorbed in work upon one (or more) of his manuscripts of the Despair Group. In the light of the other evidence to the effect that he was working on "Eseldorf" at about this time, it is reasonable to think that he had been writing some of it during those "long hours."[44] Indeed, by working "all the days, Sundays included," he could have written all of the 12,350 words of the ninety-five buff pages during the first two weeks of January.[45] But it is likely that at least the initial chapter, so much of which is devoted to Lueger, had been written somewhat earlier and thus closer to the events that prompted its composition. Quite possibly he began writing "Eseldorf" on December[39] 9, 1897. In a part of Chapter I that has been deleted from the published text, it is related that the bad priest had even schemed to cheat the devil out of a Christian that, according to a pact, was to be his in return for the building of a bridge. The previously quoted working notes evidently refer to such an incident: "Bridge—Satan built it." He had cleverly waited for word of someone dying, so that he might deliver only a dead Christian: "Towards midnight the 9th of December" the desired word was brought, and the devil was summoned and required to provide the bridge. Mark Twain, after dwelling upon the people's boundless admiration of this trick, wrote that it was turned into a proud cere-

[43] *Mark Twain–Howells Letters*, ed. Henry Nash Smith and William M. Gibson, with the assistance of Frederick Anderson (Cambridge, Mass.: Harvard University Press, 1960), II, p. 670.

[44] Paine, *Mark Twain: A Biography*, III, p. 1067, observes: "A good deal of work done at this period did not find its way into print," and, in his further discussion of Twain's work at the beginning of 1898, refers to his "interest in Satan" and mentions the "three bulky manuscripts in which he has attempted to set down some episodes in the life of one 'Young Satan.' "

[45] An indication of his probable output per day may be found in his observation, made in April, 1904, that he was then averaging "fourteen hundred words per sitting of four or five hours" (*Mark Twain's Autobiography*, I, p. 246). In early January, 1898, he would by working "long hours" have been producing considerably more. Even after allowance for his tendency to overestimate his output— see Walter Blair, "When Was *Huckleberry Finn* Written?" *American Literature*, XXX (March, 1958), p. 5—it appears that he could have written 12,350 words in less than two weeks. The estimated wordage of these 95 pp. has been computed using an average of 130 words per page, based upon a word count. These figures are higher than those that Blair found to be representative of Twain's practice at an earlier time (*Ibid.*); however, the handwriting became decidedly smaller in the later years.

mony "repeated every 9th of December, to this day."[46] The pointed and iterated reference to the 9th of December may have been a strictly contemporary one. In bringing "Stirring Times in Austria" to an end, he had taken occasion to make a point of that date, writing "We are well along in December now," and adding as a footnote, "It is the 9th.—M.T."[47] His concluding remarks in that essay had made it clear that he considered Austrian affairs were in a state of crisis at that particular time—that they were in fact in a deplorable and shameful condition. If, finding himself free from other writing commitments, he did then plunge into the composition of that first "Eseldorf" chapter, he would likely have done just what he *has* done in it: employ satiric inversion and, in mockery, celebrate this date as one marking events worthy of the highest praise.[40]

There is no indication that, after writing the part of the manuscript that is on the buff-colored stationery, he did any more work on "Eseldorf" that winter, or indeed during the rest of 1898. It is true that there is a notebook entry, made in July of that year, which in irony praises the executive abilities of Satan "who for untold centuries has maintained the imposing position of spiritual head of 4/5 of the human race."[48] This passage was, however, used not in any version of *The Mysterious Stranger* but in "Concerning the Jews."[49] Furthermore, it can be shown that by November, 1898, he was planning and in all probability writing the "Hannibal" version.

His notebook contains the following entry of November 11–12, 1898:

> Story of little Satan Jr. who came to Hannibal, went to school, was popular and greatly liked by those who knew his secret. The others were jealous and the girls didn't like him because he smelled of brimstone. He was always doing miracles—his pals knew they were miracles, the others thought they were mysteries.[50]

Paine published only this beginning of the note, the full version of which runs to about five hundred words. The entry closely parallels sixteen pages of working notes, which have been designated as Group C.[51] These notes are a plot-summary for "Hannibal" as Twain probably intended to write it. He did not, however, carry the story as far as he had plotted for it. In fact, the manuscript amounts to little more than the start of the intended draft. In this beginning, the "little

---

[46] "Eseldorf," pp. 14–16. Copyright 1963, Mark Twain Company.
[47] *Writings,* XXII, p. 243.
[48] *Mark Twain's Notebook,* p. 343.
[49] *Writings,* XXII, p. 265.
[50] *Mark Twain's Notebook,* p. 369.
[51] Notes for *The Mysterious Stranger,* DV 327c.

Satan" appears one morning at the village school and promptly startles everyone by giving his name as "44." He then performs astonishing feats of learning (such as[41] incredibly rapid reading and infallible recall). After finding a home with the Hotchkiss family, he materializes himself at a spiritualist séance and then accomplishes other wonders such as rescuing many people from a terrible snowstorm. After explaining about his ancestry, he summons a little devil to serve Mr. Hotchkiss. At this point the manuscript breaks off.[52] According to the plot, "44" was to walk through fire to save a child and then come out unharmed after the burning building had fallen in upon him. He was to explain that he couldn't feel any kind of pain and that he believed it to be imaginary. He was thereafter to fall in love with the pastor's daughter, and to try to convince her father that all human actions are prompted by selfishness. And he was to go to church and by and by get converted and become a Methodist, only to be put out of the church after he had been caught praying for Satan, his father. Later on, "44" was to decide to rid man of the Moral Sense, so that the race might be guiltless and happy; to this end, he was to start his own Anti-Moral Sense Church and to have his little devil brothers print his "bible" for him—proclaiming such ideas as Mark Twain expressed in *What Is Man?* (which in his later years he often termed his "gospel"). Also, "44" was to fall in love with Hellfire Hotchkiss (possibly Twain intended this episode as an alternate for the one involving the preacher's daughter) and get more than he had bargained for, finding that the intellectualized love of immortals was tame in comparison to earthly love.[53]

There is no evidence to show that Twain ever wrote any more of "Hannibal" than now survives. Containing only about 15,300 words, this manuscript would have required perhaps not quite two weeks of work at his usual pace. That he did this writing soon after making the notebook entry concerning little Satan, Jr., is suggested by the fact that page 5 of Group C of the working notes has on the reverse side an uncompleted letter by Twain to Henry H. Rogers, dated November 17, 1898. There is a probability that he was drafting these notes at about that time, only a few days after the entry of November 11–12. He would thus have been at work upon "Hannibal" either at that time or shortly thereafter, writing it in the latter part of November, and perhaps the early part of December, 1898. It is hard to say why he carried the draft no further. It may be of significance that he had tried to write "Hannibal" from the omniscient point of view,[42] rather than that of a boy-narrator. Tom and Huck never really came into the story, in the fragment that he wrote, except as mere allusions. He may have found that they did not belong

---

[52] "Hannibal," pp. 1–136.
[53] Notes for *The Mysterious Stranger*, DV 327c.

in the same story with the phantom-boy, Philip Traum, and could not be made to associate with him. Or perhaps Mark Twain, the Solon of an unofficial world "court of final conclusions," could no longer write from the viewpoint of a boy—a real boy, as Sam Clemens of Hannibal had been. In creating Philip Traum he had found a character who could be at once a youth and a sage: an angel-boy sixteen thousand years old.[54] Satan, Jr., who comes off mainly as an unusually brilliant schoolboy in the "Hannibal" manuscript, probably did not so well meet Twain's literary needs.[55] In any case, it is evident that he had made another start upon the story of a young Satan but had not found it to be the right one. These facts take on an added significance when related to what he wrote to Howells on May 12–13, 1899. Reporting that he was working on "a book without reserves" in which he meant to say his say and "take account of no one's feelings, no one's prejudices, opinions, beliefs, hopes, illusions, delusions," he explained:

Twice I didn't start it right; & got pretty far in both times, before I found it out. But I am sure it is started right this time. It is in [story] tale-form. I believe I can make it tell what I think of Man, & how he is constructed, & what a shabby poor ridiculous thing he is, & how mistaken he is in his estimate of his character & powers & qualities & his place among the animals.

So far, I think I am succeeding. I let the madam into the secret day before yesterday, & locked the doors & read to her the opening chapters. She said—

"It is perfectly horrible—and perfectly beautiful!"

"Within the due limits of modesty, that is what I think."

I hope it will take me a year or two to write it, & that it will turn out to be the right vessel to contain all the ordure I am planning to dump into it.[56]

His comment that he had twice started wrong and had twice gotten "pretty far in" seems an apt reference to his writing of the initial 12,350 words of "Eseldorf" and of the 15,300 words of "Hannibal" in his previous attempts at telling the tale that was to become *The Mysterious Stranger*. To be sure, if the "pre-Eseldorf" draft were to be counted as a separate version, the number would be three; but inasmuch as he had adapted it for "Eseldorf" and had even inserted some of its pages, he might very[43] well have thought of both drafts as just one try at getting the story told.

It may be further considered that at some time he had to set aside the ten pages written on the buff sheets (84–93) and then write al-

[54] *Writings*, XXVII, p. 17.

[55] The initial working notes for "Eseldorf" seem to reveal that Twain had in that version identified himself quite closely with the boy-narrator; as has been shown above, he wrote "Theodor Fischer [Tom] Huck (I)." Copyright 1963, Mark Twain Company.

[56] *Mark Twain–Howells Letters*, II, pp. 698–699.

most three hundred additional pages of "Eseldorf" before bringing in the deferred portion as pages 377–386. It seems likely that what he did in May, 1899, to get the tale "started right" was to reserve for later use that part in which he had used up his plot much too quickly in presenting the trial of Father Peter and its ironic—and tragic—outcome.

This interpretation is supported by the evidence of a single page of working notes, on paper matching that of pages 86–376 and 387–392 of "Eseldorf," which is clearly his plan for continuing the story from the point to which it had been carried in the first eighty-five pages. The first several items read:

> S. will come "every day."
> Jealousy of Wil.
> S. after 3 days furnishes details of the 4 games, with notes to Wil, whose envy & jeal are further inflamed.[57]

On page 85, the tale had reached the point at which Father Peter had been put in jail and his family had been left without support. Although momentary relief had been provided by a coin that the housekeeper Ursula had been given for washing, or attempting to wash, some clothes, and that she had thereafter pretended she had found in the road, she "could not find a coin in the road every day—perhaps [the sentence is completed on page 86, on a cream-colored paper and in a gray ink] not even a second one." In the next paragraph, Satan comes again—as he does repeatedly thereafter; he soon has the lucky cat, Agnes, providing "four silver groschen ... every morning."[58] Thereafter, Satan exhibits to the village boys many instances of human cruelty while preaching to them a continuing sermon on the degrading effect of man's "Moral Sense."[59] In this material Mark Twain seems to be speaking without reserve in the way that he had contemplated in the letter to Howells of May 12–13. Apparently he was drawing upon "The Lowest Animal" for story material. Probably it was that satiric essay, written ... at the time of the revolt in Crete, that he had had in mind when he told Howells that he was planning to "dump" much "ordure" into his tale.[44]

After such material had actually been dumped into the story, he needed additional subject matter. In his working notes he had referred to the jealousy of Wilhelm. He next developed this plot-element in the long passage (about eight thousand words, mostly deleted from The Mysterious Stranger) in which Wilhelm and the brewer Joseph Fuchs become intensely jealous of Satan. The latter captivates the girls Marget and Lilly by reciting marvelous poetry,

---

[57] Notes for The Mysterious Stranger, DV 327bb. Copyright 1963, Mark Twain Company.
[58] See Writings, XXVII, pp. 40–44.
[59] "Eseldorf," pp. 110–139.

getting splendid orchestral effects out of a tuneless old piano, and effortlessly defeating Wilhelm in chess—even though Wilhelm is the champion of that region. And to cap his performance, Satan, as Twain had planned, makes Wilhelm even more envious by later setting down from memory, in an instant's time and with perfect accuracy, the records of their games.[60]

That it was at the time of this continuation of the story that he put aside the ten pages presenting the trial scene is confirmed by the last item appearing on this same sheet of working notes:

Trial of Peter—he not present. Is begged by the boys to go & confer an immense happiness upon him to pay for his captivity & make him forget it. He confers a happy insanity—imaginary kingship. Will not restore him—*knows* a happy insanity is best for all men. . . .[61]

He was here looking forward to using, only after writing through the rest of his noted plot-ideas, a trial scene which he had almost certainly written before making these notes. He had probably recognized that, by delaying this outcome, he was making it possible to indulge in any amount of digressive moralizing and yet make the plot come out as he intended. He had a "finisher" laid by and waiting. He might well have felt sure that this time his story was "started right."

Some evidence makes it appear probable that by the fall of 1899 he had written through the part devoted to the love-rivalry theme, but not much further. A very little of this sequence has survived in the published tale: in the middle of Chapter VII it is related that Satan charmed Marget when he "branched off into poetry, and recited some," but that "Wilhelm was not as pleased as he ought to have been, and this time Marget noticed it and was remorseful."[62] It is from here that "Eseldorf" continues with nearly eight thousand words, all deleted before publication, in which Satan further arouses the love of Marget and Lilly and the jealousy of their beaux. Twain had, in writing to the end of this plot-sequence,[45] reached a total of about 29,500 words in the manuscript. The figure agrees well enough with one which he reported in what is probably a reference to his work upon "Eseldorf," in his letter to Howells of October 19, 1899:

Ah, if I could look into the insides of people as you do, & put it on paper, & invent things for them to do & say, & tell *how* they said it, I could write a fine & readable book now, for I've got a prime subject. I've written 30,000 words of it & satisfied myself that the stuff is there; so I am going to discard that MS & begin all over again & have a good time with it.[63]

[60] *Ibid.*, pp. 167–229.

[61] Notes for *The Mysterious Stranger*, DV 327bb. Copyright 1963, Mark Twain Company.

[62] *Writings*, XXVII, p. 76.

[63] *Mark Twain–Howells Letters*, II, p. 710.

In writing the love-and-jealousy episodes, he had apparently lost the thread of what little plot he had had going. It is true that he had brought a little of the same kind of material into the initial part of "Eseldorf"—mainly in the pages that he had retained from the Hannibal-oriented "pre-Eseldorf" draft. Theodor, he had written, had "passed through the parlor," finding Marget at the piano giving a lesson to Marie Lueger.[64] And in the garden he had found "Wilhelm Meidling sitting there waiting, for it was getting toward the edge of evening, and he would be asking Marget to take a walk along the river with him when she was done with the lesson. He was a young lawyer, and succeeding fairly well and working his way along, little by little. He was very fond of Marget, and she of him."[65] For these scenes, Twain was very likely using recollections of the Clemens household at about 1850 (when he was in his fifteenth year). Samuel C. Webster is no doubt right in thinking that this passage in *The Mysterious Stranger* is based upon memories of the kind of home life described in Jane Clemens' letter of January 30, 1850, to Orion:

Since I commenced writing an invitation came for Pamela to spend the evening out but she is in the dining room giving Margaret Blesser a lesson on the Guitar, Sarah Fuqua and I are in the parlour, Sarah is pract[*ic*]ing and I writing. . . . Tomorrow evening the music scollars meet again. Margaret Saxon, Sara Fuqua and Mary Buckhannan all play dewets, the scollars are improving very fast. When you come I think they will play well.[66]

Webster comments that "Sam, coming back from the printing house for an evening at home, must often have seen the picture of Pamela and her scholars that Jane Clemens describes."[67] In carrying the story of "Eseldorf" to almost thirty thousand words, Mark Twain introduced a great deal more matter of this kind. It seems that he[46] had again tried to use Hannibal material and had found that the attempt did not work out very well. Satan, when placed in the social context of the author's own village, tended to become a bright and talented lad who pleased the girls with parlor tricks—very much as "44," the young Satan of the "Hannibal" version, had shown himself to be a schoolboy paragon. Certainly the mood, tone, and subject matter of this attempt in 1899 were not in keeping with the greater part of the beginning portion of "Eseldorf." He might well have seen that the story was floundering; that he needed to "invent things" for his

[64] *Writings*, XXVII, p. 34. The reference to Marie Lueger appears on p. 73 of the manuscript. This page was not a part of the "pre-Eseldorf" draft and was not repaginated as were the sheets borrowed from that draft.

[65] *Ibid.*, p. 34. This passage is on p. 74 of the manuscript and was originally numbered 34 in the "pre-Eseldorf" draft.

[66] In *Mark Twain, Business Man* (Boston: Little, Brown and Company, 1946), pp. 15–16.

[67] *Ibid.*, p. 14.

characters "to do & say." It would not have been surprising had he then thought of discarding the manuscript and starting again. And it appears that he did make some plans for a rewriting of "Eseldorf." There are five pages of working notes in which it may be seen that he was reviewing pages 1 to 85, which he had written almost three years previously: he noted the characters and incidents along with the pages upon which they appear and added his plans for further development of many episodes. For example, at the point at which Satan fashions the tiny castle which he thereafter destroys, Twain noted, "Make him build a whole city and then drown it with a bucket of water."[68] But these revisions were never made, and the contents of the following part of the story show that he presently found a new impetus which prompted him to continue the existing manuscript instead of beginning anew. Immediately after the love-rivalry passage, a new plot-sequence is initiated in which there soon begin to appear references to contemporary events that probably, and in some cases certainly, could not have been made before the summer of 1900.

At once, Satan takes Theodor to China. And there is this curious allusion to current happenings—or rather what seems to stop just short of being that:

It was wonderful, the spectacles we saw; and some were beautiful, others too horrible to think. For instance—However, I may go into that by and by, and also why Satan chose China for this excursion instead of another place; it would interrupt my tale to do it now.[69]

The author virtually tells the reader outright that outrageous things are going on in China at the time of writing. He does not say enough about them to make a positive identification possible. But it is evident that the reference would fittingly apply to the Boxer uprising—particularly to the extremes of violence that occurred[47] during the latter part of June and the early part of July, 1900, when China was invaded by international troops and, by order of the Empress Dowager, hundreds of foreigners (chiefly missionaries) were slain.[70] Before following up his first cryptic comment upon the situation in China, Twain wrote an additional 9,200 words of "Eseldorf" (as he had given notice he would do rather than "interrupt" his story).[71] Then, by having

[68] Notes for *The Mysterious Stranger*, DV 327bb. Copyright 1963, Mark Twain Company.

[69] "Eseldorf," p. 229 *verso; Writings*, XXVII, p. 76.

[70] See Philip S. Foner, *Mark Twain: Social Critic* (New York: International Publishers, 1958), p. 253, but also *Britannica*, V, p. 532.

[71] This 9,200-word sequence includes Satan's exposition of deterministic doctrines, the episode of Nikolaus's and Lisa's drownings, and Frau Brandt's blaspheming and her subsequent execution by fire at the stake. ("Eseldorf," pp. 229–291; *Writings*, XXVII, pp. 76–107).

Satan show Theodor and Seppi a vision of the history of mankind, including an exhibition of the future, Twain found his chance for contemporary allusions.[72] Much of this material has not survived editing; that which was retained does, however, include Satan's sardonic prophecy that "the pagan world will go to school to the Christian not to acquire his religion, but his guns," and that "the Chinaman will buy those to kill missionaries and converts with."[73] In the deleted portion, the reference is more explicit: the Chinese, it is said, after becoming exasperated by foreign interference will "rise in revolt against the insults and oppressions of the intruder. This will be Europe's chance to interfere and swallow China, and her band of royal Christian pirates will not waste it."[74] Some sixty-three pages later, Satan is still predicting the future in a similar fashion, with probable reference to both the Boer War and the occupation of China by the Allied Powers: "Two centuries from now . . . the Christian civilization will reach its highest mark. Yet its kings will still be, then, what they are now, a close corporation of land-thieves."[75] The references to events in China may be compared with Twain's letter to J. H. Twichell of August 12, 1900, in which he spoke of recent news reports:

It is all China, now, and my sympathies are with the Chinese. They have been villainously dealt with by the sceptered thieves of Europe, and I hope they will drive all the foreigners out and keep them out for good. I only wish it; of course I don't really expect it.[76]

The evidence thus supports the view that Twain, after stopping work upon "Eseldorf" in the fall of 1899 with the intention not of continuing it but of rewriting from the beginning, found by the summer of 1900 that imperialism had given him new subject matter and a new impulse to go on with the tale.[77]

[72] To bring such materials into a tale of events in Austria in 1590 (see *Writings*, XXVII, p. 3) required, of course, some contriving. See n. 162 below.

[73] *Writings*, XXVII, p. 111.

[74] "Eseldorf," p. 301. Copyright 1963, Mark Twain Company.

[75] *Ibid.*, p. 364. Copyright 1963, Mark Twain Company. In writing "Eseldorf," Twain first indicated May, 1702, as the time of the action; thereafter, he deleted that date and changed the time to the winter of 1490. Then, in the typescript copy, he struck out "1490" and inserted "1590." As a result of these changes, the published story now begins, "It was in 1590—winter" (*Writings*, XXVII, p. 3), though the action, as Twain had planned and written "Eseldorf," began "one May night" (*Ibid.*, p. 10) in 1702. In predicting events of 1900, Satan was thus looking forward approximately two centuries.

[76] *Mark Twain's Letters*, II, p. 699.

[77] For an excellent study of Twain's views and writings concerning imperialism, see William M. Gibson, "Mark Twain and Howells: Anti-Imperialists," *New England Quarterly*, XX (December 1947), pp. 435–470. With reference to Twain's letter of August 12 to Twichell, quoted above, Gibson comments that "on the day before international troops relieved the legations in Peking, not many weeks before he sailed for the United States, Mark Twain clearly aligned himself with 'the person sitting in darkness' " (p. 444).

His own circumstances in the summer of 1900 were right for sustained work at composition. On June 17 the New York *World* printed a cabled report describing him as "steadily working on his[48] new book during his stay in London, living very quietly and keeping away from society so as not to be interrupted in his writing."[78] It was about two weeks thereafter, early in July, that he moved to Dollis Hill House, London, which was to be his home until his return to the United States in October, 1900. There he found even better conditions for writing, for Dollis was a secluded, peaceful place; he wrote to Twichell that he was "working & deep in the luxury of it."[79] By the end of July, he seems to have been far along in writing "Eseldorf," which must have been the manuscript to which he referred in a letter to Richard W. Gilder of July 31, 1900. He reported himself "25,000 words deep" in the writing of a story which he had, he thought, begun a good while before in Vienna; he also stated his intention of finishing it before turning to any other writing.[80] The phrase "25,000 words deep" could very well mean the amount of manuscript he had turned out during his latest, still sustained working period, rather than the total wordage of that and his earlier spurts. This larger total would then be the sum of the 29,500 words he had probably written by October, 1899, and the other 25,000—or 54,500 words. He would then, if these figures could be taken as accurate, have been within some five hundred words, or about four pages, of the end of the 423-page "Eseldorf" version, which has about 55,000 words. (These calculations are based upon word counts indicating an average of 130 words per page of the "Eseldorf" holograph.) Actually, as will be seen in a moment, he could not have been quite that far until the third week of August, 1900. But in view of his habit of overestimating his output (and in this case he was speaking in round figures and not necessarily trying to be precise), a somewhat reduced total is a more probable one. If he had written 22,500 words by the end of July, 1900, "Eseldorf" would then have totaled some 52,000 words and he would have reached approximately page 399. He could not at that time have written any further: beginning on page 399 and continuing through page 403, he made direct references to the assassination of King Humbert of Italy, which had occurred on July 29, 1900, and to certain related events which took place during the following three weeks. In particular, he commented upon an action taken by the Vatican on August 18, condemning (after having previously sanctioned) a prayer composed by the widowed Queen Margherita for her

[78] *Mark Twain: Life as I Find It,* ed. Charles Neider (Garden City: Hanover House, 1961), p. 325. Neider has reprinted selected press interviews of Twain.

[79] This letter is quoted in part in *Mark Twain: A Biography,* III, p. 1109; Paine says it was written "in midsummer." Twain reported that his wife Olivia was "enchanted with the place," which had large, attractive grounds. He was writing regularly and was "the only person . . . ever in the house in the daytime."

[80] A copy of this letter is in the Mark Twain Papers.

late husband the King, who had been excommunicated. This action was[49] reported in the London *Times* of August 20; Twain, who regularly read the *Times*, would probably have known of the matter by that date. That he devoted some considerable amount of word-age to it suggests that he was writing while the incident was fresh in his mind. Moreover, the manner in which it was brought into the story indicates, in itself, a strictly contemporary reference: "A newspaper flashed into his [Satan's] hand,"[81] Theodor reports.

At this point Satan makes some pointed remarks about papal vacillation and the doctrine of infallibility, and he criticizes mankind for not seeing the humorous aspects of the cancellation of Queen Margherita's prayer. It is this incident to which Mark Twain is referring in the often-quoted passage, shorn of its particular application, which Paine and Duneka retained in editing *The Mysterious Stranger:*

This multitude see the comic side of a thousand low-grade and trivial things—broad incongruities, mainly; grotesqueries, absurdities, evokers of the horse-laugh. The ten thousand high-grade comicalities which exist in the world are sealed from their dull vision.[82]

It seems likely that Mark Twain wrote this passage on or soon after August 20, and that he also wrote the remaining twenty pages of "Eseldorf" at that time. After relating an incident concerning a magic, many-fruited tree and the punishments inflicted by Satan upon its greedy owner, Twain continued for a few pages, not used in the published text, giving an account of Satan's performance of some conjuring tricks. Again, it seems, he had run out of plot. He may have been led into carrying the story beyond his intended conclusion (the outcome of the trial, presented on pages first numbered 84–93) by a desire to speak his mind about the condemnation of the Queen's prayer. Once he had expressed himself on that matter, he apparently had nothing to fall back upon except Satan's magic-tricks. He probably reached this point, thereby doing his last work upon "Eseldorf," some time late in August, 1900.

The evidence of the materials agrees with these findings. He had and used for other holographic manuscripts produced at Dollis Hill the two kinds of paper that he used for all of "Eseldorf" following page 85 (except, of course, pages 377–386). His "Letter to Times on Missionaries in China," for example, matches in its materials the greater part of "Eseldorf" (pages 86–376, 387–392);[50] not only the paper but the ink and the handwriting are, or appear to be, the same.[83]

---

[81] "Eseldorf," p. 399. Copyright 1963, Mark Twain Company.

[82] *Writings*, XXVII, p. 131.

[83] This unposted letter of 14 pp., actually an essay titled "The Missionary in World-Politics," is addressed to Moberly Bell and dated "Dollis Hill House, Kilburn N. W. Monday [summer–fall, 1900]." The holograph is in the Mark Twain Papers.

Likewise, his article "Dollis Hill House, London, 1900" as closely matches the concluding part (pages 393–423) that is on the ochre paper of slightly smaller size.[84]

When interviewed before and after his return to the United States in mid-October, 1900, he offered some comments which must have been in reference to his lately suspended work upon "Eseldorf." Before he left London, he reported, "I have a book half finished, but when the other half will be done the Lord only knows."[85] Upon reaching New York on October 15, he said more revealingly,

I rewrote one of my books three times, and each time it was a different book. I had filled in, and filled in, until the original book wasn't there. It had evaporated through the blanks, and I had an entirely new book. I shall write my story, and then lay the scene where I want it, and, if necessary, change other things to suit the places.

I shall very probably write a story with the scene laid in this country, or I shall place the scene of one of my present uncompleted stories here. This can be done rather handily, after the whole story is written.[86]

By this time he had, of course, made three attempts at writing the story of a young Satan: the first stint of work upon "Eseldorf" (including the "pre-Eseldorf" draft as well); the "Hannibal" version; and the revised and extended "Eseldorf" version. And, starting with the "pre-Eseldorf" beginning, he had first laid the scene in America, then had relocated it in Austria, then had brought it back to America (in writing "Hannibal"), and then had (in continuing "Eseldorf") returned it to Austria. He had indeed been changing scenes as readily as his reported comments would indicate. And it seems likely that he was then contemplating shifting the locale of "Eseldorf," one of his "present uncompleted stories," still another time.

Of particular interest is one further remark that he made when asked if he would "have any more like *Huckleberry Finn* and *Tom Sawyer*": "Yes, I shall have to do something of that kind, I suppose. But one can't talk about an unwritten book. It may grow into quite a different thing."[87] Some evidence may, just possibly, show that this intended Tom-and-Huck story was to be another version of *The Mysterious Stranger*—once again placed in an American setting. Some notebook entries, beginning in January, 1902, and continuing to July

[84] This manuscript (DV 239, Mark Twain Papers) may be dated by Twain's statement that he is to "begin a sea-voyage seventeen days hence" (p. 14); he sailed on October 6 (see *Mark Twain: A Biography*, III, p. 1110) and would have been writing on or about September 19, 1900.

[85] New York *World*, October 14, 1900; reprinted in *Mark Twain: Life as I Find It*, p. 331.

[86] New York *Herald*, October 16, 1900; reprinted in *Mark Twain: Life as I Find It*, pp. 335–336.

[87] *Ibid.*, p. 336.

of that year, present ideas for a story[51] to be called "Fifty Years Later."[88] The tale was to feature Hannibal characters, including Tom and Huck, first in their youth and then after half a century. And, in the margins of the original typescript copy of "Eseldorf," beside the part which tells of Satan's bringing down storm and fire upon the little people he has created,[89] there are these penciled notations in Twain's hand:

Boys privately rescue them—2 or 3—& keep them for years,—Their lifetime is a 12th of ours—they raise families, have funerals, &c, they are invisible to all but the boys—they have tragedies & conflagrations & love passages & murders[.]
Now—50 years later?—They are a very numerous [sic], & are two nations, divided by a ridge, & have wars of succession, & famous heroes, & crazy religions, & 2 languages.[90]

On the following page, after the sentence in the typescript which speaks of "not one of the five hundred poor creatures escaping," he noted, "Except a group found later."[91] He was evidently thinking of carrying on the story by enlarging and developing what is probably its most novel and most dramatic episode. The after-thought that provided for such a continuation, the idea of having the boys "privately rescue" a "group found later," is an interesting parallel of the note he had made at a crucial time in the writing of *Huckleberry Finn:* "Back a little, *change*—raft only crippled by steamer."[92] It appears that this improvisation that saved Huck's raft also saved Mark Twain's story by keeping the action on the Mississippi and in the river towns, where the author was imaginatively most at home and most in control of his material.[93] And it is at least possible that the rescuing of the diminutive race in *The Mysterious Stranger* might have taken that story in a direction which would have saved it from much of the moralistic exposition that filled the middle portion of the tale as he actually wrote it. By focusing upon the situation of the boys and their dependent race of manikins, he might have succeeded in projecting the human situation and man's moral involvement in a more appealing and convincing way than that of Satan's didacticism. . . .[52] "Fifty Years

[88] For a discussion of these notebook entries and of the evidence regarding the "Fifty Years Later" story that Mark Twain may have written, see *Mark Twain–Howells Letters,* II, n. 1, p. 748.

[89] See *Writings,* XXVII, p. 21.

[90] Typescript of "Eseldorf" (DV 327a, Mark Twain Papers), p. 24. Copyright 1963, Mark Twain Company.

[91] *Ibid.,* p. 25. Copyright 1963, Mark Twain Company.

[92] See Walter Blair, *Mark Twain & Huck Finn* (Berkeley: University of California Press, 1960), p. 253.

[93] See *Mark Twain at Work,* p. 62, and *Mark Twain & Huck Finn,* pp. 249–259.

Later," with its new plot-ideas, would have been a story quite different from "Eseldorf." And there is no evidence of any further work on the latter manuscript after Twain's return to the United States in October, 1900. Indeed, there is no more of that version to be accounted for; there is, to be sure, the six-page fragment which Paine added to "Eseldorf" as a conclusion for *The Mysterious Stranger*, but it was written as a part of the only version that remains to be considered—the "Print Shop" manuscript.[94][53]

"Print Shop" is definitely the version that Mark Twain wrote last.[95] There is evidence that it could not, before the late fall of 1902, have been carried beyond the first two chapters; that the greater part of it was written in Florence in 1904; that the "dream-ending" used to complete the published story was written for this version—almost certainly in 1904—and set aside for later use; that all but one chapter had been written by the summer of 1905; and that the last-written chapter, comprising his final work upon any draft of *The Mysterious Stranger*, was not composed until 1908.[96]

In this latest form of the story he combined some elements of both the "Eseldorf" and the "Hannibal" drafts and added to them much new material. Once again, after having perhaps most recently tried the story with an American background, he laid the scene in Austria. He began with the "Eseldorf" setting, adapting the first chapter of that version to make it serve as a beginning for "Print Shop." . . .[54]

Evidently Twain carried over from "Hannibal" the idea of introducing print-shop material that he had conceived before abandoning that draft. Also, he gave to the mysterious stranger of this version the same number-name that he used in "Hannibal": "44." In the story, "44," in the guise of a penniless young stranger, comes to the castle in search of work and is favored by the kindly Master Stein but per-

---

[94] This six-page fragment is presently placed with "Eseldorf" (DV 327, Mark Twain Papers.)

[95] Internal evidence . . . shows that the greater part of "Print Shop" could not have been written until 1902 or thereafter. Beginning on p. 145 of this manuscript, he introduced clippings from a religious pamphlet that had been issued by the Benedictine Sisters of Perpetual Adoration of Clyde, Missouri. The pamphlet explains that their chapel had been extensively damaged by repeated strokes of lightning. Twain represented the clipped passages as a speech by Father Peter (who had been brought into "Print Shop" in the borrowed first chapter of "Eseldorf") maintaining that these destructive bolts were actually providential and miraculous and expressed the Lord's will that the Sisters should have a new chapel. The rest of the pamphlet has also survived, and it contains a testimonial letter dated February 10, 1902; it is thus certain that Twain wrote this and the following part of "Print Shop" after that date.

[96] [Some evidence in support of these statements, omitted from this present excerpt, may be seen in *Mark Twain and Little Satan*, pp. 54–75.]

secuted by the latter's wife and step-daughter, as well as by most of the print-shop workers. . . .

August Feldner, the narrator of "Print Shop" and one of the shop workers, also befriends "44." The other workers, who become disgruntled when the master makes the stranger an apprentice, go[55] on strike, refusing to get out the order of Bibles he has contracted to produce. But "44," who already has privately displayed to August his ability to do miracles, contrives to keep the work going by bringing in doubles—"duplicates"—of the striking printers. The duplicates are at first ghostly and invisible, but "44" presently materializes them, to the astonishment and confusion of all. He also performs various other incredible feats, letting an old magician take credit for them. (The "mysterious stranger" of "Print Shop" is just that: whereas the "44" of "Hannibal" reveals that he is Satan, Jr., this one guards the secret of his identity.) He then goes out of his way to stir up resentment and make enemies for himself (for no apparent reason); after finally being burned at the stake, he appears again, alive and unchanged. At this point, the plot shifts abruptly. Love-complications are introduced, as well as other problems resulting from the splitting of several characters into multiple selves—waking self, dream self, and immortal spirit. It has already been noted that he had explored this idea of multiple selves some years earlier, in an extended notebook entry of January 7, 1897. With the help of "44," August discovers hitherto unused powers within himself; he enjoys a new independence of time and space, roams at will throughout the universe, and seems to be coming close to supplanting "44" in such a role in the story. However, "44," still the master illusion-maker, thereafter presents a pageant-in-reverse, turning back the clocks and making history roll backward. Then, for a final grand review, he summons a spectral procession of the illustrious dead; just at the last, he waves away the vision he has conjured, and he and August stand alone in a vacant and silent world.[97]

The procession of the dead is presented in the separately paginated fragment of eight pages which is a part of "Print Shop"; the foregoing part of the above summary refers to pages 23–587 of that manuscript. To this summary there might have been added the incidents of the other fragment of six pages, used as the conclusion of *The Mysterious Stranger*. . . .[56]

[T]he greater part of the manuscript was not written until 1904, after Mark Twain settled in Florence.

That he worked upon the story at Florence may readily be established by looking ahead for a moment to the time of his stay at Dublin, New Hampshire, in the summer of 1905. During most of that June he had been writing "3,000 Years Among the Microbes,"[98] but he had

97 "Print Shop" (DV 328, Mark Twain Papers), pp. 23–587.
98 See *Mark Twain: A Biography*, III, pp. 1238–1239; IV, pp. 1663–1670.

discontinued work upon that story a few days before the end of the month. On June 29 he wrote to his daughter Clara:

I have spent the day reading the book I wrote in Florence. I destroyed 125 pages of it, & expect to go over it again tomorrow & destroy 25 more. Then I think I will take hold of it & finish it, dropping the microbe book meantime.[99]

And, on page 432 of "Print Shop," a note at the bottom in the Clemens holograph reads, "June 30/05 Burned the rest (30,000 words) of the book this morning[:] too diffusive." It is clear that this manuscript, which he went over on the following day, destroying[57] pages as he had said he would do, is the one identified as the book written in Florence.

He had taken his family to Florence late in 1903, in the hope that the climate would benefit his wife, Olivia Langdon Clemens, who was then in what proved to be her last illness. . . .[100][58]

Some help in dating his . . . work upon "Print Shop" at Florence is afforded by the evidence of [Twain's] materials. . . .[59] [He] wrote pages 215–432 in [a] purplish blue ink [that he was using] between the latter part of February and the end of his period of residence at Florence. . . . [This] purplish blue shade also appears in the notebook he kept at Florence, beginning with an entry of April 3 and continuing until June 20, 1904, when he left Florence; thereafter the entries are in black ink and the purplish blue color does not appear any more.[101] The use of this[60] latter color of ink seems to have occurred only during the last four months of his stay at Villa di Quarto, Florence, thus fixing the time of composition of the middle part (pages 215–432) of "Print Shop" and of the previously-mentioned six-page fragment which furnished a final chapter for *The Mysterious Stranger*.

This fragment, in which the story arrives at the solipsistic conclusion, "*Life itself is only a vision, a dream*,"[102] is paginated 1–6 and is headed on the first page, "Conclusion of the book." It has been noted that the materials of "Eseldorf" do not at all match those of this ending. The latter is, however, matched exactly by pages 215–432 of "Print Shop"—in the paper, the handwriting, the fineness of the pen-point, and, most significantly, the purplish blue ink. . . . Mark Twain almost certainly wrote the "dream-ending" at Florence, and . . . as an anticipated conclusion, while he was more or less in the middle of composition of the story. Such an anticipation was probably no unique event in his composition. The short chapter that he wrote as the ending for *Christian Science* is a similar frag-

[99] A typescript copy of this letter is the Mark Twain Papers. Copyright 1963, Mark Twain Company.

[100] See *Mark Twain: A Biography*, III, pp. 1205–1211.

[101] Notebook 37 (1904). Some of the entries made between the above-mentioned dates have been published in *Mark Twain's Notebook*, pp. 386–387.

[102] See *Writings*, XXVII, p. 138.

ment, headed "Conclusion" and separately paginated 1–7; this unit presumably was not written in sequence with the part just preceding, and it could easily have been drafted before that part had been written.[103]

The characters named in the solipsistic conclusion, as written by Twain, are those of the "Print Shop" version. The manuscript shows the editorial changes that were made by Paine to make the fragment fit "Eseldorf": where the names "44" and "August" occur, these have been deleted and "Satan" and "Theodor" inserted. The last paragraph of Chapter X and the first paragraph of the concluding Chapter XI of *The Mysterious Stranger* were also supplied as editorial additions to make the "Print Shop" fragment serve for the completion of "Eseldorf."[104] By such editorial carpentry, the ending that Twain had intended for his latest form of *The Mysterious Stranger* was joined to a form of it that he had almost certainly not worked upon since the summer of 1900. . . .[61]

[103] Paine, No. 42, Mark Twain Papers; *Writings*, XXV, pp. 262–264.
[104] *Writings*, XXVII, pp. 136–137.

PART FOUR/A SAMPLING OF THE CRITICISM

The Devil and Samuel Clemens

COLEMAN O. PARSONS

LIFE BECAME FOR SAM CLEMENS A BRIEF AND HAPPY TRUDGING ALONG the right road, followed by an inexplicable wandering from it and by long years of futile, unutterable yearning to return. The waters of the Mississippi, gliding from mysterious reaches north of Keokuk to fabulous realms south of St. Louis, were for a time free from insistent adult values and provided sanctuary for the natural boy. From the river banks, young Clemens surveyed a domain of primal simplicity, in which refreshment from the sun's rays, incidental cleansing, a fish diet,[587] and shaded slumber temporarily banished all niggling duties. Thaumaturgically sealed by south-running water, Glasscock's Island beckoned the swimmer—a Garden of Eden saved from the world's complexities and corruption.

But just as the cool retreat of the cave became entangled in the boy's mind with thoughts of being lost, frightened, hungry, near dead, so the river took on more somber meanings. Two of Sam's friends were drowned in the Mississippi. And in winter its glittering appeal became as treacherous as the song of the Lorelei. One night, Sam and the postmaster's son, Tom Nash, stole away from home to skate "without permission." When the river began to break up about midnight, the boys took an hour to make their fearful way back to shore over floating fields of ice. All perspiring, Tom fell short in his last leap, struggled to shore in a bitter bath, took to bed, and had "a procession of diseases" culminating in scarlet fever. His doom was to go through life stone deaf and ludicrously impaired in speech. Sam Clemens never recovered from the shock of this confutation of ideal justice, this horribly disproportionate punishment of a small sin. Indeed, he himself might have been the victim of cosmic cruelty. The incident turned over and over in his mind until it emerged in three different forms in his *Notebook* (May 27, 1898) and *Autobiography* and in *The Mysterious Stranger*.

From Coleman O. Parsons, "The Devil and Samuel Clemens," *Virginia Quarterly Review*, XXIII (Autumn 1947), 582–606, by permission of the author and the publisher.

The need for him to understand why each individual's earthly paradise is lost, why life becomes sullied, led Samuel Clemens from his own baffling experience to mythology, philosophy, and religion. In "Genesis" he read that Eve, forbidden to eat of the tree of the knowledge of good and evil, succumbed to the wiles of a serpent: "In the day ye eat thereof, then your eyes shall be opened; and ye shall be as gods, knowing good and evil." Having eaten of the fruit of wisdom, Eve and compliant Adam immediately became ashamed of their nakedness and of their disobedience. Besides toil and sorrow, the punishment of[588] the greedy pair was banishment from Eden before they had a chance to plunder the tree of everlasting life.

This was the supreme decision of human history, the moment at which the sense of guilt entered consciousness. That Clemens saw Adam and Eve's dilemma in the light of his own is made clear in "The Turning-Point of My Life." Circumstance and man's natural disposition work together inexorably. Temperament is *born* in a man, "and he has no authority over it, neither is he responsible for its acts. . . . By temperament I was the kind of person that *does* things. . . . I still do the thing commanded by Circumstance and Temperament, and reflect afterward. Always violently." In a deterministic sense, Clemens would have agreed with the Calvinists, "In Adam's fall, we sinned all." But if Adam and Eve had only been asbestos-temperamental like Luther and Joan of Arc instead of helpless and butter-temperamented, the catastrophic apple would have remained on its branch!

Clemens was not satisfied until he had written his own version of "That Day in Eden" in the form of a passage from Satan's Diary. Adam and Eve had an understandable curiosity about good, evil, and death, but, lacking experience, they could not possibly comprehend Satan's explanation that innocence is the inability to distinguish right from wrong and that the Moral Sense, which makes that distinction possible, "is a degradation, a disaster . . . the *creator* of wrong; wrong cannot exist until the Moral Sense brings it into being." In answer to heedless Eve's question, Satan admitted that the Moral Sense could be acquired by eating the forbidden fruit, but he did not urge the indulgence. When Eve ate and uninterested Adam followed her lead, Satan felt sorry: "Poor ignorant things. . . . It was pitiful."

Thus was the search for the cause of mortal misery delayed by the Moral Sense, the acid which sometimes curdled Samuel Clemens' milk of human kindness. This faculty of differentiating between right and wrong he found discussed in W. E. H. Lecky's *History of European Morals,* of which he owned a well-worn copy. Opposed to the stoical, intuitive assertion[589] of a genuine benevolence was the Epicurean, experiential insistence that every action is selfish, being rooted in the impulse to avoid pain and to pursue pleasure. Clemens borrowed the phrase and its capitalization from such men as Shaftes-bury and Francis Hutcheson, pernicious revivers of a classical doc-trine (*sensus decori et honesti*), but he sided with George Berkeley and other anti-Moral Sense writers in debunking the concept.

With the opposition's attempt to substitute more realistic and objective guides for what it considered muddled, individualistic enthusiasm, Clemens was only occasionally in sympathy. Both thought and a fantastic ethical sense, in conflict with natural necessity, have adulterated all human impulse and action. Rebellion against the Moral Sense, a fraud which the rare good man would try to see through, makes it imperative to reverse practically all its decisions. Thus a crusty doctor, "the *Only* Christian" of "Was It Heaven? Or Hell?" persuades twin maiden ladies to override conscience and to do good by telling lies. Self-righteous townsmen, conventionally "good" men who boast of the Moral Sense, are attacked with Burnsian vigor in "The Man That Corrupted Hadleyburg." The comic extreme of Clemens' wistful moral anarchy is achieved in "The Facts Concern-ing the Recent Carnival of Crime in Connecticut"; the author out-lives his morbid scrupulousness and slays his shrunken, persecuting Conscience. Unfortunately, the denial of man's ethical capacity may leave the need to choose as persistent as ever.

In his protest, the American was temperamentally at one with Nietzsche in his attack on "bad conscience," with Ibsen in his charac-terization of modern man as suffering from "sickly conscience," and with Sudermann in his derision of the "conscience of the race." Clemens' chief intellectual defense of his position was that of the relativity of morals: the Creator has given man no moral code; our laws and our conscience, man-evolved and based on finite experience, have empirical validity at best. But most of the time his reaction was one of unreasoning trust in something like Rousseau's natural man and, if that creature[590] eluded search, in a blessed Noah's Ark menagerie of sinless beasts, on a par with Swift's invariably right Houyhnhnms. With Oliver Goldsmith, who wrote "The Logicians Refuted" in imitation of Swift, he could fancy

> . . . that this boasted lord of nature
> Is both a weak and erring creature.
> That instinct is a surer guide
> Than reason-boasting mortal's pride;
> And that brute beasts are far before 'em,
> *Deus est anima brutorum.*

The Moral Sense is ridiculed by the Old Man of Clemens' mechanistic gospel, *What Is Man?* but it also turns up in more imagi-native works. Huckleberry Finn is a more mature creation than Tom Sawyer because he emerges from a boy's carefree paradise into a sadly real world. He is the protesting battle-ground on which conscience, custom, and law (the Moral Sense in different aspects) clash with primal sympathy, the impulsive will to freedom, over the question of aiding or preventing Negro Jim's flight. The Moral Sense goes down in defeat. In contrast, the boys of *The Mysterious Stranger*, as Van Wyck Brooks has pointed out, have neither sufficient courage nor generosity to stand up against the witchcraft mores of their day. Sam Clemens had at last lost faith even in boys; a sustaining ideal had degenerated into an illusion, sorrowfully recognized as such. If adolescent nature was weak and corrupt, he was ironically thrown back on Calvinism. Having already transformed predestination into determinism, he now accepted total depravity—for all but the animals. So it is appropriate that his spokesman, Satan, who is beyond good and evil, beyond pain and happiness, should sneer at the Moral Sense:

No brute ever does a cruel thing—that is the monopoly of those with the Moral Sense. When a brute inflicts pain he does it innocently; it is not wrong; for him there is no such thing as wrong. And he does not inflict pain for the pleasure of inflicting it—only man does that. Inspired by that mongrel Moral Sense of his! A sense whose function is to distinguish[591] between right and wrong, with liberty to choose which of them he will do. Now what advantage can he get out of that? He is always choosing, and in nine cases out of ten he prefers the wrong. There shouldn't be any wrong; and without the Moral Sense there couldn't be any. And yet he is such an unreasoning creature that he is not able to perceive that the Moral Sense degrades him to the bottom layer of animated beings and is a shameful possession . . . He [the bullock] is not besmirched with the Moral Sense, but is as the angels are, and knows no wrong, and never does it.

When Clemens lost an ideal, he suffered for it himself and, through satire and irony, he made others suffer too. We may remember that Thomas Gray, in his Eton Ode, sees "the little victims" playing, "regardless of their doom" of adult woe and evil. Yet to the question whether these innocent boys should be warned that all men are alike condemned to groan comes the forbearing reply:

> Thought would destroy their paradise.
> No more; where ignorance is bliss,
> 'Tis folly to be wise.

Not so Clemens in his blighted mood. Entering into Satan, he does a cruel thing. He perseveringly demonstrates to the boys of Eseldorf that life is utterly miserable. At the conclusion of the events, the narrator, Theodor Fischer, is a sadder and a wiser adolescent, but a far less happy one: Satan-Clemens "vanished and left me appalled, for I knew, and realized, that all he had said was true." It is as if Sam Clemens had finally come to resent Tom's, Huck's, and his own brief squatters' rights in a fool's paradise.

Clemens was not satisfied to end his enquiry with the excrescent Moral Sense. Someone must have been responsible for the consciousness of sin. Milton had sung of sin and redemption in *Paradise Lost* and *Paradise Regained*, accepting sin as a reality and tracing it to Satan. Denying the reality of sin, Clemens[592] wrote of guilt and blamed God for the horrible affliction. Whereas Milton's emphasis was ethical, that of Samuel Clemens was psychological. In "Eve Speaks," the first mother pronounces it unjust of God to punish and debase mankind for an act of unreflecting disobedience which could only have been bad if the Moral Sense had been functioning before the apple was eaten. In this interpretation, our first parents and Satan appear not as enemies but as common victims of impulses and compulsions beyond their control. All three were insanely punished for not exercising a perfectly illusory free will. Satan, in fact, is like a drugged, fate-driven commentator on the human tragedy. He foreknows, yields information, and sorrowfully observes the consequences of a cruel God's planting the Moral Sense tree, or tree of the knowledge of sin, in a garden inhabited by the unwary. In Milton, Satan actively plots, initiates stratagems, and corrupts mankind for vengeance's sake, while God foreknows, forbears from any saving gesture, and comments. Clemens was consciously reversing the rôles of divine autocrat and rebel, for in a letter of 1858 he exclaimed to Orion, "What is the grandest thing in *Paradise Lost*—the Arch-Fiend's terrible energy!" Sam Clemens might at last say with the old Indian chief in Mary Johnston's *The Witch*: "But devils' [white men's] devil not what I call devil. Devil's god what I call devil." The marginal comments in Clemens' copy of the *Memoirs of the Duke of Saint-Simon* repeat the condemnation: "God made these animals. He must have noticed this scene [of pretended grief]; I wish I knew how it struck Him . . . We have to grant that God made this royal hog [Louis XIV]; we may also be permitted to believe that it was a crime to do so."

What aroused Clemens' theological wrath was the God of the Old Testament. As a married man, Clemens could not continue the concession of Bible-reading because the fables and myths contradicted reason, besides playing up a tribal God who was irascible, vindictive, and fickle. He would probably have expanded the remark of New England's Samuel Johnson, that Calvinism reflected "dishonour upon the Best of Beings," to[593] include all religious isms. Like the monster in Browning's "Caliban upon Setebos; or, Natural Theology in the Island," a satire on Calvinism and the anthropomorphic idea of God (Setebos), he conceived of a supergod, Caliban's Quiet and Clemens' Creator:

> There may be something quiet o'er His [Setebos'] head,
> Out of His reach, that feels nor joy nor grief,
> Since both derive from weakness in some way.

Samuel Clemens' Creator of the Universe may owe something to Voltaire's *Zadig:* "All that you see on the little atom where you were born had to be in its place and in its fixed time according to the immutable orders of Him who embraces all. . . . There is no chance." The same celestial determinist turns up in the discourse of Macfarlane, a Cincinnati boarding-house friend of Sam's during the winter of 1856–1857. The Scotsman traced everything back to "a few microscopic seed germs, or perhaps *one* microscopic seed germ," planted by the Creator; from that point on, as Sam recalled the doctrine four decades later, life had evolved progressively until it encountered a snag in envious, selfish, vengeful, drunken, unclean, thieving, persecuting, murderous, patriotic man.

Clemens' ideas also derived from eighteenth-century rationalism, which imported for American consumption the English and French deistic conception of a Supreme Geometrician, deviser of a perpetual motion machine which ran according to the laws of its own structure. Once the springs had been wound up, this many millennia clock ticked on, and none of its cogs could be held accountable for grating against other cogs. Sam Clemens' brand of deism is reminiscential of Tom Paine's *The Age of Reason*, with its substitution of mind for myth, and unconsciously of the youthful Ben Franklin's extremism: God the mechanic, the questionableness of sin and personal immortality, the denial of divine providence and human free will. Although these doctrines were mouthed "in Satan's cause," as orthodox Timothy Dwight protested, they persisted.[594]

In an article of 1870 which his wife dissuaded him from publishing, Clemens explained that the Creator, without making any promise to mankind, had ordered the machinery of the universe beneficently, exactly, changelessly. The unwritten laws are equal and impartial to all men, and if the Creator does choose to ordain immortality for man (a thing immaterial), he will not be unjust to the beneficiary. When Samuel Clemens let his mind dwell on God, he was likely to be pessimistic, but when he contemplated a Newtonian-deistic Creator, as in his *Notebook* of 1899, he swung toward optimism. And no wonder! for a perfect artisan and artist rules the magnificent universe by means of materials, thoughts and character, forces and laws which He alone originated. The only trouble with the Creator was that He kept on withdrawing from the dust-fleck earth and its atrocious gadfly gods until He became infinitely remote—almost lost, in fact—in the immensities of the universe, in the austerities of cosmic harmony. Hence Clemens' thinking tended to shift its focus from the nebulosity, inscrutability, and indifference of the Creator to his manifestation on earth in that "automatic machine," the mind, and in the workings of law: "I believe that the universe is governed by strict and immutable laws." Against such Icarian flights of reason the Young Man protests in *What Is Man?*: "This is an infernal philosophy of yours."

The Clemens theology was trinitarian. It involved contempt for the Old Testament God, championship of the insulted and injured

Satan, and immense respect for the universal Creator. But at no time does the American theologian manage to keep these three necessary persons of his trinity in mind at once. His animosity against God throws him into a despair which obliterates the Creator or which confuses man-made deity and aloof deistic reality; his support of the underdog Satan may lead to the transfer of some of the Creator's attributes to the great rebel; or absorption in the austerely efficient Creator[595] makes both God and Satan fade out of sight. The tenets of Clemens' creed were achieved separately and were never integrated; thus the creed itself was unstable and seldom consolatory. The earth is at one gloomy moment of reflection a "forgotten potato"; at another, the Creator's laws "inflict pain and suffering and sorrow. . . . Without a doubt He had an object, but we have no way of discovering what it was"; and at still another, man's purposeless evolution is "probably matter of surprise and regret to the Creator." These Hardy and Kafka moods certainly brought no comfort. Like Ivan Karamazov, Clemens challenged God on the score of injustice, thought suicide a legitimate exit from the spectacle of cosmic wretchedness, and dared suspect that God and Satan were only *emanations* of the thinker. In fine, he was a God-struggler, too much a "child of unfaith," as Janko Lavrin says of Dostoevski, to believe fully in God or Satan.

Satan was the most dynamic and meaningful figure in the new trinity. In comparison to him God simply wasn't good enough and the Creator wasn't definite enough to fill a mortal's religio-philosophic life. I shall trace in some detail the rehabilitation of Satan, as he ascends from the position of terrifying devil to that of Clemens' and the Creator's *alter ego*.

The news of the real Injun Joe's death reached Sam Clemens accompanied by nocturnal thunder, lightning, and deluge. During that wild summer rumpus, as church and local lore made unhappily clear, Satan had come in his spectacular way to hale a great sinner to the nether world. In "mortal terror" over his own "lost condition," poor Sam repented his many sins, energetically resolved to do better, and supplicated for "just one more chance." But Satan was almost immediately to appear in a different—and more appealing—light. A Hannibal boy was expelled from Sunday School as beyond control. When he disappeared from town, it was rumored that he had been snatched away by the devil at night. Then, after a long time, he turned up as a glorious small functionary on a steamboat. Thus the "notoriously worldly" scapegrace, the devil's own, gained[596] eminence, whereas Sam Clemens was punished for his orthodoxy by "obscurity and misery." This "shook the bottom" out of Sam's religious teachings—as well it might.

Although the devil of Negro slaves and white churchgoers in Hannibal remained frightful, he became an object of concerned pity in the Clemens household. Sam's mother, like Robert Burns in "Address to the Deil," unconsciously followed in the footsteps of Origen and St. Thomas Aquinas in conjecturing that Auld Nickie-Ben might still have a chance of amnesty: "I'm wae to think upo' yon den, Ev'n for your sake!" She asserted that, although "wicked and abandoned," Satan was but a sinner among sinners. As such he had been treated most unfairly. Despite the irrefutable fact that he was "our one fellow and brother . . . who had the highest and clearest *right* to every Christian's daily and nightly prayers," no petitions ascended to the heavenly throne for him. Later, in *Concerning the Jews*, her son, being no great hand at praying, imagined himself a literary man of law presenting Satan's case:

I have no special regard for Satan; but I can at least claim that I have no prejudice against him. It may even be that I lean a little his way, on account of his not having a fair show. All religions issue bibles against him, but we never hear his side. We have none but the evidence for the prosecution, and yet we have rendered the verdict. To my mind, this is irregular . . . Of course Satan has some kind of a case, it goes without saying. It may be a poor one, but that is nothing; that can be said about any of us. As soon as I can get at the facts I will undertake his rehabilitation myself, if I can find an unpolitic publisher. It is a thing which we ought to be willing to do for any one who is under a cloud.

In "Is Shakespeare Dead?" after linking the Bard and Satan as "the two Great Unknowns," Clemens launches into a fabulous account of his own very precocious collecting of data about the Arch Enemy. Insisting that his Sunday School teacher, a stone mason, supply him with materials for a biography of Satan, the child prodigy was rebuffed because of his irreverent, even flippant, attitude. Actually Sam felt "the highest respect[597] for Satan" and had no desire to scoff at him; instead, his attack was to be directed against "the Satanic Traditioners." Despite his teacher's horror of this even greater sacrilege, attention-craving Sam wrote the life at the age of seven and forever lost the entrée to respectable homes.

Milton aided in the formation of Samuel Clemens' idea of Satan. In the ringing lines of *Paradise Lost*, the proud Archangel displays very impressive originality and "go," for which heaven afforded no expression, because a heartless, stuffed-shirt autocrat demanded an unvarying celestial routine. Urged on by a natural desire for prestige, Satan rebelled and was rusticated like Italo Balbo to a Dark Continent. Once in his new realm ("Better to reign in hell, than serve in heav'n"), he showed how the burden of sin and guilt could be defiantly borne or courageously ignored. Milton's "fall'n Cherub" gives birth to Sin, cohabits with her, and sires Death. In "Eve Speaks," Satan comments that the Moral Sense at least brought death, which would one day seem good to Adam and Eve. In less serious vein, Clemens recalled Milton's allegory when he named two black cats Satan and Sin.

To Clemens, who felt no reluctance about reinterpreting Milton, the obvious leader in a crusade against the Moral Sense (or sin) was Satan, whom he began to reinstate with humorous verve. By shuffling assorted personages, he took Satan out of the company of imps and master devils. Thus he could venture the opinion that Huck's character "is no better than those of Solomon, David, Satan, and the rest of the sacred brotherhood." He early docked Satan's silly tail and tricked him out like the operatic Mephistopheles, even adding a body of radium and a skin of polonium in order to make him as modern and scientific as the Curies. Clemens wrote several friendly letters to Satan, an interview with his nether majesty, and early drafts of the adventures of that worthy's celestial nephew—all unpublished. "A Humane Word from Satan" was conveyed by human agency to the readers of *Harper's Weekly*. In his *Notebook* of May 27, 1898, and in *Concerning the Jews*, Clemens requests[598] respect for Satan's lofty executive abilities as "spiritual head of four-fifths of the human race, and political head of the whole of it. . . . I would like to see him . . . and shake him by the tail." Ignoring the *faux pas* of allowing the tail to grow back, he hopefully attempted in published "Letters to Satan" to lure his tropical highness out of a three-century retirement for "a pleasure tour through the world in person, instead of doing it by proxy through me. You have many friends in the world; more than you think."

As the Mysterious Stranger, Satan does visit the world in the guiltless person of his nephew. The Creator type brought back from infinite space and slightly humanized, he is also Samuel Clemens in eloquent defense of determinism, innocence, and solipsism. The composite picture sketched in all of Clemens' writings is that of a being who is less transstellar than the Creator and less hardhearted than God; Satan emerges as God of This World, a truly daring, free, and inquisitive spirit in opposition to factitious theologies and illusory realities. As for a god of evil called Satan, the monstrosity never existed. After several thousand years, "our fine race" has been convinced "that there is no such thing as a witch . . . no such person as Satan," no such place as hell. The American's laudation of his own particular Satan contains a suggestion of Canon Docre's worship of Satan in Huysmans' *Là Bas* as a reasonable and just god, "King of the Disinherited, Son who art to overthrow the inexorable Father!" But Clemens' paradoxes arise from partially frustrated love of humanity; Canon Docre's, from warped egotism and sadistic hatred. In the nineteenth century, Clemens' regard for Satan is more akin to that for the honest, "progressive, inquiring," democratic "Bon Diable" of popular fancy described in his friend Moncure D. Conway's *Demonology and Devil-Lore*, and it is most akin to that expressed by Jules Michelet in *La Sorcière*. The French historian finds Satan, after being "unjustly driven out of Heaven," occupying himself in this world as a champion of reason, compassion, liberty, science, and progress against human and divine authoritarians:[599]

"We are bound to pay him homage, to admit he may well be after all one of the aspects of God."

While he was doing a workmanlike job of setting Satan on his feet, Samuel Clemens did not neglect Satan's own,—Negroes, heathens, witches, and the daughters of Eve. Just as he resented the tyranny of God in the macrocosm, so did he cry out against oppression in the microcosm. His sympathy flowed forth to Negro slaves. The "nigger trader" who bought his merchandise in Missouri for consumption on Southern plantations was a "human devil" conveying mortals to. hell. Every humiliating aspect of slavery revolted Clemens, but his quintessential fury was concentrated against the supreme brutality of lynching. In "The United States of Lyncherdom," he speaks of lawless executions as increasing until they are almost an American *mania*. The secret places of every community's heart foster a "deep disapproval of lynching," but eagerness to imitate ringleaders and lack of moral courage keep it suppressed. Men of spirit are needed to form better mores. The reasoning is the same that Satan uses in *The Mysterious Stranger* to explain the witch mania in sixteenth-century Austria. In both essay and novel, the Moral Sense, from which the other animals are of course free, is arraigned. Whether the person being hanged, stoned, or burned was a Negro or a supposed witch, Clemens saw the same sheepish malice at work, and horror filled his soul.

Lynching represented the acme of modern cruelty to Clemens' mind, and witchcraft persecution that of feudal and Renaissance times. The link between the two was perhaps the Maid of Orleans and not the Hannibal slaves' witch-voodoo lore which Bernard DeVoto describes with great insight in *Mark Twain's America*. The slaves' narrative stressed the processes of witchcraft, not the mob violence they aroused. As a boy in Hannibal, Sam Clemens read the martyrdom of Joan of Arc and became a lifelong partisan, idealizing her as persistently as he did Olivia Langdon. In deciding whether Joan[600] was commissioned of God or of Satan, English and Burgundian Catholics gave credit to the latter, accusing the peasant girl of reverencing not saints "but devils in disguise" and of doing homage to the Arch Fiend. Thus she was burned at the stake as a witch, "the very child of Satan." The reader of *Personal Recollections of Joan of Arc* finds himself emotionally involved with the author in the cause of Joan against her Christian accusers; if godly men can do such wrong to the most extraordinary person in the world, then welcome, Satan, as an ally! The seven long narratives, the autobiography, and the two travel books in which Clemens introduces witchcraft associate persecution chiefly with England, France, and Austria. The classic witchcraft hysteria of Salem, Massachusetts, seems to have interested him only slightly, although he did write this note in his copy of Cotton Mather's *Magnalia Christi Americana:* "The wise man of one age is the idiot of the next."

Samuel Clemens also abominated the forcible Christianizing of the heathen—the Blessings-of-Civilization Trust's moving in on "the person sitting in darkness." But whether he was wrought up over a converted Moro, a rabbled witch, or a hanged Negro, he was tempted to gloat over these outrages as irrefutable proofs that the human race was utterly brutal, damned, and depraved.

Fortunately for Clemens' sanity, humanity fell into two categories —the lifebearing, nourishing, protective female, and the competitive, grasping, destructive male. The distinction is least unfavorable to man in *Adam's Diary*, for the hero, though unimaginative, blundering, and comical, is not actively malicious. In *Eve's Diary*, the first mother, like Sam's Jane and Olivia Clemens, is inquisitive, resourceful, loving, and pathetically victimized by uncontrollable forces. Scorning those forked radishes misnamed lords of creation and feeling that his mother, wife, and daughters had been much kinder to him than his fallen nature deserved, Clemens was misanthropically disappointed in Adam, father, self, and mankind at the same time that he idealized Eve, mother, wife, and womankind. With Byron he "despised the human race because he despised himself.[601] I feel as Byron did, and for the same reason." Maddening knowledge of one sex was balanced by reassuring ignorance of the other sex. As the knightly champion of injured womankind, Clemens broke a lance *In Defense of Harriet Shelley*, stood up for Joan of Arc, and became almost hysterical over Mrs. Minor Morris' mistreatment in Teddy's White House. Like Jonathan Swift, Clemens populated his Lilliputs chiefly with men.

In the psychic malaise induced by a sense of guilt, Samuel Clemens tried to gain control of the consciousness of sin by understanding his own experience, by penetrating the meaning of Biblical mythology and revising myth in the light of his own knowledge of psychology and the accursed Moral Sense, and by creating a neo-trinitarian theology. He exchanged the customary functions of God and Satan and entered into defenses of Satan's supposed allies on earth,—the black man, the witch, the misbeliever, and the weaker vessel. Additional evidences of one of the most fertile neuroses a genius ever fostered are Clemens' incessant narcotic activity of composition, reading, billiards, and engagements; blind dependence on the Moral Sense of others; occasionally ostentatious shouldering of his burden, followed by assertions of unworthiness; disclaimers of responsibility; conjectures as to God's responsibility and the Creator's indifference; emphasis on man's insignificance in relation to the immensities of space and time; attacks on business cheats and verminous mankind in general, with a suggestion for exterminating the pest by shutting off the supply of oxygen; compensatory hero-worship (General Grant) and elation over his own power, prestige, and wealth; and a fixation on "kind, benignant" death, suicide, and madness.

Bernard DeVoto comments on the Clemens domestic tragedies in *Mark Twain at Work:* "He walked the narrow edge between sanity and madness." And Clemens, in his own *Notebook,* observed: "When we remember that we are all[602] mad, the mysteries disappear and life stands explained." But interpreting life as nothing more than a bedlamite's vision did not satisfy Sam Clemens as long as it did Luigi Pirandello. A much more pleasing fancy was that, as Calderón expresses it in the title of a play, *Life Is a Dream.* Pater, Schopenhauer, and Pascal fondled the same idea, which achieved classic utterance in lines which Clemens quotes in "Is Shakespeare Dead?": "We are such stuff As dreams are made on, and our little life Is rounded with a sleep." Clemens' final statement on dream philosophy is supposed to be pronounced by Satan, whose incognito is Philip Traum or Dream, in *The Mysterious Stranger:*

Life itself is only a vision, a dream.... Strange, indeed, that you should not have suspected that your universe and its contents were only dreams, visions, fiction! Strange, because they are so frankly and hysterically insane—like all dreams: a God ... who created man without invitation, then tries to shuffle the responsibility for man's acts upon man, instead of honorably placing it where it belongs, upon himself; and finally, with altogether divine obtuseness, invites this poor, abused slave to worship him! ... There is no God, no universe, no human race, no earthly life, no heaven, no hell.... Nothing exists but you. And you are but a *thought*—a vagrant thought, a useless thought, a homeless thought, wandering forlorn among the empty eternities!

Having dethroned God and exalted Satan as a necessitarian, anti-Moral Sense divinity, Clemens then called on Satan to abdicate. But the abdication speech is not actually Clemens' final word on dreams. It is rather one of his final words, for he liked to have two such words —a hopeful and a hopeless one. Much of his unpublished work has to do with the relativity of reality, the transcending of illusions like time and space, and the confusion of dream and waking. In "The Great Dark," the vindictive Superintendent of Dreams plants in ship passengers' minds a doubt of waking reality and a belief in dreams. The whole voyage, in fact, is a vision in which the malevolence and purposelessness of life are projected into a brief, intense nightmare. The boundary is traced more distinctly and more cheerfully[603] in Clemens' *Notebook* jotting of January 7, 1897. In dreams his "unhampered spiritualized body flies to the ends of the earth in a millionth of a second. Seems to—and I believe, *does....* It was not a dream—it all *happened.* I was actually there in person—in my spiritualized condition." To the question of dreams being conterminous with mortality comes the heartening answer: "When my physical body dies my dream body will doubtless continue its excursion and activities without change, forever." Thus immortality, one of the egotistic values of orthodoxy which Clemens had scrapped because of reason, antagonism to God, and conviction of the Creator's lack of interest, was regained through dreams.

In these thoughts Clemens agrees with other dream sages. Henry Holt advances similar theories in *On the Cosmic Relations:*

The dream has claims to be considered part of an eternal life. ... Most savages, and not a few savants, think the soul actually does go to the place where, in dreams, it seems to go. ... The dream life contains so much more beauty, so much fuller emotion, and such wider reaches than the waking life, that one is tempted to regard it as the real life, to which the waking life is somehow a necessary preliminary. So orthodox believers regard the life after death as the real life. ... For one, I would infinitely prefer my dream life to any fancied heaven I know of.

The companion piece to *The Mysterious Stranger,* steeped as it is in pessimism, is the optimistic, autobiographical narrative, "My Platonic Sweetheart," both of which were conceived in Austria in 1897–1898. The shorter tale covers the years 1854–1898, in which on an average of once every two years, a spiritually changeless girl of fifteen met and loved the author, an invariable seventeen, in his dreams. The *Notebook* also emphasizes the Peter Pan nature of Sam Clemens' dream self: "I was never old in a dream yet." "My Platonic Sweetheart" presents this wistful sketch of a faith:

In our dreams—I know it!—we do make the journeys we seem to make; we do see the things we seem to see; the people ... are real, not chimeras; they are living spirits, not shadows; and they are immortal and[604] indestructible. They go whither they will; they visit ... even the twinkling suns that wander in the wastes of space. ... When we die we shall slough off this cheap intellect, perhaps, and go abroad into Dreamland clothed in our real selves, and aggrandized and enriched by the command over the mysterious mental magician who is here not our slave, but only our guest.

Being a unique solipsist had become a bore to Clemens, just as Byron felt out of sorts until he created the Byronic heroine. The author and his platonic sweetheart, both equally real, existed in a paradise of uninhibited innocence resembling that of "Paul and Virginia." And again a dream philosopher is on Clemens' side, this time Hornell Hart: "It has been shown that a person may create a more or less elaborate dream-world of his own, and that by telepathy he can share to a greater or less extent the dream-creations of others."

An advantage of dreams which Clemens does not discuss is that they emancipate the sleeper from the Moral Sense. In "A Chapter on Dreams," Robert Louis Stevenson tells how his Brownies brought him scenes of *Dr. Jekyll and Mr. Hyde* in his sleep: "My Brownies have not a rudiment of what we call a conscience." Sam's close friend, William Dean Howells, discussed the subject in *Impressions and Experiences:*

The dreamer is purely unmoral—good and bad are the same to his conscience; he has no more to do with right and wrong than the animals; he is reduced to the state of the merely natural man; and perhaps the primitive men were really like what we are all now in our dreams.

Howells conjectures that our waking consciousness is "the off-spring of conscience" and that dreams show us "what we would be without our souls, without their supernal criticism of the mind." To Howells the mind was without pity or remorse in dreams; to Clemens it was reinstated in its kingdom of sinlessness, for it was the supernal heckling of the soul that made waking life seem intolerable to him. . . .[605]

The Microscope and the Dream

GLADYS CARMEN BELLAMY

THE BOOK CALLED THE MYSTERIOUS STRANGER PRESENTS MARK TWAIN'S final expression of the village and its inhabitants. Bernard DeVoto believes that this book resulted from the personal disasters which engulfed Mark Twain in the late eighteen nineties. His publishing firm failed; the Paige typesetting machine wrecked his fortune in its debacle; his youngest daughter, Jean, was discovered to be afflicted with epilepsy; his eldest daughter, Susy, closest to him in talent and spirit, died of meningitis; and Livy, after Susy's death, was an invalid the last eight years of her life. "The gods had turned against their darling," says Mr. DeVoto in *Mark Twain at Work;* and he believes that the tragic writings which include "The Great Dark" and *The Mysterious Stranger* constituted an attempt by Mark Twain to reintegrate his writing talent, almost destroyed by these disasters, and to still the accusing voice of his conscience by proving to himself that he was not to be blamed.

Mark Twain was always among the most autobiographical of writers. Yet, studying the record, it seems impossible to escape the conclusion that *The Mysterious Stranger* must some day have been written, substantially as he wrote it, with or without his personal calamities. As a matter of fact, the earliest hint of the story appears in a "Mr. Brown" letter of June 2, 1867. There Mark Twain reports an Apocryphal New Testament, seen in a New York library. In Chapter 15, according to Mark Twain, the boy Jesus plays with other boys; he makes clay animals that come to life and "clay birds

From *Mark Twain as a Literary Artist,* by Gladys Carmen Bellamy, pp. 352–362. Copyright 1950 by the University of Oklahoma Press.

which he causes to fly." Believing Jesus to be a sorcerer, the parents of the other boys forbid them to play with him. In Chapter 16, Joseph is seen to be unskillful at his carpenter's trade; young Jesus assists him by touching the ill-shapen articles, thus giving them the proper dimensions. In Chapter 19, Jesus is charged with causing the death of[352] various boys who have displeased him. Mark Twain summed up the activities of this apocryphal lad:

The young Savior's resentments were so frequent . . . that Joseph finally grew concerned about the matter and gave it his personal attention:
"16. Then said Joseph unto Mary, henceforth we will not allow him to go out of the house, for every one who displeases him is killed."
His society was pleasant, but attended by serious drawbacks.

Remembering Mark Twain's view of life, even in his happiest years, remembering too the fascination which the figure of Satan had always held for him, it seems inevitable that he would write *The Mysterious Stranger.* In the writing of *Huckleberry Finn,* he had already experimented with beauty tinged with strangeness and horror. A passage in *A Tramp Abroad,* which he wrote while *Huckleberry Finn* lay unfinished, anticipates an important bit in the presentation of young Satan as the Stranger. The passage describes the "prismatic colors" of clouds over the Alps, clouds resembling "gossamer webs" of a "lovely phantom fabric, . . . a fabric dainty enough to clothe an angel with." Soon he realized that the continuous movement of those delicate opaline colors reminded him of "what one sees in a soap-bubble that is drifting along." Both the Apocryphal account of the boy Jesus and the description of a soap-bubble as fit clothing for an angel were to furnish details for the earthly visits of Satan in *The Mysterious Stranger.*

The essence of tragedy in this book lies not in any malevolence against mankind exhibited by the Superior Powers in the person of young Satan, for there is little, although it appears. The chief tragedy lies in the utter indifference towards mankind which Satan exhibits. And this idea appears in Mark Twain's writings dating from his halcyon days. On August 12, 1883, a time of great personal happiness, he wrote in his *Notebook:* "I think we are only the microscopic trichina concealed in the blood of some vast creature's veins, and it is that vast creature God concerns himself about and not us." In the notes of 1885–86, just before the time of *A Connecticut Yankee,* he wrote:

Special Providence! That phrase nauseates me—with its implied importance of mankind and triviality of God. In my opinion these myriads of globes are merely the blood corpuscles ebbing and flowing through the[353] arteries of God and we but the animalculae that infest them . . . and God does not know we are there and would not care if He did.

Later, he recorded in *Following the Equator* a "large dream" in which he dreamed "that the visible universe is the physical person of God," with vast worlds as the blood corpuscles of His veins, and all living creatures are the microbes that infest the corpuscles. These passages are curiously reminiscent of the theories of Robert Fludd, as well as those of eighteenth-century Deists whom Mark Twain probably never read. The notes seem more closely connected with "3,000 Years Among the Microbes" than with any of his other fiction; yet they are linked, too, with *The Mysterious Stranger*. A note of August, 1897, labeled by Paine as probably for *The Mysterious Stranger*, reads:

He had but one term for that large body which has such a fine opinion of itself—"the little stinking human race, with its little stinking kings and popes and bishops and prostitutes and peddlers."

He said: "The globe is a living creature, and the little stinking human race and the other animals are the vermin that infest it—the microbes." . . .

One fine May morning when the boy Theodor, the narrator [of *The Mysterious Stranger*],[354] was on a hilltop with his friends Nikolaus and Seppi, a handsome youth came strolling along, "easy and graceful and unembarrassed, not slouchy and awkward and diffident like other boys." He sat down and talked to the boys in a simple, gentle way, winning their friendship at once. As he talked, he made a tiny squirrel out of clay, and it ran up a tree; he made a mouse-sized dog that barked at the squirrel, and birds that flew away singing. At last Theodor asked who he was. " 'An angel,' he said, quite simply, and set another bird free and clapped his hands and made it fly away." Then he formed tiny men and women from clay; they went to work, cleared a small space, and began to build a little castle. The three boys made horses and cannon and halberdiers, but dropped the figures and broke them in the astonishment of learning that their visitor's name was "Satan." Young Satan mended them with a touch, as the boy Jesus had mended Joseph's ill-formed work in the passage copied in Mark Twain's *Notebook* in 1867. Satan explained that only his uncle, for whom he was named, had been affected by the Fall; the rest of the family were still untouched by sin. At that moment two of the tiny workmen began to quarrel "in buzzing bumblebee voices" and fell to fighting. Momentarily annoyed,

Satan reached out his hand and crushed the life out of them with his fingers, threw them away, wiped the red from his fingers on his handkerchief, and went on talking . . . : "We cannot do wrong; neither have we any disposition to do it, for we do not know what it is."

The boys were shocked and grieved at "the wanton murder he had committed," but he talked on, switching his young listeners quickly from horror to beauty:

somehow . . . charming us in spite of the pitiful scene that was now under our eyes, for the wives of the little dead men had found the crushed . . .

bodies and were crying over them . . . and a priest was kneeling there . . . praying; and . . . pitying friends were massed about them . . . a scene which Satan paid no attention to until the small noise of the weeping and praying began to annoy him, then he . . . took the heavy board seat out of our swing and brought it down and mashed all those people . . . just as if they had been flies.

But he soon enchanted the boys again "with that fatal music of his voice. . . . He made us drunk with the joy of being with him."[355]

This fluctuation of mood between beauty and horror continues. The boys were always expecting beautiful things to happen when they were in Satan's presence. He told them of "the daily life in heaven" and also "of the damned writhing in hell." The vision of hell was so horrible, with condemned persons shrieking in their anguish, that the boys could hardly bear it; but Satan was "as bland about it as if it had been so many imitation rats in an artificial fire."

Whenever Satan's conversation turned to the human race, one would think he was talking "about bricks or manure or any other thing that . . . hadn't feelings." Presently he had the tiny castle finished, and it was beautifully done. He offered to create a miniature storm and earthquake around it, as entertainment, but warned the boys to stand back out of danger. They wanted to warn the tiny people, too, but "he said never mind them; they were of no consequence, and we could make more, some time . . . if we needed them." The tone of contemptuous indifference is only slightly more exaggerated than that of Mark Twain's Western sketch of 1864, "The Case of Smith vs. Jones," in which the ignorant, lying witnesses are shown in a sorry light, with a witness box in a corner "where more can be had when they are wanted." This time, however, Mark Twain's sympathy seems to be with the creatures in the box—here, the castle. A small cloud settled over the castle, and the little people flocked inside for shelter, but lightning blazed out and set it on fire. They "came flying out, shrieking, but Satan brushed them back, paying no attention to our begging and crying and imploring." Then an earthquake rent the ground, and the castle toppled into the chasm, which "closed upon it, with all that innocent life, not one of the . . . poor creatures escaping. . . . 'Don't cry,' Satan said; 'they were of no value. . . . we can make plenty more.' " . . . [356]

Throughout his life, Mark Twain derided man's belief that he is the favored creature of the universe; and the irony basic in this story appears in the relationship of the boys and Satan. When Satan takes Theodor to China on a tour of inspection, Theodor is "drunk with vanity and gladness." The three boys feel themselves to be the pets of Satan: yet he destroys Nicky and blasts the happiness of the other two by opening their eyes to what human life really is.

To entertain the two surviving boys, Satan shows them "the progress of the human race...its development of that product which it calls civilization." Mark Twain passed the ages in review: the boys saw the murder of Abel by Cain; then a long series of wars, murders, massacres; Sodom and Gomorrah; more wars. Christianity finally came into existence, but always there were wars, "hideous drenchings of the earth with blood." Then Satan exhibited the future, showing them "slaughters more terrible,...more devastating in their engines of war." Apparently, the chief progress had been, and would continue to be, in instruments for the mutual destruction of men. " 'And what does it all amount to?' said Satan with his evil chuckle. 'You gain nothing; you always come out where you went in.' "

A peculiar mingling of the beautiful and the horrible pervades *The Mysterious Stranger.* Once, departing, Satan dissolved himself and let the boys see him do it:

> He stood up and...thinned away until he was a soap-bubble, except that he kept his shape. You could see the bushes through him...as you see things through a soap-bubble, and all over him played and flashed the delicate iridescent colors of the bubble....You have seen a bubble strike the carpet and lightly bound along two or three times before it bursts. He did that. He sprang—touched the grass—bounded—floated along—touched again—and...presently exploded—puff! and in his place was vacancy. It was a strange and beautiful thing to see....[358]

As manifested in Mark Twain's fiction, his conceptions of good and evil, beauty and ugliness, are closely connected with the philosophy of escape displayed in the travel books. There, ugliness is reality; beauty is dream. But in his late fiction the urge towards escapism enlarges the dream motif until the dream finally engulfs the whole of life, the ugliness as well as the beauty. The difference, however, is of degree rather than of kind. When Mark Twain at last arrives at the nihilism of *The Mysterious Stranger,* he arrives by a path on which his feet have been set since the Sandwich Islands letters of 1866, with their siren song of escape from an active life to an isle of dreams.

The Mark Twain of *The Mysterious Stranger* even affirms, in an elevated form, the creed of that Mark Twain of Western journalism who had insisted that "one can deliver a satire with telling force through the insidious medium of a travesty." Satan tells Theodor that laughter can destroy certain "juvenilities":

"For your race, in its poverty, has unquestionably one really effective weapon—laughter. Power, money, persuasion, supplication, persecution—these can lift at a colossal humbug—push it a little—weaken it a little, century by century; but only laughter can blow it to rags and atoms at a blast. Against the assault of laughter nothing can stand."

Satan continued to take Theodor about the world, showing him wonders reflecting the "triviality of our race....not out of malice...it only seemed to amuse and interest him, just as a naturalist might be amused and interested by a collection of ants."[359]

The Mysterious Stranger is Mark Twain's greatest use of the device of diminishing humanity to microscopic proportions. By means of Satan he employs the Olympian detachment of a god and at the same time, by means of Theodor, reports it through the lips of a [360] boy. Thus he is twice-removed from the rage-provoking perversities of mankind. After studying early manuscripts of this story, Mr. DeVoto wrote that at first young Satan was "no more than a vehicle for Mark's derision of that God whose vengefulness creates human pain and for his scorn of the ant-like race pain is inflicted on. . . . But he became more than that." Yes, for the artist in Mark Twain would demand more than that—some sense of the alleviation that art requires to give a feeling of conclusiveness, as well as to make the tragic thing tolerable. He would not feel that need in a Socratic debate such as *What Is Man?* but in fiction he would be more alert to the obligations of the artist.

Unfortunately, by the time of *The Mysterious Stranger* he can no longer depend upon his boys for the saving grace. For Theodor confesses:

Naturally there were some who pitied Marget and Ursula for the danger that was gathering about them, but naturally they did not say so; it would not have been safe. . . . We boys wanted to warn them, but . . . when it came to the pinch . . . [we] found that we were not manly enough nor brave enough to do a generous action when there was a chance that it could get us into trouble.

Huck had often protected Nigger Jim at the risk of his own safety. But Mark Twain's boys have now become "like all the one-horse men in literature" and seem bent on earning the reader's contempt. By this time he cannot close the arc of his artistic circle by a realistic acceptance of human nature, even though he is dealing with boy nature; for these boys, through Satan, have had their eyes opened to the futility of human existence. And what does Mark Twain do to give the requisite sense of alleviation? As an artist, he does two things: he first presents the tragedy of life as a spectacle of the human race in miniature, with, as Mr. DeVoto says, "the suffering diminished to the vanishing point since these are just puppets, unreal creatures moving in a shadow-play"; and then he moves the reader on into a sense of dream. For anything can be endured in a dream.[1][361]

---

[1] Commenting upon the use of the dream in *The Mysterious Stranger,* Mr. DeVoto says that for Mark Twain the dream had "closed the arc," that in this story the dreadful things alleged against mankind in *What Is Man?* are said again, "but now they are tolerable, conformable, acceptable, for they have been removed far away, over them broods the peace of distant dream" (*Mark Twain at Work,* 129).

Escape as Nihilism:
The Mysterious Stranger

ROGER B. SALOMON

IN HIS SIGNIFICANT LITTLE BOOK "MARK TWAIN AT WORK," BERNARD DE Voto notes how Mark Twain's image of himself was impaired by the personal catastrophes of the 90's and goes on to describe the influence of this impairment on the form and themes of his later writing. "The gods had turned[191] against their darling," says DeVoto (p. 108). Twain's response to their betrayal was a sharper sense of personal guilt, which at the same time strengthened his conviction that *all* human nature was weak and fallible—indeed, hopelessly damned by corruption within and the iron chain of causality without. With his already meager belief in man thus further compromised, Twain's faith in civilization (the progress of man in society) could not long survive. By the early 1900's, in fact, pessimism regarding the "damned human race" had almost completely corroded away this faith.

In *Following the Equator* this corrosive process can most clearly be seen at work. During his trip around the world (1895–96), Twain's pessimism had found ready confirmation in the excesses of later nineteenth-century imperialism. He had abundant opportunity to contrast the values and actions of men of widely varying positions on the cultural scale. The resulting book was bitterly ironic; the ideal of civilization that Twain had so confidently held up in his early travel books, in *Following the Equator* is everywhere exposed as a sham and a delusion. The ideal, however, is exposed, as a whole, indirectly. The conception of progress still lingers on as the dominant image of social development, and no alternative theory of history is seriously proposed, though Twain is led to the very brink of a theory of recurrence. Certainly the faith which had, at least to some extent, animated the conception in his previous writings has disappeared....[192]

Far more characteristic of *Following the Equator* than qualified hopes is Twain's growing conviction that history was empty of *any*

From Roger B. Salomon, *Twain and the Image of History* (New Haven, Conn.: Yale University Press, 1961), pp. 191–192; 199–210, by permission of the publisher.

redemptive value. In an extraordinary passage, which looks far ahead into the twentieth century, he describes the fascination of India, with its "monotony of dust-colored dead levels and scattering bunches of trees and mud villages. It is not a beautiful country, yet there is an enchantment about it." The cause of the spell cast by India, Twain goes on to say, is history. "It is that that affects you, a haunting sense of the myriads of human lives that have blossomed, and withered, and per-ished here, repeating and repeating, century after century, and age after age, the barren and meaningless process; it is this sense that gives to this forlorn, uncomely land power to speak to the spirit and make friends with it; to speak to it with a voice bitter with satire, but elo-quent with melancholy" (21, 139).[1] The touches of romantic rhetoric in this passage (even more in evidence further on when Twain talks about "man and his vanities") should not blind us to the significance of its main contention: that history is a "barren and meaningless process"—change that is no change, recurrence without purpose.

Because his gaze was fixed so intently at this time on the supposed immutability of human nature, Twain had thus reached a position far more drastic even than that of Henry and Brooks Adams, whose theories of decline were really a long lamentation for the values of a political[199] Golden Age in the past.[2] In his comment on India, Twain, for all his rhetoric, was much closer in spirit to Eliot's Thomas Becket, who ironically describes the past as "not worth forgetting" and who does

> ... not know very much of the future
> Except that from generation to generation
> The same things happen again and again.
> Men learn little from others' experience.[3]

For Becket, as for his creator, history is without teleological signifi-cance because of the radically defective nature of man. This essentially is the conception of history (implied in *Huckleberry Finn*) which

---

[1] Parenthetical references by volume and page are to *The Writings of Mark Twain* (New York, Gabriel Wells, 1922–1925), 37 vols.

[2] Theoretically, Brooks Adams' "law" was cyclical: i.e. any society moved from an imaginative, agrarian, decentralized stage to one which was intellectual, materialistic, and centralized. The latter eventually brought about its own dis-integration through sterility, and presumably the whole process would be repeated again. Yet Adams' *Law of Civilization and Decay* ends ominously. We are more materialistic than the Romans ("the Romans were never wholly sordid, nor did they ever niggle") and "we lack the stream of barbarian blood which made the Middle Ages" (New York, Vintage, 1955, p. 308). Clearly what Brooks, like Henry, was interested in stressing was the long (and probably irreversible) decline from the Middle Ages. Written during the free silver controversy, his book is a curious commingling of the Jeffersonian-Agrarian tradition with the romantic medievalism of Ruskin.

[3] *Murder in the Cathedral* (New York, Harcourt, Brace, 1935), p. 24.

Twain was working toward in *Following the Equator* and which he was to develop explicitly at some length in *The Mysterious Stranger*. But Eliot's vision is Christian and apocalyptic; although we must start with temporal, ever-changing experience, we come to see its dependence upon the timeless—"Only through time time is conquered."[4] For Twain, on the other hand, those very forces which were pressing on him an agonizing awareness of the world of flux, were, at the [200] same time and by their very nature, destroying the imaginative and spiritual validity of his own center of the turning wheel. Indeed, it is this dilemma which presented itself to him when he sat down to write *The Mysterious Stranger*.

"Would you like to see a history of the progress of the human race? —its development of that product which it calls civilization?" Satan asks his young companions in *The Mysterious Stranger*. Upon their affirmative answer, he presents a vision of Cain murdering Abel, followed by an endless vista of wars, murders, and massacres—Hebrew, Egyptian, Greek, Roman, and those of the "ages of Europe." "It is a remarkable progress," he adds:

In five or six thousand years five or six high civilizations have risen, flourished, commanded the wonder of the world, then faded out and disappeared, and not one of them except the latest ever invented any sweeping and adequate way to kill people. They all did their best—to kill being the chiefest ambition of the human race and the earliest incident in its history—but only the Christian civilization has scored a triumph to be proud of. Two or three centuries from now it will be recognized that all the competent killers are Christians; then the pagan world will go to school to the Christian—not to acquire his religion, but his guns.   (27, 108–11)

Satan goes on to portray the future explicitly for the boys: "before our eyes nation after nation drifted by, during two or three centuries, a mighty procession, raging, struggling, wallowing through seas of blood, smothered in battle smoke . . . and always we heard the thunder of the guns and the cries of the dying." The ultimate cause of the endless cycle of slaughter, he concludes, finally, is human nature: the usurpations of minorities; the acquiescence of the majority.[201] "The first man was a hypocrite and a coward, qualities which have not yet failed in his line; it is the foundation upon which all civilizations have been built" (27, 111–12).

Here human corruption is envisaged as a quality inherent in Adam; no fall is involved. <u>Corruption, in other words, is not the result of but anterior to civilization—the First Cause of all social forms.</u> Elsewhere in the book, corruption and the historical evils resulting

[4] T. S. Eliot, *Four Quartets* (New York, Harcourt, Brace, 1943), p. 5. My comment on Eliot's conception of time is a close paraphrase of Morris Weitz, "T. S. Eliot: Time as a Mode of Salvation," *Sewanee Review, 60* (1952), 58–9.

from corruption are blamed on the Moral Sense; man does wrong because of false notions of right and wrong inevitably inculcated by society. The torture of a heretic, for example, is compared to the exploitation of factory workers by "rich and very holy" proprietors, who "pay to these poor brothers and sisters of theirs ... only enough to keep them from dropping dead with hunger." Significantly, in this passage Twain directly attacks the technology he had so long celebrated and actually goes on to argue that the factory system is even *worse* than medieval torture: "They broke him [the tortured man] on the wheel and smashed him to rags and pulp after we left [says Satan], and he is dead now and free of your precious race, but these poor slaves here [the factory workers]—why they have been dying for years and some of them will not escape from life for years to come" (*27*, 50–3).

Such is the conception of human history in *The Mysterious Stranger*—a conception that contributes heavily to the total pessimism of the book. It is, however, only one aspect of this pessimism, just as Twain's belief in progress in the 1880's was only part of his vision of human experience during that period. What of his dream of escape from history—his complex image of goodness, stasis, freedom that had coalesced in the figure of the boy floating down the Mississippi on a raft? Clearly, in *The Mysterious Stranger* as in *Following the Equator*, a coherent primitivism was impossible for Twain because of his overwhelming sense of[202] the evil inherent in man. As Gladys Bellamy has noted, "he can no longer depend upon his boys for the saving grace."[5] Nikolaus and Seppi and Theodor in *The Mysterious Stranger* have more pity than their elders but they are just as cowardly. On one occasion, for example, the boys want to warn Marget and Ursula that the community suspects them of witchcraft, but, as Theodor admits: "we backed down when it came to the pinch, being afraid. We found that we were not manly enough to do a generous action when there was a chance that it would get us into trouble" (*27*, 59–66). On another occasion Theodor stones a woman being hanged because if he "had not done as the others did it would have been noticed and spoken of." In his heart he is sorry for her, but "all were throwing stones and each was watching his neighbor" (*27*, 114–15). To be sure, Theodor leaves one witch-burning because "it was too dreadful," and at another he gives the victim an apple (*27*, 60); but these gestures remain his nearest approach to independent moral action. In such scenes Twain preserves the situation so common in his writing of the cruel mob observed by a boy who either pities and (if possible) aids the victim or is himself the victim. The sole—though crucial—difference in *The Mysterious Stranger* is the shift in the moral stance of the boy: pity has been rendered impotent by fear.

[5] *Mark Twain as a Literary Artist* (Norman, Univ. of Oklahoma Press, 1950), p. 361.

Unfallen, free from the Moral Sense, master of "time and distance" (27, 26, 114), Satan is the one explicitly Adamic figure in the book. His "innocence," however, leads not so much to goodness as to indifference—indeed, to what, at least to mortal eyes, seems very close to callousness. If nothing else, his name and the curious fact that he is nephew to the great fallen angel would suggest Twain's deeply ambivalent feelings toward him. Time was[203] cruel, but eternity was insensate and capricious.[6] Only in animals could Twain still locate innate goodness, and they merely served to illuminate more sharply the horror of man. A dog, for example, who tries to save the life of the master who has misused him, exhibits the same enduring and instinctive loyalty and sense of responsibility that Twain in other books had associated with Edward, Huck, and Jim (27, 54–7).

Yet as the paths of escape narrowed for Twain, the need increased. "Raft" imagery keeps reappearing in his writing of the 90's. "If I had my way I would sail on forever and never go to live on the solid ground again," he remarks in Following the Equator (21, 290–1). Stasis predicated on physical isolation, however, was inadequate for obvious reasons; even Huck and Jim's paradise had been invaded by the Duke and the Dauphin—those grotesque symbols of the very civilization from which the boy and the Negro were attempting to flee. By 1890, for Twain as for the rest of the country, the frontier was closed; in the years ahead, symbolic as well as literal escape to the wilderness would become increasingly difficult. Social stasis was an equally futile hope. On the first page of The Mysterious Stranger, Austria in 1590 is described as "far away from the world, and asleep." The boy narrator goes on to note that Eseldorf, his village, was "in the middle of that sleep, being in the middle of Austria. It drowsed in peace in the deep privacy of a hilly and woodsy solitude where news from the world hardly ever came to disturb its dreams, and was infinitely content." Here Twain instinctively (not, I think, ironically) evokes the Jeffersonian idyl, but, of course, its validity is contradicted by the whole drift of the story—even by the[204] very name of the village. It is significant that, in reworking his story, he transferred it from Hannibal, as if the lingering associations of Hannibal prevented him from giving free vent to his nihilism. Certain medieval practices, moreover, always remained his ultimate images of inhumanity. In his "Eddypus" manuscript Twain carefully makes the distinction between a "dully dozing" southern village and its medieval counterpart; even with slavery, he says, the southern village had no Inquisition and no burning of heretics (p. 29). Death by fire (which figures prominently in The Mysterious Stranger) has an important psychological meaning for Twain. It is clearly related to his feelings of guilt about his brother

[6] Twain's ambivalent feelings toward the Deity in The Mysterious Stranger have been aptly compared with those of Hardy by Edwin S. Fussell, "The Structural Problem of 'The Mysterious Stranger'," Studies in Philology, 49 (1952), 97.

Henry, who perished in a steamboat tragedy, as well as those about the drunk who burned up in jail because Twain had given him matches.[7]

In the face of such terrible visions, escape was conceivable only on far more drastic terms: nothing less than severance of the direct relationship between the mind and the world. It was, indeed, impossible unless one or the other were totally destroyed. Thus insanity was a possible means of escape. "Are you so unobservant as not to have found out that sanity and happiness are an impossible combination?" asks Satan after he has made the kindly Father Peter insane. "No sane man can be happy, for to him life is real and he sees what a fearful thing it is. Only the mad can be happy." Death, naturally, was equally effective. The narrator says of Satan with more truth than he is aware of at the time: "He didn't seem to know any way to do a person a favor except by killing him or making a lunatic out of him" (27, 130-1). The alternative to death and insanity was to destroy the world while leaving the mind intact; and this Twain tried to do by means of a curious extension of the dream image—his image of "unreality."[205] According to Bellamy, "the urge toward escapism enlarges the dream motif until the dream finally engulfs the whole of life, the ugliness as well as the beauty."[8] "Nothing exists but you," says Satan to Theodor. "And you are but a thought—a vagrant thought, a useless thought, a homeless thought, wandering forlorn among the empty eternities" (27, 140). In his desire to escape the shock and disillusionment of life in time, Twain had arrived close to the modern existentialist position.

Such a solution to life's problems may have had an immense therapeutic value for Twain; it may, indeed, as DeVoto has suggested, have brought him back from the brink of insanity.[9] As an artistic device, however, it is less successful. Twain makes his escape by fiat not by art, because his image of escape had been destroyed in the process of its transformation and he had nothing concrete to substitute for it. A literary image is a complex of sensuous, compelling, and value-laden associations. In *Huckleberry Finn*, Twain's image of escape is compounded of the naive innocence of childhood, the godlike stature of the raftsmen, and the sense of release (with its possibility of moral freedom) and stasis attendant on sleep, drifting, and physical isolation from society. His image is "unreal" only in the sense that it describes a reality transcending the flux of empirically centered experience—a source of values beyond the reach of life in time and history though constantly in conflict with it.

In *The Mysterious Stranger* the components of this complex image are systematically rejected as themselves being without value. The "unreality" of the dream concept is retained but this "unreality"

---

[7] Dixon Wecter makes this point in *Sam Clemens of Hannibal* (Boston, 1952), pp. 253–6.

[8] *Mark Twain as a Literary Artist*, p. 360.

[9] *Mark Twain at Work*, pp. 129–30.

now is not the unreality of transcendence mirrored in concrete images but the unreality of total negation; the dream, in other words, has[206] become a device for exorcism rather than artistic creation. The sole remaining "reality" is the existential "I," but Twain makes no serious attempt to conceive of this "I" imagistically as certain twentieth-century writers have done. It is, moreover, even debatable whether the ending of The Mysterious Stranger works out in intellectual terms. Edwin Fussell has attempted to show how Twain prepares for the ending through various "levels of dreaming" in the book, but he as much as admits that to take the ending at its face value is to turn the rest of the book into an epistemological nightmare.[10]

But if Twain fails to develop a coherent imaginative response to what Camus has called the "absurdity" of life, he succeeds, nevertheless, at the more modest level in making this absurdity vivid, albeit in nineteenth-century terms. The real theme of The Mysterious Stranger —the theme which, as it is developed concretely, gives to the book its enduring value—is not the literal unreality but the meaninglessness of life. Life is insubstantial only in its futility, its lack of stable and enduring values; only in the face of the indifference (if not the malice) of God, the weakness and the limited vision of man, the sense of the monotony and repetition of human events. Camus' "absurdity" is Twain's "vanity," a note sounded again and again in the book. Satan's laughter reaches out to embrace all human pretensions. On one such occasion Theodor recounts how Satan suddenly sobers up a little and says: "But, after all, it is not all ridiculous [i.e. man's pride in his deeds]; there is a sort of pathos about it when one remembers how few are your days, how childish your pomps, and what shadows you are" (27, 53). To the extent that men were "shadows"—without the dignity of enduring substance and final ends—they were "unreal." But this is, of course, a far cry from solipsism.[207]

What is the meaning of history, asks Satan rhetorically in The Mysterious Stranger? What does the endless, empty cycle of civilizations amount to? He answers his own question by remarking that it amounts to "nothing at all." "You gain nothing," he explains; "you always come out where you went in. For a million years the race has gone on monotonously propagating itself . . . to what end? No wisdom can guess" (27, 111–12). Twain leaves the problem of an adequate conception of history—of visible images of the past, present, and future or viable images of the transcendence of time—at exactly the point at which the contemporary artist has been forced to construct new hypotheses and new artistic forms in accord with these hypotheses. Driven by a similar impulse to recover an order and stasis beyond time or simply to portray the sterility of a time-ridden world, certain modern writers have abandoned naturalism for deliberate anachronism, iso-

10 Fussell, pp. 95–104.

lated image groups (i.e. the blurring or complete denial of narrative and even syntactical sequence), extravagant use of myth, symbolic characterization, and stream-of-consciousness techniques—all of which tend to work against the normal, chronological structure of the literary medium. For these writers, as Joseph Frank has noted, the mythical imagination has supplanted the objective historical imagination.[11] Twain's work can be most fruitfully viewed as a significant step down the long road to this transformation. In *The Mysterious Stranger*, the movement away from a naturalistic style is obvious and explicit.

At the same time, the relative success of the modern writer in meeting the imaginative challenge occasioned by the failure of history throws a good deal of light on certain of the root causes of Twain's artistic imperfections: on the one hand, a frequent failure to bring his deepest vision[208] into focus or even to acknowledge it completely (e.g. *A Connecticut Yankee* and *The Prince and the Pauper*); on the other, the unfulfilled attempt to wed vision to substantial form (e.g. *Joan of Arc* and *The Mysterious Stranger*). Even in *Huckleberry Finn*, although Twain succeeded brilliantly in suggesting a mode of being apart from history, he was still a slave to the time-sequential structure of his naturalistic narrative and the logical demands of a "social problem" plot. However long he allowed Huck and Jim to loaf on Jackson's Island or to float on the bosom of the river, Twain was committed to taking them somewhere else; they could not forever drift downstream, least of all into the deep South. Here, indeed, is the core of Twain's dilemma in the book and the reason why the final chapters seem such a drastic falling off from the central episodes.

The fact is that Huck cannot be meaningfully separated from his river surroundings *because* his largest dimension is mythological. For the mythological imagination "place, not time ... [is] the crucial form of perception ... For mythical thinking the relation between what a thing 'is' and the place where it is situated is never purely external and accidental; the place is itself a part of the thing's being, and the place confers very special ties upon the thing."[12] It is "place" in this sense which gives Huck his real significance, yet it is place which Twain is eventually forced to violate because of the growing absurdity of the plot after the raft has passed Cairo. That he hesitated so long to remove Huck from the river suggests Twain's intuitive awareness that Huck would lose stature and meaning were he to be separated from the images which define him—indeed, which are an integral part of his being. The best that can[209] be said of the final scenes is that they are a

---

[11] Pages 379–92. My comments in this paragraph draw heavily on Frank's excellent article.

[12] Isabel G. MacCaffrey, *Paradise Lost as "Myth"* (Cambridge, Harvard Univ. Press, 1959), pp. 69–70, and n. 25. The quotation dealing with mythical thinking is taken by MacCaffrey from Ernst Cassirer, *Mythical Thought*, trans. Ralph Manheim (New Haven, Yale Univ. Press, 1955), p. 92.

grotesque and heavy-handed parody of the true romance of the river. But Huck's loss of stature—his sudden descent from mythical hero to little boy—is jarring, disorienting, and anti-climactic. A complete victim of the plot, he is only freed from its effects when Twain arbitrarily dissolves it by announcing that Jim has been emancipated all along. Then and only then can Huck return to his appropriate place. Or can he? His plan "to light out for the Territory ahead of the rest" (13, 405) betrays its weakness in its very phraseology, for it acknowledges that the "sivilizing" Aunt Sallys will always be close behind. Huck's place, in other words, was too geographical, too localized; it was threatened by both the chronological demands of the conventional novel and the larger chronology of history. Thus the image of the river was productive of one great book but of no enduring vision, point of view, or style because it was everywhere vulnerable to the very time it sought to transcend. Tormented by history, which for most of his life he alternately sought to embrace and cast away, Twain was finally driven in *The Mysterious Stranger* to a passionate, frantic, arbitrary denial of its power to hurt him: "It is all a dream—a grotesque and foolish dream" (27, 140). For the Twain of *The Mysterious Stranger*, as for so many later writers, history (to paraphrase Stephen Dedalus) had become a nightmare from which one must—somehow—awake to live and write.[210]

Nightmares and Dreams

ALBERT E. STONE, JR.

TOGETHER WITH SOME SLIGHTER PIECES LIKE "LETTERS FROM THE EARTH" and "Little Bessie Would Assist Providence" (both unpublished fragments), *The Mysterious Stranger* presents us with the "symbols of despair" (to use DeVoto's appropriate phrase) of a village agnostic grown old and bitter. The novel exhibits Twain's mind at one extreme of its violent oscillation, at that pole where a meaningful universe is now rejected and one in which human freedom (hence human responsibility) is seen as illusion.

From Albert E. Stone, Jr., *The Innocent Eye: Childhood in Mark Twain's Imagination* (New Haven, Conn.: Yale University Press, 1961), pp. 231–250, by permission of the publisher.

We know there always existed an opposite pole to Mark Twain's misanthropy. At the other end of his mind Twain was a man with strong emotional attachments not only to specific human beings but to the potential dignity of the human condition itself. Strongest of all his intuitive sympathies, of course, was his feeling for children. This predilection persisted right alongside his burgeoning pessimism. Thus only a few years before *What Is Man?* he wrote *Tom Sawyer, Abroad;* a few years later he was busy with "Eve's Diary" and " A Horse's Tale." Such vacillations characterize the writer's whole career. . . . Hence the persistence of a sentimental impulse throughout his period of blackest despair should not be wondered at. Like the Angel Fish Club which he established about this time, his attachment to childhood and his special fondness for young maidens survived even the onslaught of his rage against the cosmos.

Since virtually all of Twain's last works which exhibit this[231] sentimental side deal with girls, one is tempted to wonder whether the aged writer did not unconsciously divide his allegiance along sexual lines. "The Death Disk," "A Horse's Tale," "Eve's Diary," and "Marjorie Fleming, the Wonder Child" are, on the surface at least, happy pieces in which the power and beauty of girlhood are celebrated. *The Mysterious Stranger,* on the other hand, attempts to demonstrate "what a shabby poor ridiculous thing" man is, and does so principally in terms of boyish characters. Closer scrutiny shows, however, that in spite of attractive plausibility this notion does not do justice to the inner coherence which Twain's bifocal vision actually had. Though *The Mysterious Stranger* manifests superficially a nihilism that totally contradicts the mood of idyllic, innocent happiness of the other stories— notably, "A Horse's Tale"—a closer look at the fabric of both sorts of fiction uncovers a sympathetic thread running through the story of young Satan's visit to Eseldorf and, conversely, a melancholy, elegiac tone underlying the saccharine narratives of Cathy Alison and her cousins. In other words, Twain allowed both spirits to enter and form a necessary element of both stories. Despair *and* sentimentality are inseparable here, as in the novels and stories of earlier years, because they formed consistent and complimentary aspects of his view of reality. In this fundamental respect his imagination was entirely static.

More than any other factor, I believe, the unchanging dualism of his mental temper explains why he continued, long after the nostalgic appeal of Hannibal had evaporated, to select boys and girls as favorite fictional characters. To the last, he saw the world of childhood as the appropriate battle ground upon which his violently contradictory views of human nature and destiny could deploy themselves without ever reaching a definitive outcome. As had been the case with *Joan of Arc,* he could not bring himself, either in *The Mysterious*[232] *Stranger* or in the genial little tales of these last years, to deny the hopeless determinism of the one or the fond idealizing of maidenhood so typical of the other. All his life Mark Twain found it difficult to settle down. . . . [233]

As the century waned, however, . . . Twain's cast of mind steadily darkened. . . . His growing rigidity of thought manifested itself in many ways. Two of the most revealing forms it took were *What Is Man?*, the "gospel" of pessimism he began writing also in 1898, and in Twain's private reading, particularly in books about psychology and popular science. One of the more revealing of these latter expressions of his cosmic philosophy is his own copy of James Mark Baldwin's popular introduction to psychology, *The Story of the Mind*, which appeared in 1899. Twain's marginal comments in this little volume reinforce the doctrine of man as a machine—the doleful answer to the query of *What Is Man?*.

Cast in the form of a dialogue, *What Is Man?* repeats in [237] skeletal form the double perspective of many of Twain's novels. That is, a Young Man, as naive as the greenhorn in *Life on the Mississippi*, asks questions of an Old Man who is as cynically wise as Sieur Louis de Conte after his career as page to a saint is over. Inevitably not much dramatic interest is generated. Over and over again the refrain is repeated: "Man the machine—man the impersonal engine. Whatsoever a man is, is due to his *make,* and to the *influences* brought to bear on it by his heredities, his habitat, his associations. He is moved, directed, COMMANDED, by *exterior* influences—*solely*. He *originates* nothing, not even a thought." The Old Man will not even allow Adam the least bit of freedom to think originally. "Adam probably had a good head," he admits, "but it was of no sort of use to him until it was filled up *from the outside*. He was not able to invent the triflingest little thing with it . . . A man's brain is so constructed that *it can originate nothing whatever*. It can only use material obtained *outside*. It is merely a machine; and it works automatically, not by will-power" (*26*, 5, 7).[1]

The impotence of the human mind to act independently—that is the melancholy message the Old Man asserts and which the Mysterious Stranger echoes with sardonic insistence. They are, of course, voicing the convictions of Twain himself. By the mid-nineties, he had come to rest in a philosophy which, rejecting the Christian explanation of human freedom of the will, accepted uncritically those aspects of popular evolutionary thought that regarded man as caught in a cul-de-sac of environmental forces from which there is no escape. In *Mark Twain at Work* Bernard DeVoto has explained Twain's private reasons for adopting such a form of environmentalism, one far starker in its human prospects than formulations of Herbert Spencer or William Graham Sumner. DeVoto argues that Twain's whole purpose as a writer during his last years was to absolve himself from imagined

[1] Parenthetical references by volume and page are to *The Writings of Mark Twain* (New York: Gabriel Wells, 1922–1925), 37 vols.

guilt for[238] the dire family calamities that engulfed him. "Art is the terms of an armistice made with fate," DeVoto asserts, and goes on to analyze Twain's determinism in these terms: "He had tried to say: it was not my fault, I was betrayed. But the accusation could not be stayed so easily. He had tried to say: it was not my fault, for the fixed universe of inescapable law intended from the beginning that this should happen."[2]

To see Twain's determinism as psychologically rather than intellectually necessary is doubtless a sound insight; it helps, for one thing, to bridge the apparent gap between the two sides of his mind. But to such an explanation must be added evidence for the writer's honest wrestling with the intellectual problems of his generation. Though uneducated in a formal sense and hence like all self-taught men full of surprising depths and shallows, Twain nevertheless was generally familiar with the fields of popular science, philosophy, and, as it emerged, psychology. From what we know of his conversation and letters and from the contents of his library he followed the Darwinian dialogue of his age. He owned and read with attention some, at least, of the works of John Fiske, Andrew D. White, and William James, as well as more popular formulations like C. W. Saleeby's *Evolution, the Master-Key*.[3]

One of these books which Twain read carefully was James Mark Baldwin's *The Story of the Mind*, a copy of which its author sent with the affectionate inscription "From one Mark to Another."[4] Twain's underlinings and marginal comments indicate that his imagination responded vigorously to Baldwin's explanations. Moreover the form these responses took[239] is strikingly similar to the language of *The Mysterious Stranger*. In the introduction, for instance, Baldwin remarks upon the genesis of human mentality, "we must think of it [the Mind] as a growing, developing thing, showing its stages of evolution in the ascending animal scale, and also in the unfolding of the child . . . and as revealing its possibilities finally in the brutal acts of the mob, the crimes of the lynching party, and the deeds of collective righteousness performed by our humane and religious societies." Twain marked this whole passage, for the author of *Huckleberry Finn* knew at first hand man's capacities in the direction of mobs and lynching parties. He twice underscored the word "brutal" and underlined (very likely with grave reservations) "humane" and "deeds of collective righteousness." *The Mysterious Stranger*, on which Twain may well have been work-

[2] DeVoto, *Mark Twain at Work*, pp. 129, 130.

[3] See *Mark Twain Library Auction Catalogue*, April 10, 1951, in MTP, especially Items 15a, 28a, 61a, 7c, 69c, 74c, D3, D47.

[4] MT's copy of James Mark Baldwin, *The Story of the Mind* (New York, D. Appleton and Company, 1899), is in the Mark Twain Library, West Redding, Connecticut.

ing as he read Baldwin, contains (like the earlier novels) a number of graphic depictions of mobs and lynching parties.[5]

To be sure, Twain did not need a Princeton professor to inform him of man's inhumanity to his fellows. The question raised by *The Story of the Mind* is not literary influence, but rather evidence of intellectual awareness on Twain's part of scientific opinion concerning man's freedom as a thinking animal. On this score, Baldwin both reassured and upset him. The psychologist presented the latest theories linking all forms of life into one organic chain; at one place he wrote, "there is the rise of the evolutionary theory, which teaches that there is no absolute break between man and the higher animals in the matter of mental endowment; and that what difference there is must itself be the result of the laws of mental growth."[6] Twain more or less accepted this; "no frontier" he wrote carefully in the margin. Then Baldwin continued, "the more adequate the science of the human mind has become[240] the more evident has it also become that man himself is more of a machine than has been supposed." Twain emphatically agreed. In fact, he went further; "He is wholly a machine" he asserted at the edge of the page. "Man grows by certain laws," Baldwin continued; "his progress is conditioned by the environment, both physical and social, in which he lives; his mind is a part of the natural system of things." Here Twain differed completely. Twice underscoring "growth," he wrote indignantly in the margin, "There is no mental *growth*. There is extension of mental *action*, but not of capacity."[7]

"Man is wholly a machine. There is no growth or change, only more of the same automatic, inevitable response to external stimuli." This, in essence, is the intellectual position Twain held during the period in which *The Mysterious Stranger* was written. Since there are clear indications in earlier works of his tendency to think in these terms, one must be careful about ascribing all of the writer's rigid determinism, as DeVoto is inclined to do, to an attempt to rationalize guilt feelings arising from the death of loved ones. Like all works of the fictional imagination, *The Mysterious Stranger* is the product of Twain's total experience. . . .[241]

We learn Eseldorf's true status only gradually, and do so through the innocent eye of Theodor, the last boyish narrator in Twain's fiction. In a manner not unlike *Moby-Dick* Twain's novel has a divided focus. Philip Traum (like Ahab) is ostensibly the chief figure. However, it speedily becomes clear that all of Traum's actions are not only perceived through Theodor's mind but are directed toward illuminating that Ishmael-like mind with a sense of the true nature of things.

[5] *The Story of the Mind,* pp. 6–7.
[6] *Ibid.,* p. 24.
[7] © Mark Twain Company.

What is happening is a cosmic initiation, with Theodor as the neophyte and Philip Traum the master of ceremonies.

The relation between the divine boy and the human is a complex one. Theodor's reaction to young Satan's instructive miracles—as, for instance, when he creates a crowd of tiny human figures, sets them to work, but casually crushes the life out of them when they begin quarreling—is a mixture of wonder and revulsion. To Theodor's young and naive mind, Satan's nonchalant murder of the tiny creatures is literally a brutal act. But Philip shows him that brutes never behave as badly as humans. Like Satan himself, animals lack a moral sense, and hence they cannot wrongfully inflict pain. "When a brute inflicts pain," he explains to the three boys,

he does it innocently; it is not wrong; for him there is no such thing as wrong. And he does not inflict pain for the pleasure of inflicting it—only man does that. Inspired by that mongrel Moral Sense of his! A sense whose function is to distinguish between right and wrong, with liberty to choose which of them he will do. Now what advantage can he get out that? He is always choosing, and in nine cases out of ten he prefers the wrong. There shouldn't be any wrong; and without the Moral Sense there couldn't be any.[242]   (27, 50–51)

These are indeed confusing words and deeds for Theodor to comprehend. On the one hand Philip Traum has the attributes of God—he creates effortlessly all forms of good things, and elicits the most ecstatic adoration from the boys. But just as effortlessly he commits the most inhumane deeds and does them in the same spirit of innocent ruthlessness a leisurely cat would display in devouring a mouse. He appears genuinely to like Theodor, Seppi, and Nikolaus, and yet his scorn for humanity is comprehensive. He blames men for misusing their miserable moral sense, but in the next scene will prove that man has absolutely no freedom of choice to exercise that sense. Satan by turns laughs and rages at human behavior; he will at one moment consider man's frailties so contemptible as to be beneath notice and then launch into a detailed diatribe against the evils of colonialism. Philip Traum is a thinly masked mouthpiece for the contradictions of Twain's own tortured mind. Philip Traum is one part Bad Boy, one part God, and one part Mark Twain.

As he had done many times before, Twain uses children as the chief vehicle for his cosmic allegory. Thus when he is anxious to demonstrate the inevitability that Man's moral sense will produce pain and suffering, he shows the villagers of Eseldorf dealing with a suspected witch. "They chased her more than half an hour, we following to see it," Theodor tells us,

and at last she was exhausted and fell, and they caught her. They dragged her to a tree and threw a rope over a limb, and began to make a noose in it, some holding her, meantime, and she crying and begging, and her young daughter looking on and weeping, but afraid to do or say anything.

They hanged the lady, and I threw a stone at her, although in my heart I was sorry for her; but all were[243] throwing stones and each was watching his neighbor, and if I had not done as the others did it would have been noticed and spoken of. Satan burst out laughing.   (27, 114–15)

This scene, which echoes earlier episodes in *The Prince and the Pauper, Huckleberry Finn,* and *A Connecticut Yankee,* marks a fictional high-water mark in Twain's misanthropy. Never before had the writer taken such explicit pains to show that boys are no different in their moral cowardice from other people. Theodor's confession (so different in its implications from Huck's unconscious lapses) pinpoints with dismaying clarity the end of Twain's belief in children's moral superiority.

Boys are as craven as grown-ups for several reasons. For one thing, they have the moral sense, that well-nigh infallible human instinct to do wrong and inflict pain. Moreover, boys cannot fail to throw stones at witches because, like everyone else, they are slaves to public opinion. "Monarchies, aristocracies, and religions are all based upon that large defect in your race," Traum tells Theodor, his words ringing with the same scorn Colonel Sherburn's had for Huck Finn, "the individual's distrust of his neighbor, and his desire, for safety's or comfort's sake, to stand well in his neighbor's eye" (27, 118).

But Theodor throws a rock at the unfortunate woman for a more comprehensive reason than either of these. This boy lives in a world in which this act, like all others, is absolutely predetermined and inevitable. "Among you boys you have a game," Satan explains, "you stand a row of bricks on end a few inches apart; you push a brick, it knocks its neighbor over, the neighbor knocks over the next brick—and so on till all the row is prostrate. That is human life. A child's first act knocks over the initial brick, and the rest will follow inexorably. If you could see into the future, as I can, you would see everything[244] that was going to happen to that creature; for nothing can change the order of its life after the first event has determined it" (27, 81). Such determinism, Satan tells the three boys is neither ordered nor foreordained by God. "No. The man's circumstances and environment order it." Even were a person to try to assert his own will in opposition to the predetermined condition of things, such an act would itself be part of the pattern, "a thought bound to occur to him at that precise moment, and made certain by the first act of his babyhood" (27, 82–83). Satan does not bother to notice how this assertion flatly contradicts his earlier remark about man's liberty to choose whether he will do right or wrong. *The Mysterious Stranger* contains so many such ambiguities that as a coherent *Weltanschauung* it can be regarded only as the end-product of a tired mind grappling with ideas foreign or inaccessible to it. Twain was no philosopher. But he *was* a literary artist; and while no reader can fail to notice the metaphysical fuzziness, neither can one miss the imaginative intensity generated at several points in the narrative. The emotional impact thus produced—and it occurs, as might be expected, most frequently in connection with Theodor and his friends, not with Satan—signals both the book's success as fiction and its inadequacy as philosophy. As the reader's sympathies are aroused, the world of Eseldorf is seen through Theodor's eyes. Gradually it is perceived that the various intellectual confusions spring from Twain's dramatic structure as well as from metaphysical imprecision. As Edwin Fussell has convincingly demonstrated, *The Mysterious Stranger* is the fictional representation of the mental process of a boy thinking his way from the mistaken belief that the material world is real to final awareness that the only reality lies in dreams.[8] That is Satan's objective in[245] Theodor's initiation. "It is true, that which I have revealed to you," Satan says at the last; "there is no God, no universe, no human race, no earthly life, no heaven, no hell. It is all a dream—a grotesque and foolish dream. Nothing exists but you. And you are but a *thought*—a vagrant thought, a useless thought, a homeless thought, wandering forlorn among the empty eternities!" To which Theodor adds, "He vanished, and left me appalled; for I knew, and realized, that all he had said was true" (27, 140).

Philosophically speaking, of course, solipsism can be a coherent system only in a deaf-mute; even to assert it is to deny it. But Twain creates the illusion of order by constructing his story so that, at each stage of Theodor's enlightenment, both character and author accept as "real" that segment of experience being tested. This is the reason, among others, for Twain's reiterated use of his tried-and-true device, the divison of his chief character into two distinct personalities. Satan and Theodor Fischer are two boys, one of whom represents the intellectual, amoral, and nihilistic side of Twain's mind and the other embodies the emotional and moral values that are in process of dissolution. In rough fashion, therefore, the two fit the classic pattern of earlier novels first established by Tom and Huck and repeated, with minor variation, by the pauper and the prince, Tom Driscoll and Chambers, Sieur Louis and Joan.

Within this dramatic and ideological framework, changes taking place in Theodor's innocent imagination are both accepted as valid and shown to be simply the illusion of change. Thus though we come to recognize that nothing *actually* exists, that literally everything is a dream, yet we cannot help sympathizing with the boy's dismayed reactions to Satan's revelations. For instance, one of Traum's favorite lessons is to demonstrate how an apparent tragedy like the death of[246] a loved one is, in the omniscient mind, often known to be a happier fate than others that might have occurred. He proves this by telling Theodor that Nikolaus will die by drowning two weeks hence, that this

[8] See E. W. Fussell, "The Structural Problem of *The Mysterious Stranger*," *Studies in Philology*, 49 (1952), 95–104.

death is far preferable to, say, forty-six years of painridden paralysis. Poor Theodor and Seppi (who learns the grisly secret) go through torments of pity and remorse during that fortnight. Twain's evocation of that grief (so close to his own experiences) is genuinely moving. "No, my mind was filled with Nikolaus," Theodor relates,

> my thoughts ran upon him only, and the good days we had seen together at romps and frolics in the woods and the fields and the river in the long summer days, and skating and sliding in the winter when our parents thought we were in school. And now he was going out of this young life, and the summers and winters would come and go, and we others would rove and play as before, but his place would be vacant; we should see him no more. Tomorrow he would not suspect, but would be as he had always been, and it would shock me to hear him laugh, and see him do lightsome and frivolous things, for to me he would be a corpse, with waxen hands and dull eyes, and I should see the shroud around his face . . .   (27, 89)

In imagery Huck Finn might have used, Twain here voices his private grief and says a requiem on a writing career spent as the champion of childhood. Theodor's elegy indirectly mourns the lost world of Cardiff Hill and Jackson's Island. "It was an awful eleven days," he goes on to remark, "and yet, with a lifetime stretching back between today and then, they are still a grateful memory to me, and beautiful. In effect they were days of companionship with one's sacred dead, and I have known no comradeship that was so close and precious" (27, 94). The dream of innocence is dead, as we realize when Theodor confesses that he is an old man recalling the[247] past and not the young boy actually living through Nikolaus' last days.

The emotional charge infused into this and other scenes argues eloquently, though surreptitiously, that cynicism and solipsism are not *really* Twain's most deeply felt convictions. His more genuine sentiments are expressed by various characters in *The Mysterious Stranger*, one of whom is the mother of the dead [Lisa], Frau Brandt. Accused of blasphemy and witchcraft (the medieval equivalents, in a sense, of Twain's own sin in writing this book), the grief-stricken woman is led to the stake. Turning to the people of Assville, she delivers a farewell. "Pronounce your sentence and let me go; I am tired of your society," she says.

> So they found her guilty, and she was excommunicated and cut off from the joys of heaven and doomed to the fires of hell; then she was clothed in a coarse robe and delivered to the secular arm, and conducted to the market-place, the bell solemnly tolling the while. We saw her chained to the stake, and saw the first thin film of blue smoke rise on the still air. Then her hard face softened, and she looked upon the packed crowd in front of her and said with gentleness:
> "We played together once, in the long-agone days when we were innocent little creatures. For the sake of that, I forgive you."   (27, 107)

This pardon in the name of childhood for society's inhumanity evokes at once the whole of Mark Twain's past. Hannibal and its various fictional images, similar scenes of sacrifice in *The Prince and the Pauper* and *Joan of Arc*, Twain's lifelong interest in history and in the roles innocence and integrity had played therein—all of these are implied or recalled in the tired martyr's speech. Symbolically, at least, Prospero is laying down his wand.[248]

When, therefore, Twain reaches the solipsistic climax of *The Mysterious Stranger* and asks his reader to accept in all seriousness that none of these experiences is actual but only the merest figment of dreamy illusion, the demand is too great. The story of Theodor Fischer's initiation is too convincing as fiction to persuade as philosophy. Its maker has dramatized the divided camps of his own imagination so effectively that Satan's revelation of the cosmic joke of existence cannot erase or diminish the memory of certain boys and their friends—a mother, a kindly old priest, a good-hearted lawyer, all figures out of Twain's earlier fiction. These characters, though not without their flaws as literary creatures, are more "real" than Philip Traum, whose name suggests not merely his symbolic significance but also the limits of his dramatic potentiality.

Though they disliked each other's work, Mark Twain and Henry James would surely have agreed on this one point: to function at all, the artist must celebrate life. James expressed it once in the preface to *The Wings of the Dove* (a novel also begun in the last years of the waning century): "The poet essentially *can't* be concerned with dying ... The process of life gives way fighting, and often may so shine out on the lost ground as in no other connexion."[9] By virtue of a similar commitment, Twain's achievement—of sustaining until the final page a desperately delicate balance between despising mankind and loving certain individuals, between intellectual assertion of a meaningless universe and intuitive awareness of love's reality—makes *The Mysterious Stranger* a work of very modern dimensions. Characteristically, Twain was able to bring off this feat by viewing once again the bitter truths of human life from the double perspective of boyhood and old age. Looking through the innocent eye as well as through the[249] tired mind enabled him, in a nostalgic sense at least, to keep writing worthwhile fiction right to the end of his unhappy life.[250]

[9] Henry James, *The Art of the Novel, Critical Prefaces,* ed. R. P. Blackmer (New York, Scribner's, 1946), pp. 289–90.

A Supernatural Spectator

HENRY NASH SMITH

IN ADDITION TO PUBLISHED WORK DURING THESE YEARS [THE 1890's AND early 1900's] Mark Twain began dozens of manuscripts he was unable to finish. Bernard DeVoto's memorable essay entitled "The Symbols of Despair"[1] interprets this body of unpublished material as a series of efforts by Mark Twain to free himself from responsibility for the misfortunes he believed he had brought upon his family. De Voto regarded *The Mysterious Stranger*, the most important of the unfinished manuscripts, as "a minor masterpiece," largely because he saw in it an act of self-healing. He found the meaning of the book in the fact that it gathers all the unbearable scenes of man's meanness and cowardice and cruelty, the whole bloodstained panorama of history, into a single vision which then is declared to be but a dream. Placed at such a psychological distance, the spectacle that had previously been too painful to be mastered by the artist's imagination became tolerable; even the torment of his own guilt was assuaged by the pronouncement of young Satan that "there is no God, no universe, no human race, no earthly life, no heaven, no hell. It is all a dream—a grotesque and foolish dream. Nothing exists but you. And you are but a *thought*,—a vagrant thought, a useless thought, a homeless thought, wandering forlorn among the empty eternities!"[2]

This speech of Satan comes in the last chapter, which Paine discovered separately in Mark Twain's papers after the writer's death and added to one among several incomplete versions of the story in order to make the book he published as *The Mysterious Stranger*. The ending does not[185] unequivocally belong with the version Paine chose: in the manuscript of the chapter as he found it Satan is called by the curious name "44" borne by a cognate figure in a quite different ver-

---

From Henry Nash Smith, *Mark Twain: The Development of a Writer* (Cambridge, Mass.: Harvard University Press, 1962), pp. 185–188. Copyright, 1962, by the President and Fellows of Harvard College. Reprinted by permission of the publishers.

[1] The essay is in *Mark Twain at Work* (Cambridge, Mass.: Harvard University Press, 1942), pp. 105–130.

[2] *The Writings of Mark Twain* (New York: Gabriel Wells, 1922–1925), XXVII, 140.

sion of the story.[3] The question is however not crucial, for in all the versions Mark Twain clearly intends to adopt the perspective of a transcendent observer in order to depict human experience as meaningless.

Such a procedure does provide an imaginative escape from his sense of guilt. But it has a significantly close relation to ideas and themes that appear not only in *Pudd'nhead Wilson* and "The Man That Corrupted Hadleyburg" but in *A Connecticut Yankee,* which was written before any of the misfortunes mentioned by DeVoto. The despair expressed in Mark Twain's late work had its origins in an intellectual crisis antedating the period of his personal misfortunes.

Mark Twain declared to Howells that in *The Mysterious Stranger* he intended to "tell what I think of Man, & how he is constructed, & what a shabby poor ridiculous thing he is."[4] When Satan says that mankind is "dull and ignorant and trivial and conceited, and . . . a shabby, poor, worthless lot all around"[5] he is voicing the author's disillusionment with the glittering promise for man's continuous moral improvement held out by the doctrine of progress. Just as Mark Twain had poured all the capital he could muster into the typesetter, he had invested all his political enthusiasm, his humanitarian emotion, and his hope for the future of his country in the idea that the common man was the prime creative force in history. Hank Morgan's conclusion that the mass of the nation in Arthur's Britain was only "human muck," which was of course a judgment on the mass of the American nation in the 1880's, proclaimed the bankruptcy of the writer's idealisms. The outcome had been in sight since the moment when Mark Twain confronted the fact that Huck's and Jim's quest for freedom was doomed to failure. For these protagonists had become the bearers of the vernacular system of values that had sustained his writing career. Hank Morgan's doctrinaire republicanism in *A Connecticut Yankee* translated into ideological terms the broader, deeper, subtler affirmations that had been frustrated in *Huckleberry Finn.* Since Mark Twain was trying to sustain by force of will a belief that had already lost its intuitive solidity, the outcome of the story was latent in it from the beginning.

The most significant trait of Satan in *The Mysterious Stranger* is his lack of a moral sense and of sympathy for mere human beings. The pressures[186] that finally drove Mark Twain to conceive of an observer thus protected against suffering are neatly expressed in a scene that recalls the traumatic spectacle of the young husband on the rack in Morgan le Fay's dungeon. Satan miraculously transports himself and Theodor, the boy who tells the story, to the interior of a prison.

---

[3] The manuscript of the last chapter is in DV 327, Mark Twain Papers.

[4] In a letter from Vienna, 13 May 1899, *Mark Twain–Howells Letters,* ed. Henry Nash Smith and William M. Gibson (Cambridge, Mass.: Harvard University Press, 1960), II, 698–699.

[5] *The Writings of Mark Twain,* XXVII, 20.

We were in the torture-chamber, Satan said. The rack was there, and the other instruments, and there was a smoky lantern or two hanging on the walls and helping to make the place look dim and dreadful. There were people there—the executioners—but as they took no notice of us, it meant that we were invisible. A young man lay bound, and Satan said he was suspected of being a heretic, and the executioners were about to inquire into it. They asked the man to confess to the charge, and he said he could not, for it was not true. Then they drove splinter after splinter under his nails, and he shrieked with the pain. Satan was not disturbed, but I could not endure it, and had to be whisked out of there.[6]

Satan explains that the spectacle illustrates the moral sense, which causes man to inflict pain for the pleasure of it. Theodor is next shown a French factory in which the workers, "little children and all," are forced to work fourteen hours a day, with a four-mile walk to and from "the pigsties they inhabit." The torture undergone by these unfortunates, Satan declares, is worse than that of the young man in the prison, for his agony lasted but a few hours, whereas the agony of the workers lasts through years and decades. "It is the Moral Sense," he adds, "which teaches the factory proprietors the difference between right and wrong—you perceive the result."[7]

Given this image of human society, a rational observer could have but one wish—to carry out Hank Morgan's impulse by hanging the race and ending the farce. Satan performs such an act in an early chapter of *The Mysterious Stranger*. He has created little men and women of clay and brought them to life for the amusement of Theodor and his friends. Two of the men quarrel and begin to fight one another. "Satan reached out his hand and crushed the life out of them with his fingers, threw them away, wiped the red from his fingers on his handkerchief, and went on talking where he had left off." When the wives of the dead men find the bodies of their husbands and fall to weeping a crowd collects about them, and the noise attracts Satan's attention; "then he reached out and took the heavy board seat out of our swing and brought it down and mashed[187] all those people into the earth just as if they had been flies, and went on talking just the same."[8]

Satan's destruction of the mimic world he has created is the symbolic gesture of a writer who can no longer find any meaning in man or society. Mark Twain's only refuge is to identify himself with a supernatural spectator for whom mankind is but a race of vermin, hardly worth even contempt. And this marks the end of his career as a writer, for there was nothing more to say.[188]

[6] *The Writings of Mark Twain,* XXVII, 50.

[7] *The Writings of Mark Twain,* XXVII, 52–53.

[8] *The Writings of Mark Twain,* XXVII, 16–17. I have discussed this passage in "Mark Twain's Images of Hannibal: From St. Petersburg to Eseldorf," *Studies in English* (University of Texas), 37; 3–23 (1958).

The Mysterious Stranger

JAMES M. COX

THE EXTENT TO WHICH MARK TWAIN WAS BEING THREATENED BY THE repression implicit in the dominant figure of the ironic stranger becomes fully explicit in the direction he took upon completing *Pudd'n-head Wilson*. His next book was *Joan of Arc*. It is inaccurate, however, to say simply that *Joan of Arc* was "by" Mark Twain, for not until after the book was serialized was Mark Twain's authorship acknowledged. This hesitation is the central fact about *Joan of Arc*, revealing more, perhaps, than the entire two volumes which chronicle the history of the saintly maid. For Samuel Clemens' reluctance to acknowledge Mark Twain's authorship was not a mere modest withdrawal but an almost total denial of his humorous genius and was inseparably related to the very conception of the pure and white Joan of Arc.

The terms under which Mark Twain was being stifled were as clear as they were simple. *Joan of Arc* was to be a "serious" book. The whole project had about it a fatal reverence perhaps best figured forth in Paine's unctuous account of his master's transition from Pudd'nhead to Joan. "With [*Pudd'nhead Wilson*] out of his hands," averred Paine, "Clemens was ready for his great new undertaking. A seed sown by the wind more than forty years before was ready to bloom. He would write the story of[274] Joan of Arc."[1] The wind to which Paine referred was that which, blowing along the main street of Hannibal in 1849, supposedly wafted a leaf from a book about Joan of Arc in the path of the highly imaginative thirteen-year-old Samuel Clemens. This event, according to the sixty-year-old writer, marked the beginning of his *literary* ambition. Ever since that memorable day, he maintained, the figure of Joan of Arc had stood like a beacon in his imaginative landscape—a light which at once signified the source as well as the goal of his inspiration.

From James M. Cox, *Mark Twain: The Fate of Humor* (Princeton: Princeton University Press, 1966), pp. 247–284. Copyright © 1966 by Princeton University Press. Reprinted by permission of the publisher. Chapter XI is here reprinted entire.

[1] Albert Bigelow Paine, *Mark Twain: A Biography* (3 vols.; New York, 1912), II, 957.

The entire story of the wind, the leaf, the book, and the fledgling author is every whit as conventional in conception as *The Personal Recollections of Joan of Arc*, whose advent it presumably foretold. Moreover, no direct evidence exists to prove that the episode transpired. Although both Paine and Dixon Wecter cite it prominently in the life of Samuel Clemens, there is no reason to believe in it any more than in any of the other dubious memories of Mark Twain.[2] The story gives every evidence of having come to prominence after the writing of the book and is but one more of Samuel Clemens' testimonials to his lifelong faith in the maid whose history he had written.

The story is a fabrication, not a tall tale. Instead of reconstructing the past of Samuel Clemens under the humorous exaggeration of Mark Twain, this anecdote set about transforming the tall tale of Mark Twain into the invention of the boy-author Samuel Clemens. As the story was designed to present the emergence of literary ambition in the untutored but sensitive boy, so *Joan of Arc* was to be the ultimate fruit borne from the chance seed planted so long ago. The book was to be, above everything else, serious literature. Once again, Paine's narrative[248] sets the tone admirably, revealing the particularly decorous scene in which the genteel undertaking was conceived.

Walking the floor one day at Viviani, smoking vigorously, he said to Mrs. Clemens and Susy: "I shall never be accepted seriously over my own signature. People always want to laugh over what I write and are disappointed if they don't find a joke in it. This is to be a serious book. It means more to me than anything I have ever undertaken. I shall write it anonymously."

So it was that that gentle, quaint Sieur de Conté took up the pen, and the tale of *Joan* was begun in that beautiful spot which of all others seems now the proper environment for its lovely telling.[3]

Securely located in a picturesque Italian villa, surrounded by wife and daughter, the humorous artist piously announces his intention of embarking upon a work which will be the culmination of a lifetime ambition, heretofore rendered impossible by his impure and worldly journeywork. He is, in other words, undertaking to write a literary "masterpiece"—a work which, identified with the very birth of literary ambition, is to be triumphantly serious in intention and executed in an idealized and sequestered setting. It was not enough that the book be serious; it must be unstained with commerce—a labor of pure love, untouched by money. Writing to Henry Huttleston Rogers, the Standard Oil tycoon who was mightily assisting him through his financial

[2] *Ibid.*, 1, 81–82. Dixon Wecter, *Sam Clemens of Hannibal* (Boston, 1952), p. 211. But Wecter notes (p. 309n) that Mark Twain failed to mention this supposedly significant turning point in his sketch "The Turning Point of My Life" which was written long after *Joan of Arc*.

[3] Paine, *A Biography*, II, 959.

crisis, Samuel Clemens could note with pride: "Possibly the book may not sell, but that is nothing—it was written for love."[4]

He went out of his way to insist that it had been in the process of creation longer than any of his other productions. On his seventy-third birthday when, as Paine observes, "all his important books were far behind him, and he could judge them without prejudice," he announced with finality: [249]

I like the *Joan of Arc* best of all my books; & it *is* the best; I know it perfectly well. And besides, it furnished me seven times the pleasure afforded me by any of the others: 12 years of preparation & 2 years of writing. The others needed no preparation, & got none.[5]

This proclamation was no casual verbal aside to be quoted by his biographer, but a formal note left by its author as an unmistakable testimonial to his most serious literary effort. Paine dutifully reproduced the facsimile of the document in his biography as incontrovertible evidence of Mark Twain's preference.

Such high esteem for the work and its saintly subject did have some basis in Mark Twain's imagination. That Joan of Arc may have long been a subject of interest to him is revealed in a love letter he wrote his wife during their courtship. There he specifically linked Olivia with Joan, observing that though his frail lady might not lead men into battle, she would, in her own exquisite way, command all the power of Joan of Arc. Yet there are by no means enough references to Joan in Mark Twain's earlier letters or other writings to warrant the passionate involvement with her story he later professed to have had. Moreover, a scrutiny of his account of the birth and progress of the book tends to disclose the slightness rather than the profundity of his engagement. When he said much later that the book was twelve years in preparation and two years in the writing, the point to remember is that *Huckleberry Finn* was eight years in the writing. Despite his insistence that he began the story five times, even Paine could find no direct evidence that he had done enormous work on the project before he actually began the book.[6] In the preface of *Joan of Arc*, eleven sources are cited, all of which, Mark Twain says, were carefully "examined in verification of the truthfulness" of the narrative.[7] This is hardly the extensive [250] bibliography that either Mark Twain or Paine thought it was. Furthermore, the whole notion of a bibliography was but one more way of puffing *Joan* as a serious book resting upon solid literary scholarship. Actually the scholarship

[4] Albert Bigelow Paine, *Mark Twain's Letters* (2 vols.; New York, 1917), II, 624.

[5] Paine, *A Biography*, II, 1,034.

[6] *Ibid.*, p. 959.

[7] Samuel L. Clemens, *The Writings of Mark Twain*, Author's National Edition (25 vols.: New York, 1907–18), XVII, vi. Hereafter referred to as *Writings*.

amounted to little more than a dependency: the books, rather than proving a stimulus for narrative discoveries, provided an arrangement of events on which Mark Twain's torpid imagination could rely. And rely he did. Having invented the Sieur Louis de Conté as his narrator, he could let this invented voice move easily along the ready-made sequence of events which the previous histories recorded. Such a procedure relieved him of the burden of conceiving a plot. Instead of reconstructing the past, as he had done in his great narratives, he was actually leaning upon it.

If his insistence upon the length of time and amount of research devoted to *Joan of Arc* actually conceals how modest were his endeavors, what of his claim that Joan was not commercially tainted? Here again there is every indication that Mark Twain did not lose sight of the commercial possibilities of his great, pure project. When the book was finished and being serialized in *Harper's,* he disclosed his usual determination to exploit the financial possibilities of the book. In 1895, writing from Vancouver to J. Henry Harper—he had just undertaken his world tour to pay his way out of bankruptcy— Mark Twain expressed the wish that his identity as author of *Joan* be revealed. He thought it would help the lecturing tour by keeping his name before the public. He wrote later, however, that Olivia was troubled about the matter and wanted Harper to decide when the time was right. Harper decided that the time to capitalize on Mark Twain's name was when the book was to be published.[8]

These conflicting responses disclose that Mark Twain's elaborate statements about the birth and writing of *Joan* hold no more weight— possibly even less—than his casual dismissals of his humorous productions. Both attitudes[251] were in a sense lies, but the humorous attitude exposed the truth, whereas the serious attitude denied the character and concealed the truth. Yet they are attitudes, not facts, and primarily lead us to demand the truth concealed behind them. If this truth is concealed, it is by no means buried. Indeed, the facts concerning the writing of *Joan of Arc* are, like Poe's purloined letter, remarkably evident, and they confirm the course Mark Twain's repression of himself was taking as he made his way from *Pudd'nhead Wilson* toward *The Mysterious Stranger.*

Although the primary fact about *Joan* is Mark Twain's attempt to deny his identity as its author, there are two other facts which stand out in the history of his writing during this period. First, throughout the entire time following *A Connecticut Yankee*—the time during which *Joan* was written—Mark Twain was heading into bankruptcy, a shameful experience for anyone who has taken pride in his rise from poverty and obscurity to wealth and prominence. For Mark Twain it was much more than business failure. His discovery of his genius in Virginia City had literally been a substitute for the silver he could not find, and all his life he tended to see his creative productions in terms of the capital into which he could convert them. Possessed of a truly speculative imagination, he invariably saw his literature as invention and enterprise.

Just as his literary efforts were related to speculative enterprise, his speculative enterprises became concentrated upon two ventures intimately related to the act of writing: the Webster Publishing Company and the Paige Typesetter. Into the publishing concern and the Paige Typesetter Mark Twain literally poured all his available capital, and by 1892 he had actually put his own capacity for invention in the service of Paige's machine. He was, as he himself once said, a slave of business, for his books were being written to obtain immediate capital to sustain his sinking projects. Mark Twain, investor in [252] the automatic writer, was converting himself into a writing mechanism in an effort to satisfy the appetite of what he came to call the "diabolical machine."

But there was a second major fact of this phase of Mark Twain's career. The seminal story of this entire period—the story which in effect generated all the others—was "Those Extraordinary Twins." Mark Twain clearly explained how the farce released *Pudd'nhead Wilson*. He did not make clear how much it had to do with the other two major productions, *Tom Sawyer Abroad* and *Joan of Arc*. His letters of the period cast interesting light on the relationship between the sketch and all his work during the years his fortunes were failing.

On August 10, 1892, he wrote to Fred J. Hall, who had assumed direction of the Webster Company after Charles L. Webster had died:

I have dropped that novel I wrote you about, because I saw a more effective way of using the main episode—to wit: by telling it through the lips of Huck Finn. So I have started Huck Finn and Tom Sawyer (still 15 years old) and their friend the freed slave Jim around the world in a stray *balloon*, with Huck as narrator, and somewhere after the end of that great voyage he will work in the said episode and then nobody will suspect that a whole book has been written and the globe circumnavigated merely to get that episode in in an effective (and at the same time apparently unintentional) way.[9]

The novel he had dropped was, according to Paine, "Those Extraordinary Twins."[10] His turning toward Huck Finn becomes apparent later in the same letter when he casually observes that when he had been in New York "the other day," Mary Mapes Dodge, editor of *St. Nicholas,* had offered him $5,000 for a boys' story of 50,000 words. What he had evidently done was to fall back into the capital style of

[9] *Letters,* II, 565.
[10] *Ibid.,* p. 566.

Huckleberry Finn, with the intention[253] of converting what he had already written on the "Twins" in Huck's narrative.

But Tom Sawyer's adventures apparently would not sustain his imagination, and on September 18—five weeks later—he wrote Mrs. Theodore Crane, his wife's adopted sister,

I have been driving this pen hard. I wrote 280 pages on a yarn called "Tom Sawyer Abroad," then took up the "Twins" again, destroyed the last half of the manuscript and rewrote it in another form, and am going to continue it and finish it in Florence. "Tom Sawyer" seems rather pale to the family after the extravagances of the Twins, but they came to like it after they got used to it.[11]

This indicates that his original work on the "Twins" had been extensive and that he could not manage or did not wish to integrate it into Huck Finn's narrative. During the ensuing weeks—amid moving to the Villa Viviani above Florence, collecting fugitive tales for a volume, and taking care of Olivia—he not only finished *Tom Sawyer Abroad* but continued to make headway with the "Twins." And on December 12, 1892, he was able to write to Hall:

I finished "Those Extraordinary Twins" night before last—makes 60 or 80,000 words—haven't counted.

The last third of it suits me to a dot. I begin, today, to entirely re-cast and re-write the first two-thirds—new plan, with two minor characters, made very prominent, one major character cropped out, and the twins subordinated to a minor but not insignificant place.

The minor character will now become the chiefest, and I will name the story after him—"Pudd'nhead Wilson."[12]

He had thus managed to capitalize on *Tom Sawyer Abroad* and was in the process of realizing *Pudd'nhead*[254] *Wilson,* which was evolving from the farce of the twins. On January 28, 1893, he wrote to Hall:

My book is type-written and ready for print—"Pudd'nhead Wilson—A Tale." (Or, "Those Extraordinary Twins," if preferable.)

It makes 82,500 words—12,000 words more than Huck Finn. But I don't know what to do with it. Mrs. Clemens thinks it wouldn't do to go to the Am. Pub. Co. or anywhere outside of our own house; we have no subscription machinery, and a book in the trade is a book thrown away, as far as money-profit goes. I am in a quandary. Give me a lift out of it.

I will mail the book to you and get you to examine it and see if it is good or if it is bad. I think it is good, and I thought the Claimant bad when I saw it in print; but as for real judgment, I think I am destitute of it.

I am writing a companion to the Prince and Pauper, which is half done and will make 200,000 words; and I have had the idea that if it were gotten up in handsome style, with many illustrations and put at a high enough

11 *Ibid.,* p. 568.
12 *Ibid.,* p. 574.

price maybe the L.A.L. [Library of American Literature] canvassers would take it and run it with that book. Would they? It could be priced anywhere from $4 up to $10, according to how it was gotten up, I suppose.

I don't want it to go into a magazine.[13]

This letter discloses—in a way that no amount of Mark Twain's testimonials can—that if "Those Extraordinary Twins" was the seminal book of the period, it was *Pudd'nhead Wilson* and not *Joan of Arc* which demanded all his resources as a writer. It emerges as *the* book of those difficult years. But it is upon *Joan of Arc* that the letter throws most light. First of all it shows that both *Joan of Arc* and *Pudd'nhead Wilson* had sprung into life at the time Mark Twain was working on "Those Extraordinary Twins." The letter further discloses that *Joan,* as originally[255] conceived, was a companion piece to *The Prince and the Pauper,* which amounts to saying it was a genteel historical narrative designed to make money. He makes no mention of its having been a lifelong ambition; rather, he sees it as a book which will have "handsome style," be published in an expensive edition, and be included in the Library of American Literature, that heavy-weighted "set" which was dragging the Webster Publishing Company toward bankruptcy. Finally, the letter indicates that the writing was proceeding apace. *Pudd'nhead Wilson* might be a struggle, but *Joan* was coming into being with facile and remarkable ease. That it came with ease is by no means a sign of its inadequacy, for some of Mark Twain's best work came with ease. But its ease is most significant in relation to Mark Twain's determined effort at a later time to insist upon the pains with which it was constructed.

Even so, Mark Twain did not sweep through to the conclusion of *Joan* in one sustained burst—and for a reason. He was not through with *Pudd'nhead Wilson.* Not only was he not through; he became involved in another complete revision of the book. Whether this revision was prompted by Hall's objection to the January 28th version or whether Mark Twain had found himself answering his own question is a matter of speculation. In any event he was able to write Hall on July 30, 1893:

This time "Pudd'nhead Wilson" is a success! Even Mrs. Clemens, the most difficult of critics, confesses it, and without reserves or qualifications. Formerly she would not consent that it be published either before or after my death. I have pulled the twins apart and made two individuals of them; I have sunk them out of sight, they are mere flitting shadows, now, and of no importance; *their* story has disappeared from the book. Aunt Betsy Hale has vanished wholly, leaving not a trace behind; Aunt Patsy Cooper and her daughter Rowena have almost disappeared—they scarcely walk across[256] the stage. The whole story is centered on the murder and the trial; from the first chapter the movement is straight ahead without divergence or side-play

---

13 *Ibid.,* p. 579.

to the murder and the trial; everything that is done or said or that happens is a preparation for those events. . . . When I began this final reconstruction the story contained 81,500 words, now it contains only 58,000. I have knocked out everything that delayed the march of the story—even the description of a Mississippi steamboat. There's no weather in, and no scenery—the story is stripped for flight![14]

He went on in this letter to tell Hall that he intended to complete a travelogue of a raft trip down the Rhone and to return to his Adam's diary.

All of this writing constituted Mark Twain's valiant attempt to secure enough capital to float his foundering business. Yet for all his effort, eighteen months after writing this letter to Hall, his publishing house had failed and his typesetter project had disintegrated despite his frantic battle to stem the tide of misfortune sweeping toward him. He was engulfed in business much of that time, spending the winter of 1893–94 in New York, where he could keep in touch with the ebb and flow of his fortunes. That same winter he met Henry Huttleston Rogers, the man he thought would save his business life. As Rogers firmly took the financial helm, Mark Twain was able to write Olivia of his plans to return to Europe and of his intentions of quitting business:

> When the anchor is down, then I shall say:
> "Farewell—a long farewell—to *business!* I will *never* touch it again!"
> I will live in literature, I will wallow in it, revel in it, I will swim in ink! Joan of Arc—but all this is premature; the anchor is not down yet.[15]

But the manner in which Rogers was to save Mark Twain's business life was actually to kill his businesses, thereby ending the deceptions of an illusory future. He[257] first closed out the publishing house in April, 1894, enabling Mark Twain to return to Europe early in the summer of 1894, apparently believing that Rogers would pull the typesetter through. Evidently with such a belief in mind he returned to work on *Joan* later that summer, for on September 9, he wrote to Rogers that he had driven himself too hard on the book and had been forced to rest. His taking up the book was by no means a purely literary venture. The letter to Rogers makes clear that he was determined to make a big book out of *Joan.*[16] If he had trimmed *Pudd'nhead* with a fine economy, he was expanding *Joan* into a work big enough to occupy handsome space in the literary world.

Mark Twain's reckonings on putting *Joan* into the service of the typesetter failed to take into account the actions of the remarkable Rogers, who, after giving the typesetter as much chance as he thought

14 *Ibid.,* pp. 590–91.
15 *Ibid.,* p. 607.
16 *Ibid.,* p. 616.

wise, determined to get Mark Twain completely out of business. By the middle of December he had all but accomplished the fact and wrote Mark Twain of the imminent failure of the machine. Even in face of the end, Mark Twain not only continued to concoct schemes to save the business, but turned instinctively to writing in an effort to raise capital. Thus in a calm postscript to his letter replying to Rogers' staggering news he wrote:

I am going right along with Joan, now, and wait untroubled until I hear from you. If you think I can be of the least use, cable me "Come." I can write Joan on board ship and lose no time. Also I could discuss my plan with the publisher for a *deluxe* Joan, time being an object, for some of the pictures could be made over here cheaply and quickly, but would cost much time and money in America.[17]

As long as there was the remotest hope for his business enterprise, it did not occur to Mark Twain to insist that[258] *Joan* must not be converted into literary capital. But his business world was nonetheless collapsing. Under the astute—Paine always assures us that it was astute—direction of Rogers, Mark Twain was masterfully put out of business and all his finances put in Rogers' expert hands.

If *Joan* had formerly been the book which Mark Twain had seen as a way to keep in business, it now became a means of getting out of business, and Joan herself became the figure who could be seen as "purely" literary—so literary, in fact, that Mark Twain was able to write Rogers that the book was written for pure "love." The book itself became the means by which Mark Twain could at one and the same time put his business troubles out of mind and surrender to the financial acumen of Rogers—who efficiently saw to it that Mark Twain's affairs were brought to order.

The cost of the surrender can best be measured by seeing what the settlement was. First of all, Mark Twain declared bankruptcy—which was in effect a full recognition of the failure of his speculative imagination, that imagination which had from the beginning identified art and fortune. Second, he lost possession of his works. By Rogers' astute management, his copyrights were transferred to his wife's name to prevent creditors from gaining possession of what Rogers shrewdly realized was Mark Twain's most valuable property. The transfer of copyright had its fatal significance, however. If it meant that the property would not be lost, it also meant that Olivia—who had been his play censor—now assumed outright ownership of copyright. Her emergence as independent owner of the copyright symbolized what had happened to Mark Twain. He had lost possession of his name, and his benign censor, who had hitherto been straight man to his humorous genius, was now given legal right to his name in order to protect his

17 *Ibid.*, p. 618.

family from being thrown utterly upon the mercy of his creditors. Finally, Rogers took absolute charge of Mark Twain's money until the[259] creditors were paid off.[18] During the whole of Mark Twain's round-the-world lecture tour—which he undertook in order to pay one hundred cents on the dollar and thus show himself a man of honor in the manner of Sir Walter Scott—he sent all his proceeds directly to Rogers, who saw to it that the money was applied to the debts. Though Rogers was kind and though Olivia changed no whit toward the man whose copyright she now owned, the decisions of the period disclose the surrender of Mark Twain's creative force. It was as if Jervis Langdon, in the person of Henry H. Rogers, had returned to protect his daughter and her children from his son-in-law's irresponsibilities.

These failures in the life of Samuel Clemens did not "cause" the despair and failure in the work of Mark Twain; they are instead the disasters which corresponded to the failure of *Joan of Arc*. Thus, at the same time that Samuel Clemens was losing control of his copyrights, Mark Twain was denying his identity as a writer. The ultimate irony lay in the serious lie he invented to celebrate his own self-effacement.

Against the background of *Pudd'nhead Wilson*, the figure of Joan of Arc assumes a strikingly meaningful identity. *Pudd'nhead* ironically chronicled the secret history of miscegenation; *Joan of Arc* reverently recounted a life of purity and inviolate maidenhood. In viewing these two books which literally accompanied each other in emerging from Mark Twain's imagination, the two women, Roxana and Joan, stand like contrasting sculptures on the landscape. The one—dark, voluble, and comical—who, though her sexuality is not dramatized, is nonetheless the sexual object at the mercy of a society of gentlemen; the other—pale, chaste, and serious—whose martial power and childlike purity bring her into power over a society of rude and barbarous soldiers.[260]

The sharp contrast between the dark, humorous mother and the serious, radiant maiden goes far toward defining Joan of Arc. She is the visionary embodiment of all the utterly conventional, utterly somber, utterly reverent attitudes and language upon which Mark Twain's humor had played through all the years of his career. She is the absolute epitome of the reverence against which the irreverent Mark Twain had defined his identity in *The Innocents Abroad*. More than that, she is a stranger—but not an ironic stranger, for no genuine irony can penetrate her reverent identity. She is rather the mysterious stranger—the first authentic one to appear in Mark Twain's world—and she is quite appropriately given an angelic identity.

[18] Paine, *A Biography*, II, 983–87. See also Ferguson, *Man and Legend*, pp. 258–59.

The surest way to see her is to define Mark Twain's point of view upon her. In that point of view lay whatever particularity, whatever signature, he was able to infuse into the legend and history he inherited. He left the legend and history largely intact, showing remarkably little tendency to analyze or explore its dramatic possibilities. His attitude toward the Middle Ages, particularly toward Catholicism, was one of almost undisguised contempt—so much so that he saw Joan's entire pilgrimage in extremely melodramatic terms. Because he could not see her rebellion as dangerous and perplexing, and because he would not see the churchmen as anything other than ignorant asses or hopeless devils, he could imagine no genuine resistance which would have in turn given Joan stature and complexity. He lacked the kind of dramatic intelligence by means of which Shaw was able to endow Joan's interlocutors with the wit which in turn gave Joan power. Compared to Shaw's intense Joan, Mark Twain's conception is, as Shaw himself shrewdly observed, peculiarly sterile.[19] [261]

Yet Mark Twain did have a point of view. It involved the intrusion of a fictional narrator, the Old Sieur Louis de Conté, who would relate the events of Joan's life, transforming the chronicle into a kind of pleasant firsthand view of remote history. The narrator's vantage point is one remote in time from the events he chronicles, for he is an old man recollecting the life of the marvelous girl. Yet his chronicle is personal, for his youth and young manhood were spent serving as her page.

The best way to see the Old Sieur's failure as a narrator is to compare it with Huckleberry Finn's success. Both books portray a child acting "wrongly" in an evil world. Huck is confronting the evil of slavery in the Old South and Joan is struggling against the impotence and corruption of the clergy and aristocracy in the bygone medieval world. Both are involved in actions which presumably are one hundred per cent approvable. What then is the difference between them? Joan, like Hank Morgan, is a conscious rebel, approving of her own actions. Huck Finn, however much he might rebel, could never win his own approval. Joan is never the bad girl in her own eyes, but the good girl consciously doing the worthy bidding of her voices. Presumably in an effort to "humanize" this coldly angelic good girl, Mark Twain put her story in the mouth of the Old Sieur. But in the process of the telling, he simply managed to transfer Joan's self-approval into the Old

[19] Shaw says in his preface to *Saint Joan:* "Mark Twain's Joan, skirted to the ground, and with as many petticoats as Noah's wife in a toy ark, is an attempt to combine Bayard with Esther Summerson from *Bleak House* into an unimpeachable American school teacher in armor. Like Esther Summerson she makes her creator ridiculous, and yet, being the work of a man of genius,[261] remains a credible human goodygoody in spite of her creator's infatuation. It is the description rather than the valuation that is wrong" (*Saint Joan* and *The Apple Cart,* Standard Edition [London, 1933], p. 26).[262]

Sieur's indulgent adoration of the child he had served. Instead of personalizing Joan, the narrative merely sweetens her all the more, and what was once her bold rebellion becomes in Mark Twain's point of view an old man's tiresome reverence. Indeed, the Old Sieur embodies the emotion of reverence better than any of the pious pilgrims on the *Quaker City*.

It is just this reverence which, since it is the emotion[262] of the narrative, inevitably suppresses Mark Twain's humor. In fact, all the forms of Mark Twain's humor literally appear as characters serving the martyred maid. There is first of all the Paladin, the liar Mark Twain who must exaggerate all experience into a tall tale; there is La Hire, the profane Mark Twain who cannot forswear swearing; there is Noel Rainguesson, the mimic Mark Twain who cannot resist impersonating the Paladin. Significantly all these characters are expended in Joan's high mystic mission. They are the humorist's sterile gestures in a world given over to propagating the reverent image of Joan. Their intended function in the narrative is clear. They are there to provide an earthy touch to the reverent narrative, thereby brightening up with a kind of comic relief the pathetic history of the martyred maiden. But their presence in the narrative confirms rather than threatens the essential gentility of the Sieur's reverent pose, giving his unctuous tale at best a proper whimsicality—something in the nature of a minister's anecdote to salt the sermon.

The whole performance is so dismal as to make one wish it were a parody, yet clearly it is no parody. Mark Twain is obviously serious— so serious that he cannot be Mark Twain. Which brings us back to Joan's identity. The embodiment of all the conventions which Mark Twain had humorously subverted during his career, she clearly and completely represses his humor. The end of the Sieur's story makes clear the meaning of Joan:

I have finished my story of Joan of Arc, that wonderful child, that sublime personality, that spirit which in one regard has had no peer and will have none—this: its purity from all alloy of self-seeking, self-interest, personal ambition. In it no trace of these motives can be found, search as you may, and this cannot be said of any other person whose name appears in profane history.[20][263]

This image, which evoked the pathetic old narrator to adore it, all but denied the identity of Mark Twain in the process. Huck Finn had been the narrator who at once had extended and realized Mark Twain's range of humor—he had even humorously pushed Mark Twain aside in the first paragraph to write his own book. The Sieur does not push Mark Twain aside; he does not even acknowledge his existence. His story *is* the very image of Joan which he evokes. She is not the play censor who releases Mark Twain but the serious muse who does indeed censor, enslave, and finally deny the humorist; and she appears at the precise moment when Mark Twain was releasing his copyrights to the possession of his wife. Paine, with that typical unconscious irony which makes the biography at once annoying and formidable, completed his praise of the book by observing:

It was the only book of all he had written that Mark Twain considered worthy of this dedication:

> 1870 · TO MY WIFE · 1895
> OLIVIA LANGDON CLEMENS
> This Book
> is tendered on our
> wedding anniversary in
> grateful recognition
> of her twenty-five years
> of valued service as my
> literary advisor and
> editor.
> THE AUTHOR[21]

Joan of Arc was thus the total embodiment of the conventional values and the emotional reverence against which Mark Twain's humor hitherto played. Mark Twain's identity was threatened in direct proportion to the autonomy she preempted. It is just this threat which accounts for the dramatic division of Mark Twain's later work into the sentimental on the one hand and the ironic on the [264] other. In the sentimental category, there are "A Horse's Tale," "A Dog's Tale," and "The Death Disk"—all more or less nauseating shorter fiction following the lines of *Joan of Arc*. All these stories, interestingly enough dominated by girls, deploy the same unctuous tone of the Sieur Louis de Conté. They foreshadow that turn in Mark Twain which brought him, near the end of his life, to form the Angel Fish Club, made up of girls of school age whose central function was to cast their doting gazes upon the club's founder and chief member. Mark Twain's grief over the death of Susy Clemens is usually cited as the essential motive behind the sentimental stories. But *Joan of Arc* preceded the death of Susy by more than a year, once more emphasizing how often in Mark Twain's career literature and style take precedence over life.

In contradistinction to the sentimental and conventional tales featuring juvenile heroines, there is the ironic fiction which continues the march of the ironic stranger. Chief among such tales are "The Man That Corrupted Hadleyburg," "The £1,000,000 Bank Note," and "The $30,000 Bequest," all of which hinge upon a stranger's intruding into a complacent society and, by tempting the community with money, subverting the entire social order. "The Man That Corrupted Hadleyburg" is preeminent among such stories and could well be called the

---

[21] Paine, *A Biography*, II, 1,033.

furthest extension of all the tendencies of *Pudd'nhead Wilson*. It is a story of total irony, total plot. The epigrams which stood above the fiction in *Pudd'nhead Wilson* have been assimilated into the searing conciseness of the taut, arbitrary plot and the triumphant bitterness of tone which characterize the story.

What becomes evident in considering this pronounced division between the ironic and the sentimental is that it began in "Those Extraordinary Twins." That story first set in motion the threat of absolute divison between angelic and diabolic, light and dark, ironic and sentimental. For the body joining the original twins did not bind them together so much as it defined their mortal[265] opposition to each other. Only by severing the twins could Mark Twain pursue the divergent channels this opposition heralded—which is precisely what he did, thus releasing himself from the paralysis and structural impasse represented by the antithetical impulses. From Angelo, the blond, angelic twin, he went toward *Joan of Arc;* from the dark, conscienceless Luigi toward the false Tom Driscoll and the world of Pudd'nhead Wilson. The point of such a division is not that the sentimental represses the ironic, but that the division itself is the repression. The very emergence of the opposing twins is the signal not of unity or complexity, but of division and simplification in matters of characterization, plot, and style. To be sure, the ironic dimension of Mark Twain's writing was the more basic and represented the area closest to the world of humor; not surprisingly, the ironic narratives were the ones which exacted the greatest struggle from their divided author. Yet they too involved a repression of his humorous genius, directed as they were toward serious goals. The ironic, purged of the sentimental, involved a reduction, a loss, a maiming, an incompleteness for Mark Twain— an incompleteness absolutely embodied by the fragmented and abortive seminal burlesque of "Those Extraordinary Twins," which had in effect fathered the birth of the division. Thus Mark Twain, whose very identity and name designated a union of the two worlds, was faced with the task of bringing the two worlds back together in a new union. His effort to do just that was the last great struggle of his career—the writing of *The Mysterious Stranger.*

The apparent story of how *The Mysterious Stranger* came to be is well known by Mark Twain devotees. Like Melville's *Billy Budd,* the story was found among its author's papers. And if there has been difficulty in obtaining a reliable text of *Billy Budd,* the problems attaching to *The Mysterious Stranger* are even more disconcerting. For years there seemed to be no problem, because Paine, who published the story six years after Mark Twain's[266] death, told such a beguiling story about discovering the cache that only chronic skeptics had cause to doubt. The story of little Satan, according to Paine, was one which Mark Twain had worked on intermittently for years and had said on one occasion was complete, aside from a brief ending which he could write at any time. But the ending had apparently not been written—or such seemed the state of affairs—when, long after Mark Twain's death, Paine came across the concluding chapter, happily preserved among the papers. What Paine did not say was that Mark Twain had made three separate and distinct attempts to write *The Mysterious Stranger* between 1897 and 1905, and that the concluding chapter which he, Paine, attached to the published version was clearly intended to be the conclusion of another version of the story. Paine was of course aware of the three attempts to write the story, but preferred to perform concealed editorial transitions and changes of names so that the true identity of the concluding chapter would be undetected.

For Bernard DeVoto, who succeeded Paine as editor of the Mark Twain Papers, the closing years of Mark Twain's life came to seem the years which held the real secrets of his genius, and he determined to wrest order from the chaos of unpublished manuscripts Mark Twain had left behind him. He knew, as Paine had known before him, that there were three manuscript versions of the story of little Satan coming to a world of children to perform his miracles. The three versions were, as DeVoto was to term them, the "Hannibal" version, a short and relatively unsuccessful beginning in which the action takes place in Hannibal. In this version Tom and Huck find the boredom of the schoolroom suddenly relieved by the miraculous presence of Satan, who in this version of the story goes by the name of "44." However, the story does not progress beyond exploiting "44's" magic tricks. A second version of the story, the "Eseldorf" version, is the story essentially as Paine published it, with the exception of numerous excisions and with the addition of the missing[267] last chapter, which Paine so fortuitously "found." Finally, there is the "Print Shop" version, the longest of the three, in which Satan is once more named "44," but is by no means the boyish miracle worker of the Hannibal version. He is, instead, the dream self of August Feldner—who takes the place of Theodor Fischer—and he sets about to free August from the illusions which enslave him. But in the process, the action becomes involved in a mélange of philosophic and burlesque additions to the plot and loses the simplicity and economy of the Eseldorf version.

Whereas Paine had simply chosen to exploit the papers for publication and conceal difficult discrepancies which from his point of view did seem minor, DeVoto was concerned to develop a theory of Mark Twain's despair. He intended to write a book disclosing the way in which Mark Twain arrived at his last testament. He did not live to write the book, but in the last essay of *Mark Twain at Work*, "The Symbols of Despair," he set forth the shape of his theory. As DeVoto saw it, the disasters of bankruptcy, the death of his favorite daughter Susy, the discovery that another daughter Jean was an epileptic, and the acute invalidism and approaching death of Olivia, impaired Mark Twain's image of himself. Faced with the sense of responsibility for the disasters which involved his family, Mark Twain's guilt subjected his ego to a severe assault during the years of failure and grief. At the same time, however, his imagination was struggling to find a form which would bring the disasters of experience under control. For years no such form was forthcoming. Instead, there were a series of fascinating but abortive attempts at stories which came to nothing. The most powerful of these stories—stories usually involving a man in the throes of family disaster, financial ruin, or self-accusation—projected a dream fantasy of a polar voyage which began in a microscopic drop of water and ended in the desolation of an unspeakably remote and icy sea. This and similar fantasies haunted Mark Twain's imagination between 1896 and 1905. In DeVoto's eyes,[268] *The Mysterious Stranger* was the narrative by means of which Mark Twain recovered his balance at the edge of insanity—and saved himself both as man and writer. Such a theory required that the Eseldorf version be the final of the three versions, and such was the conclusion to which DeVoto duly came.

In a recent study of the three versions of the story, John S. Tuckey, availing himself of all possible evidence and making intelligent speculations where necessary, has conclusively shown that DeVoto's guesses are untenable.[22] Rather than being the last version of the three, the Eseldorf version was, according to Tuckey, the first—except for what he terms a "pre-Eseldorf" fragment evidently incorporated into the Eseldorf manuscript.[23] Begun in the fall of 1897, when Mark Twain was in Vienna, and continued until January, 1898, the Eseldorf version was resumed from May until October of 1899, dropped, and again taken up from June to August of 1900, before being finally abandoned.[24] All work on the Hannibal version was done in November and December of 1898.[25] The Print Shop version was not begun until November of 1902, was pursued intermittently until October, 1903, intensively from January to June of 1904, and again in June and July of 1905.[26] [269]

---

[22] John S. Tuckey, *Mark Twain and Little Satan* (West Lafayette, Ind., 1963). This excellent book not only describes what Paine did and De Voto thought but offers the best account to date of Mark Twain's work during this final phase of his life as an active writer.

[23] *Ibid.*, pp. 24, 51.

[24] *Ibid.*, pp. 25–40, 43–53. Tuckey believes that Mark Twain intended the Eseldorf version to end with the happy insanity of Father Peter following the trial scene, but that satiric impulses toward particular events in the summer of 1900 led him to carry the story beyond his intended conclusion.

[25] *Ibid.*, pp. 41–42.

[26] *Ibid.*, pp. 54–61, 68–70. Mark Twain wrote a small, but significant, episode in 1908 (Tuckey, pp. 72–73). This portion—in which "44" shows August Feldner a ghostly procession of the dead of all the past, then waves it away in oblivion leaving the two alone in a soundless world—could have been intended as a conclusion for the Print Shop version, but Tuckey believes that[269] the episode would have brought the story into line with the conclusion written in 1904.

The six-page chapter which Paine discovered as a "conclusion" to the Eseldorf version was, according to Tuckey, written between February and June of 1904—when Olivia Langdon was in her last illness—and was clearly intended to be a conclusion for the Print Shop version. To make it seem a part of the Eseldorf version, Paine and F. A. Duneka, both of whom edited the story, had to change the name of "44" to Satan. This was not all. They had to write the initial paragraph of the chapter in order to link the fragment with the earlier manuscript. They also borrowed the name "The Mysterious Stranger" from the Print Shop version.[27] Yet all the editorial changes cannot make the "44" of the last chapter identical with the Satan of the first ten chapters. Satan had been bodied forth as an angel, but "44" had been narratively defined in the Print Shop version as the dream self of August Feldner. Thus his announcement that he is a dream, which comes as a revelation to both Theodor Fischer and the reader in the published story, was, in its original context, to have been a revelation only to August.

Tuckey's findings do not invalidate so much as they define Paine's text of *The Mysterious Stranger*. Though clearly edited by Paine, that text just as clearly is not going to be superseded by any future text. In one sense, Tuckey is right in concluding that Paine's version "does not represent Mark Twain's intention,"[28] since Paine[270] played fast and loose with the versions of the story. Yet the point remains that there is *no* text of the story—that, far from finding his intention as he proceeded from version to version of his story (as DeVoto wished to believe), Mark Twain clearly lost it. What he found instead was a new editor to replace the lost Olivia Langdon Clemens. If, as Tuckey believes, he wrote the ending of his book at the time of her death, he found in Albert Bigelow Paine the man who would and could take upon himself the "liberty" of editing his remains. Considered from the point of view of "principle," Paine took outrageous freedoms. But given the state of the three versions which lay before him, Paine's edition was clearly a brilliant performance. Choosing the Eseldorf version was not difficult, since it was obviously the most sustained and coherent of the three, but the changes, excisions, and transitions Paine made required a presumptuousness bordering on audacity. Finally, Paine's "discovery" of the ending was in its way a genuine discovery. What-

[27] They took even further liberties. Mark Twain had, in the original manuscript, pursued what for him was a familiar plot device—the presence of a good priest (Father Peter) and a bad one (Father Adolf). But Duneka, a Roman Catholic, strongly objected to the bad priest, and he and Paine invented the astrologer to serve as villain of the published version, leaving Father Adolf precariously present but detached from the plot—resembling in this respect the twins Angelo and Luigi whom Mark Twain left in *Pudd'nhead Wilson*. According to Tuckey, Paine and Duneka cut out about one-quarter of the wordage of the manuscript—sometimes as many as forty pages of manuscript in sequence—to give the reader a coherent tale.

[28] Tuckey, *Mark Twain and Little Satan*, p. 77.[270]

ever inconsistencies existed as a result of the transposition, the consistencies were far more striking. By the time Paine had completed his operation, the lesion had been concealed so remarkably as to leave but a gliding, almost imperceptible trick of transformation at the story's end, as if the movement were indeed a dream. And so the Print Shop ending turned out to be an Eseldorf ending after all; for if Satan's angelic identity in the Eseldorf ending was explicit, his dream identity was clearly implicit, thus allowing Paine's transposed ending to work in its new context.

That Paine's edition should be "doubted" is only true to Mark Twain's identity. But like his *Biography,* which—for all its censorship, protection, and concealment—has proved more and more difficult to supersede, his edition will, when the last word of each unpublished version has been duly edited and published, be more, not less, formidable.[29] In the last analysis, Mark Twain discovered in[271] Paine the editorial intention which he had lost; thus Paine's posthumous edition of Mark Twain's last work is the closest thing to Mark Twain's intention that we shall ever have. Paine was, in fact, able to do precisely what Mark Twain could not do—integrate and coordinate the dissipating impulse of Mark Twain's final effort as a writer.[30] That is why *The Mysterious Stranger,* even with our added consciousness of the editorial process which brought it to conclusive form, remains Mark Twain's last written work. It is what we may call the essential form of Mark Twain's "despair," and deserves analysis as such.

Perhaps the most illuminating approach to *The Mysterious Stranger* is to see it in the light of *Joan of Arc.* Joan is the good, good girl—the epitome of conventional purity, the object of the reverent style, the human saint in the process of being translated into an angel. Philip Traum, on the other hand, is the *little* Satan come down to inhabit the world of the three boys. The quality of that world is immediately defined in the opening paragraphs of the story:

[29] The published version of *The Mysterious Stranger* represents a wholeness unapproached by such unpublished manuscripts as[271] "Statement of the Edwardses," "The George Harrison Story," or "3,000 Years Among the Microbes." All of these share the thematic drift of the three versions of *The Mysterious Stranger* and show the same tendency of inventive impulse dissipating into indulgence. There is, as a matter of fact, a character named Doangiveadam who threatens at one point to take over the action of the Print Shop version. The character's name reveals nothing so much as Mark Twain's actual relationship to his story. Hopefully all these manuscripts will one day be edited and published, not only for the interest they inevitably have but also to dispel the myth, so energetically fostered by Mark Twain, that the powerful work is still to come.

[30] Having completed his biography of Mark Twain, Paine may very well have felt that his massive editorial work on the book was not really a violation of any principle but "only" what Mark Twain would have wanted anyway, in which case his fiction about the ending may not have seemed at all a fiction.[272]

It was in 1590—winter. Austria was far away from the world, and asleep; it was still the Middle[272] Ages in Austria, and promised to remain so forever. Some even set it away back centuries upon centuries and said that by the mental and spiritual clock it was still the Age of Belief in Austria. But they meant it as a compliment, not a slur, and it was so taken, and we were all proud of it. I remember it well, although I was only a boy; and I remember, too, the pleasure it gave me.

Yes, Austria was far from the world, and asleep, and our village was in the middle of that sleep, being in the middle of Austria. It drowsed in peace in the deep privacy of a hilly and woodsy solitude where news from the world hardly ever came to disturb its dreams, and was infinitely content. At its front flowed the tranquil river, its surface painted with cloud-forms and the reflections of drifting arks and stone-boats; behind it rose the woody steeps to the base of the lofty precipice; from the top of the precipice frowned a vast castle, its long stretch of towers and bastions mailed in vines; beyond the river, a league to the left, was a tumbled expanse of forest-clothed hills cloven by winding gorges where the sun never penetrated; and to the right a precipice overlooked the river, and between it and the hills just spoken of lay a far-reaching plain dotted with little homesteads nested among orchards and shade trees.[31]

Here is one of Mark Twain's finest impersonations of the style of juvenile romance—it is so good that it seems better and "richer" than anything Charlotte Yonge, Kate Douglas Wiggin, or Frances Hodgson Burnett might achieve. It is a highly stylized set piece of description, carefully wrought to convey a miniature and picturesque idyl in which pastoral and historical past are fused in a dreamy setting. All movement is stabilized as in a tableau, and all tendencies of the prose are directed toward indulging the landscape by removing it from motion. Thus, the river is tranquil, its surface is painted with cloud forms[273] and reflections. The sky and the moving boats are not perceived directly but pictured in a reflective scene. The castle, perfectly conventional, frowns from the top of its precipice, its bastions "mailed" in vines. The "tumbled expanse of forest-clothed hills" are "cloven by winding gorges," and the homesteads "dot" the plain. The entire passage seeks to evoke the indulgently picturesque scene of a literary fairy tale.

The intention of this first passage is more to set the convention than disclose the character of the narrator. That is why Theodor Fischer, the narrator, seems always more conventional than individual. His individuality can scarcely be felt against the pressure of the convention his language impersonates—the convention of juvenile romance, with its indulgent reverence for the olden time. Theodor is, in fact, an almost exact parallel of the Old Sieur Louis de Conté who narrated *Joan of Arc*. His entire stance, especially the reverent, oversweet, and somewhat effeminate tone, echoes the Sieur's voice.

There is, of course, one touch of irony in Theodor's opening

---

[31] *The Mysterious Stranger and Other Stories* (New York, 1922), p. 3.

passage, when he observes that those who said the Age of Belief still prevailed in Austria "meant it as a compliment, not a slur." The irony here, though brief, is clearly intended as an intrusive, almost sardonic observation of the experienced narrator's wry comment upon the particular innocence of his past; it is at the same time a stylistic grimace at the particular complacency the idyl indulges and sustains. At first glance such irony might seem to distinguish Theodor's style from the Old Sieur's, yet the same kind of irony is present in *Joan of Arc*. For the Old Sieur, having seen Joan killed by the world, possesses such a contempt for humanity that he frequently releases a scornful generalization about the nature of man.

But there is a deployment of ironic effect in *The Mysterious Stranger* which makes it a direct antithesis of *Joan of Arc*. The antithesis is produced not by a change of tone or narrative consciousness but by a change of[274] mysterious strangers. Joan had been the mysterious stranger of her village who, possessed by angelic voices, defied the despair and complacency which gripped the people she was to save. However rebellious she was, however scathingly she exposed the folly of the Church and government, she was the pure and martyred maid of Orleans whom Mark Twain, through the recollections of the Sieur, was joining history to revere. Little Satan is different. To be sure, he is an angel, but his name discloses his relationship to the darker powers. Not a devil or even diabolical, he is a bad boy angel come to earth for two reasons. As bad boy, he has come to please himself with the same kinds of showmanship that Tom Sawyer had sprung upon the bored community. As angel, however, he aspires to do more than engage in boyish pranks. He means to expose the paltry human scene in which his miracles are to be enacted and at the same time please himself.

And he does please himself with every exposure. Philip Traum is, after all, a kind of genie who appears to conduct the children on a series of remarkable adventures. The magician possessed of the greatest tricks, he enters the sleepy village to inject a sense of excitement and glamor into the lives of the bored boys who live there. The dream of possibility long since surrendered by the adults yet still visible to the children, he represents nothing less than the creative imagination. This symbolic status is at the core of the satiric conception of the book. For the book is satiric, and not humorous, in intent, which is to say that the impulse to expose reality dominates the impulse to play upon it. The pleasure of judgment thus supersedes the pleasure of play. Whereas Huck had rejected civilization in order to play in the territory, Satan rejects it because it is contemptible. The intent of Philip Traum's final speech is to illuminate Theodor's—and the reader's—mind by confronting him with a shocking revelation:[275]

"It is true, that which I have revealed to you; there is no God, no universe, no human race, no earthly life, no heaven, no hell. It is all a dream—a grotesque and foolish dream. Nothing exists but you. And you are but a *thought*—a vagrant thought, a useless thought, a homeless thought, wandering forlorn among the empty eternities!"

He vanished, and left me appalled; for I knew, and realized, that all he had said was true.[32]

Theodor's concluding word is the key term of the passage; it not only echoes Satan's contention in the immediate context, but provides a possible termination of the entire narrative, thereby making the chapter seem, even if it is not, the logical conclusion which Paine pretended it was. This does not mean that the book is truer than *Huckleberry Finn* or any of Mark Twain's earlier works, but that it is committed to a conceptual rather than a narrative substance. This tendency toward disclosure and concept shifts the emphasis from Satan's action to his thought. To see just how the form of the book conspires toward this end, one has but to see the nature of Satan. He is seen from the beginning to be an extension of the boys' wishes and thoughts. Thus he can both read their minds and enliven their somnolent lives. Yet he is by no means an hallucination of Theodor. He can be seen by the select society of the three boys and, under the name of Philip Traum, he has objective existence in the village. He is, and is clearly meant to be, not a private projection of the narrator but an embodiment of the creative imagination itself, affording the children excitement and adventure, even as it frees them to see the truth.

And what is the truth which Satan reveals? It is that man is a slave. His argument hinges on two revelations. First, man is a slave of circumstance; his life is a fatally fixed chain of acts brought about not by God—interestingly enough—but by his own first act.[276]

"You see, now [says Satan to Theodor], that a man will never drop a link in his chain. He cannot. If he made up his mind to try, that project would itself be an unavoidable link—a thought bound to occur to him at that precise moment, and made certain by the first act of his babyhood."

It seemed so dismal!

"He is a prisoner for life," I said sorrowfully, "and cannot get free."

"No, of himself he cannot get away from the consequences of his first childish act. But I can free him."[33]

Although Satan's philosophical exercise need not be perfect, this one is clearly so inadequate that it fails to sustain the illusion of philosophical thought. Theodor never questions and Satan never defines what he means by *act*, though presumably he means not a child's conscious choice but a baby's uncomprehending gesture; the first act is thus rooted not in the mind but in the identity. Yet Satan insists that this first act is more original than fatal. The point is not that the idea is false but that it is so sketchily presented as to fail to meet the de-

[32] *Ibid.*, p. 140.
[33] *Ibid.*, p. 83.

mands it evokes. This failure causes action to evade the thought it provokes and drift toward a miraculous demonstration of each inadequately stated proposition. Thus when Satan says that he can free man from his slavery, he proceeds to show how he, as an angel, is able to change a link in the chain and alter the lives of men.

But man is not only in metaphysical chains, he is also morally a slave—a victim of the Moral Sense. The Moral Sense is, of course, the faculty enabling men to distinguish good from evil. Satan first calls the faculty into question when he creates a tribe of little men before the boys' astonished eyes, then pleasantly annihilates them as if they were no more than ants. Confronted by the children's horror at his action, he almost laughingly avers that men are unspeakably inferior to angels by[277] virtue of possessing the Moral Sense. Discomfited by Satan's revelation, the children seek illumination from the benign Father Peter:

> There was a question which we wanted to ask Father Peter, and finally we went there the second evening, a little diffidently, after drawing straws, and I asked it as casually as I could, though it did not sound as casual as I wanted, because I didn't know how:
> "What is the Moral Sense, sir?"
> He looked down, surprised, over his great spectacles, and said, "Why, it is the faculty which enables us to distinguish good from evil."
> It threw some light, but not a glare, and I was a little disappointed, also to some degree embarrassed. He was waiting for me to go on, so, in default of anything else to say, I asked, "Is it valuable?"
> "Valuable? Heavens! lad, it is the one thing that lifts man above the beasts that perish and makes him heir to immortality."[34]

Between the innocence of childhood and Father Peter's reverence comes Satan's relentless exposure. The force of his argument lies not so much in his irreverent inversion of genteel values as in the radical orthodoxy of his position. For little Satan has the angelic, not the diabolical, point of view. Though his name suggests the experience of his old Uncle, this little Satan is unfallen. It is the children, oddly enough, who have fallen—and not into original sin but into the fatuity of adulthood. Theodor is finally just what his stilted and nice language discloses him to be—a reverent little man.

Surely Mark Twain's triumph in *The Mysterious Stranger* is the play upon this double inversion, in which Satan's apparent diabolism is actually prelapsarian innocence and the children's seeming innocence is nothing less than a complete Fall. Satan's line of logic on this[278] score is as relentless as the series of illuminations by means of which he proves his propositions. He shows with ironic innocence how man's belief in the Moral Sense inevitably manifests itself as an action of brutality. Why? Simply because the Moral Sense makes pos-

[34] *Ibid.*, pp. 33–34.

sible the identity of good and evil, right and wrong, thereby enabling man to subvert the pleasure principle. Whereas the angel—and by implication the child—knows no wrong and gains pleasure from an instinctive and instinctual relation to life itself, man gains pleasure by inflicting pain on others. In one of Satan's finest moments, he upbraids Theodor for referring to a particularly sadistic inquisitional torture as *brutal*.

"No, it was a human thing. You should not insult the brutes by such a misuse of that word; they have not deserved it. . . . It is like your paltry race—always lying, always claiming virtues which it hasn't got, always denying them to the higher animals, which alone possess them. No brute ever does a cruel thing—that is the monopoly of those with the Moral Sense. When a brute inflicts pain he does it innocently; it is not wrong; for him there is no such thing as wrong. And he does not inflict pain for the pleasure of inflicting it—only man does that. Inspired by that mongrel Moral Sense of his!"[35]

Satan is not here defending animal innocence, but indicting the Moral Sense which enables man to enjoy inflicting pain, thereby exposing him as the sole creature who gains pure pleasure from hurting his fellow man.

Not only does Satan's most effective criticism of man hinge upon his exposure of the Moral Sense; his chief force of character—his effective identity—resides in his being without it. What sustains the narrative more than any other factor is the inverted or contradictory emotional response to experience which Satan and the children have. The climax of the episode in which Satan creates[279] the race of little men occurs when he casually and innocently annihilates them before the appalled eyes of the children. And at every point in the narrative Satan's particular emotional freedom from grief and guilt is exploited. He cannot die and he cannot do wrong; he can only expose man's absurd moral sense to the children. His whole pleasure is to laugh at the pathetic figure of man, whose moral sense epitomizes the absurdity and futility of human existence. It is the sum and summary which, in the angelic view, makes man a grotesque and foolish joke.

In the face of such folly, Satan takes upon himself the burden of initiating the children into the double awareness that life is not worth living—that Death is the blessing and not the curse of man. For Death is the event which frees man from the shackles of determinism. In a dramatic demonstration of the full import of his philosophy, Satan indicates to Theodor his regard for the three children and speaks of his intention to release Nikolaus from the chain of events which await him. Certain that Satan will do generously by one whom he likes, Theodor is delighted to hear of the decision, only to be desolated by Satan's disclosure that Nikolaus, who would have lived sixty-five years under

[35] *Ibid.*, pp. 50–51.

the old dispensation, will live but twelve more days under Satan's new order. Satan blithely reassures Theodor and soothes his grief by revealing that Nikolaus "had a billion possible careers, but not one of them was worth living."[36] And so Nikolaus dies with his companions' foreknowledge grieving them at every approaching moment, yet leaving them powerless in the face of the inexorable plot which Satan has devised. Through all this section, Satan affects an innocent pleasure which at once frees him from the sentiment the little men continually indulge and dramatizes his radical innocence.

Mark Twain's success in exposing the Moral Sense brings us back to his failure in the matter of determinism. He is never able to integrate the two concepts. For the Moral Sense has to do with man's pride, folly, and self-deception,[280] whereas the deterministic thesis rests upon the undefined concept of a "first" act which determines the rest of man's existence. The Moral Sense is calculated to expose the folly of man; the deterministic thesis, on the other hand, must—if it is to be effective—be the plot of God.

But precisely here the book is reticent; hence Satan's statement that the primal act is by man, not by God. Yet if man is responsible, why is the deterministic thesis necessary? Why not simply let the Moral Sense bear the satiric burden? In a certain sense, the book does point toward an attack on God; Satan places the first act in infancy, making it a product of the instinctive rather than the conscious will, thereby implicating God more than man in the chain of events. Such, at least, is the implication when Satan says that of a billion possible careers for Nikolaus none was worth living. Even so, the book evades this issue and pursues a delaying line of action. The question comes to be: why did Mark Twain avoid the real necessity of the deterministic thesis? One possibility is that he was afraid to make the direct charge against God; yet he had said things equally "dangerous" and had made jokes equally if not more irreverent.

The real reason—or at least a more relevant reason—for Mark Twain's inability to meet the necessity of the deterministic thesis has to do with the character of little Satan; he cannot really attack God directly without losing his angelic identity. If he rebels, he inevitably becomes diabolic and takes upon himself the role of the avuncular Satan. As fallen angel he could no longer blithely ridicule the Moral Sense, for he himself would be in hot-hearted rebellion against it. Instead of laughing at Man, he would perforce have to free him from his chains. His satanic identity indicates the eternal presence of the impulse to rebel against God and thus makes necessary the deterministic thesis. But just as surely, the fact that it is *little* Satan and not the Old One keeps Mark Twain from being able to carry out the attack upon God. This inability[281] to coordinate the two lines of

[36] *Ibid.*, p. 86.

criticism—the one against man, the other against God—produces the real hiatus in the book.[37]

This central problem could well have been what drove Mark Twain to his repeated efforts to finish the manuscript. With every appearance of little Satan, whether the scene was Hannibal or Austria, Mark Twain was back in a new version of his old dilemma: what to do with little boys about to grow up. Yet if the dilemma forced him into greater and greater efforts to breach or camouflage the division in his conception, it must have made him more and more certain of his ending. For the ending which he confidently left for Paine to find was a way out of the dilemma. It was like a goal which he could see but could not reach. In it, Satan does attack God, but only at the moment of his disappearance. Visiting Theodor for the last time, he explains that everything is a dream, that he himself is but a dream and Theodor but a thought wandering alone in shoreless space. "I am perishing already—I am failing—I am passing away," he announces, whereupon he delivers his assault upon God:

"Strange . . . that you should not have suspected that your universe and its contents were only dreams, visions, fiction! Strange, because they are so frankly and hysterically insane—like all dreams: a God who could make good children as easily as bad, yet preferred to make bad ones; who could have made every one of them happy, yet never made a single happy one; who made them prize their bitter life, yet stingily cut it short . . . who gave his angels painless lives, yet cursed his other children with biting miseries and maladies of mind and body; who mouths justice and invented hell—mouths mercy and invented hell—mouths Golden Rules, and forgiveness multiplied by seventy times seven, and invented hell; who mouths morals to[282] other people and has none himself; who frowns upon crimes, yet commits them all; who created man without invitation, then tries to shuffle the responsibility for man's acts upon man, instead of honorably placing it where it belongs, upon himself; and finally, with altogether divine obtuseness invites this poor, abused slave to worship him!"[38]

This ending has the kind of perorational finality so lacking in *Huckleberry Finn*. Moreover, it has a logic in relation to the book, for it releases Satan's attack at the moment of his dissolution, in effect enabling him to destroy his own identity by delivering his pent-up attack on God. Yet the inevitability of the ending does not keep it from being a way out rather than a way through the dilemma which caused it. For little Satan's attack is what it reveals itself to be—an outburst of the pent-up indignation which the structure and style of the book could not discharge. More important, Satan's solipsism constitutes a decisive weakening of the criticism produced by his ironic innocence. Finally, the ending gives the lie to the identity of the book, for Satan in his

[37] This failure of coordination may very well have been at the heart of Mark Twain's failure during this entire phase of his career.

[38] *The Mysterious Stranger*, p. 139.

act of departing actually acquires the Moral Sense he has been remarkably and effectively free of in the successful moments of the narrative. The truth is that Satan must forego the emotion of indignation if he is to be free of the Moral Sense. There can be no hostile rebellion based on principle without acquisition of that abhorred faculty.

Mark Twain had evidently seen and understood the problem. After all, he had written the ending as a goal to be reached. Moreover, he had envisioned little Satan's dissolution in the act of releasing his pent-up indignation. What he had not been able to do was to unify the division in his conception—the division between the angelic and the diabolic Satan. That division had both plagued and motivated him from the time it formally announced itself in the seminal farce of "Those Extraordinary Twins." The writing of *The Mysterious Stranger* was his prolonged[283] struggle to breach the division and achieve the kind of wholeness which had eluded him in his waning years. But though he had seen his ending—something he had not been able to do so well in *Huckleberry Finn*—the merciless division could neither be healed nor concealed. It was there from the beginning in the very seed of the conception, making the narrative connections more and more tenuous even as the ending became more and more inevitable. Though he could end the story, he could not finish it. Instead, it finished him as a writer.[284]

QUESTIONS FOR STUDY

1. How well did Albert Bigelow Paine and Frederick A. Duneka do their editorial work in preparing *The Mysterious Stranger* for posthumous publication? Do you think that their deviations from Mark Twain's text can be justified? If so, on what grounds? If not, should their edition be rejected? Or must it be regarded as a *fait accompli*? What edition could or should take its place?

2. In particular, can you defend Paine and Duneka's reduction of the role of Father Adolf and their addition of another character, the astrologer? How effective is the device of using the astrologer as the villain in the story? Can effectiveness be any justification for the exceeding of editorial prerogatives?

3. What is a novella? What features of *The Mysterious Stranger* make it proper to call it a novella? What are some other novellas in American literature? In other literatures? How would you rank Mark Twain's novella among them?

4. How would you compare the description of the village of Eseldorf with Mark Twain's descriptions of St. Petersburg in *Tom Sawyer* and of Dawson's Landing in *Pudd'nhead Wilson*? After making your own comparisons, you should read Henry Nash Smith's "Mark Twain's Images of Hannibal: From St. Petersburg to Eseldorf," *Texas Studies in English*, XXXVII (1958), 3–23. You may also wish to consult Dixon Wecter, *Sam Clemens of Hannibal* (Boston: Houghton Mifflin, 1952).

5. How has Mark Twain characterized his narrator, Theodor Fischer? Does Theodor exhibit the same characteristics throughout the story? Does he change as a result of his association with Philip Traum? In what ways?

6. Does the mysterious stranger, Philip Traum, speak and act consistently in the story? E. S. Fussell considers this and related questions in "The Structural Problem of *The Mysterious Stranger*," one of the articles in this volume. Do you agree with Fussell that "failure to arbitrate the claims of objective and subjective phenomena ultimately explains the basic confusion in *The Mysterious Stranger*"?

7. What do you understand by Philip Traum's statement to Theodor, "I am but a dream—your dream, creature of your imagination"? Is the mysterious stranger a projection of the narrator's unconscious mind? Is the story "a testament to man's imagination as creator," as E. H. Eby asserts in "Mark Twain's Testament," *Modern Language Quarterly*, XXIII (September 1962), 254–262? Which other critics tend to agree with Eby?

8. What deterministic doctrines does Mark Twain assert in the story? Is the deterministic emphasis maintained throughout the story or only in some parts of it? What view, if any, does Mark Twain assert in opposition to determinism?

9. In what respects is Philip Traum a "transcendent" character? In what other works by Mark Twain can you find similar figures? Compare their roles in their stories with the role of Philip Traum in *The Mysterious Stranger*.

10. Ludwig Lewisohn has stated in *Expression in America* (New York: Harper & Row, Publishers, 1932), p. 226, that in *The Mysterious Stranger* (and also in *What Is Man?*) "we find the crudest and most shallow treatment of the most intricate matters; we find, quite literally, the ideas of a village agnostic." Leslie Fiedler has more recently written in *Love and Death in the American Novel* (New York: Criterion Books, 1960), p. 438, that *The Mysterious Stranger* "is finally an obvious book." How much validity do these charges seem to have?

11. Compare Mark Twain's representation of mobs and mob actions in *The Mysterious Stranger* with such representations in *Huckleberry Finn* and *A Connecticut Yankee in King Arthur's Court*. What in each case is the attitude of the narrator toward the mob and to what extent does he become involved in its actions?

12. After reading Mark Twain's essay "The Lowest Animal" in *Letters from the Earth*, ed. Bernard DeVoto (New York: Harper & Row, Publishers, 1962), pp. 222–232, compare the criticism of mankind's weaknesses and inadequacies expressed there with Philip Traum's discourses on man as a degraded creature.

13. What kinds and what amount of satire do you find in *The Mysterious Stranger?* What are the principal targets of this satire? How effective is the satire? Which of the critics represented in this volume have considered the satire in the story, and how do their views compare?

14. In what respects does Bernard DeVoto's interpretative study "The Symbols of Despair" appear to be sound, and in what respects, if any, does it seem to be unsound?

15. In what sense may *The Mysterious Stranger* be considered a hoax? For an excellent discussion of this question, read the chapter on "The Hoax as Cosmology" in Pascal Covici, Jr., *Mark Twain's Humor: The Image of a World* (Dallas: Southern Methodist University Press, 1962), pp. 213–250. Which other critics have taken notice of hoax-like aspects of the story? How do their views compare with Covici's?

16. According to James M. Cox, what dilemma did Mark Twain face in attempting to finish *The Mysterious Stranger?* Do you agree with Cox's view that the story "finished him [Mark Twain] as a writer"? Explain.

BIBLIOGRAPHY: SELECTED CRITICISM

Abel, Darrel. *American Literature*, Vol. III: *Masterworks of American Realism: Twain, Howells, James.* Barron's Educational Series, 1963. Pp. 113–116.

Allen, Charles A. "Mark Twain and Conscience." *Literature and Psychology,* VII (May 1957), 17–21.

Altick, Richard D. "Mark Twain's Despair: An Explanation in Terms of His Humanity." *South Atlantic Quarterly,* XXXIV (October 1935), 359–367.

Andrews, Kenneth R. *Nook Farm: Mark Twain's Hartford Circle.* Cambridge, Mass.: Harvard University Press, 1950. Pp. 236–237.

Arvin, Newton. "Mark Twain: 1835–1935." *The New Republic,* XX (June 12, 1935), 125–127.

Baender, Paul. "Alias Macfarlane: A Revision of Mark Twain Biography." *American Literature,* XXXVIII (May 1966), 187–197.

———. "The Date of Mark Twain's 'The Lowest Animal.'" *American Literature,* XXXVI (May 1964), 174–179.

Baldanza, Frank. *Mark Twain: An Introduction and Interpretation.* New York: Barnes & Noble, Inc., 1961. Pp. 138–140.

Bellamy, Gladys Carmen. "Samuel L. Clemens," in *Eight American Writers,* ed. Norman Foerster and Robert P. Falk. New York: W. W. Norton & Company, Inc., 1963. Pp. 1181–1184.

———. *Mark Twain as a Literary Artist.* Norman: University of Oklahoma Press, 1950. Pp. 352–376.

Blair, Walter. *Mark Twain and Huck Finn.* Berkeley: University of California Press, 1960. Pp. 31–33, 184.

Bradford, Gamaliel. "Mark Twain." *Atlantic Monthly,* CXXV (April 1920), 464–473.

Brashear, Minnie M. *Mark Twain, Son of Missouri.* Chapel Hill: University of North Carolina Press, 1934. Pp. 240, 251–252.

Brooks, Van Wyck. *The Ordeal of Mark Twain.* Revised ed. New York: E. P. Dutton & Company, Inc., 1933. Pp. 214–256.

Budd, Louis J. *Mark Twain: Social Philosopher.* Bloomington: Indiana University Press, 1964. Pp. 191–206.

Burhans, Clinton S. "The Sober Affirmation of Mark Twain's Hadleyburg." *American Literature,* XXXIV (November 1962), 375–385.

Canby, Henry Seidel. *Turn West, Turn East.* Boston: Houghton Mifflin Company, 1951. Pp. 239–257.

Carter, Paul J., Jr. "Olivia Clemens Edits *Following the Equator*." *American Literature*, XXX (May 1958), 194–209.

Covici, Pascal, Jr. *Mark Twain's Humor: The Image of a World*. Dallas: Southern Methodist University Press, 1962. Pp. 213–250.

Cowie, Alexander. *The Rise of the American Novel*. New York: American Book Company, 1951. Pp. 636–640.

Cowper, Frederick A. G. "The Hermit Story, as Used by Voltaire and Mark Twain," in *Papers . . . in Honor of . . . Charles Frederick Johnson*, eds. Odell Shepard and Arthur Adams. Hartford, Conn., 1928. Pp. 313–337.

Cox, James M. "*A Connecticut Yankee in King Arthur's Court*: The Machinery of Self-Preservation." *Yale Review*, L (Autumn 1960), 89–102.

———. *Mark Twain: The Fate of Humor*. Princeton: Princeton University Press, 1966. Pp. 247–309.

———. "*Pudd'nhead Wilson*: The End of Mark Twain's American Dream," *South Atlantic Quarterly*, LVIII (Summer 1959), 351–363.

Cummings, Sherwood. "Mark Twain's Social Darwinism." *Huntington Library Quarterly*, XX (1956–1957), 163–175.

DeVoto, Bernard. "Introduction." *The Portable Mark Twain*. New York: The Viking Press, Inc., 1946. Pp. 23–27.

———. *Mark Twain at Work*. Cambridge, Mass.: Harvard University Press, 1942. Pp. 105–130.

———. *Mark Twain's America*. Boston: Little, Brown and Company, 1935. Pp. 269–297.

Eby, E. H. "Mark Twain's Testament." *Modern Language Quarterly*, XXIII (September 1962), 254–262.

Fatout, Paul. *Mark Twain on the Lecture Circuit*. Bloomington: Indiana University Press, 1960. Pp. 241–288.

Ferguson, DeLancey. *Mark Twain: Man and Legend*. Indianapolis: The Bobbs-Merrill Company, Inc., 1943. Pp. 184–304.

Fiedler, Leslie A. *Love and Death in the American Novel*. New York: Criterion Books, Inc., 1960. Pp. 437–439.

Flowers, Frank C. "Mark Twain's Theories of Morality." *Mark Twain Quarterly*, VIII (Summer–Fall 1948), 10–11.

Foner, Philip S., ed. *Mark Twain: Social Critic*. New York: International Publishers Company, Inc., 1958.

Friedrich, Gerhard. "Erosion of Values in Twain's Humor." *The CEA Critic*, XXII (September 1960), 1–8.

Fussell, E. S. "The Structural Problem of *The Mysterious Stranger*." *Studies in Philology*, XLIX (January 1952), 95–104.

Gerber, John C. "Mark Twain's Use of the Comic Pose." *PMLA*, LXXVII (June 1962), 297–304.

Gibson, William M. "Mark Twain and Howells: Anti-Imperialists." *New England Quarterly*, XX (December 1947), 435–470.

Harnsberger, Caroline. *Mark Twain: Family Man*. New York: Citadel Press, 1960.

Howells, William Dean. *My Mark Twain: Reminiscences and Criticisms*. New York: Harper & Row, Publishers, Inc., 1910.

Jones, Alexander E. "Mark Twain and Freemasonry." *American Literature*, XXVI (November 1954), 363–373.

———. "Mark Twain and the Determinism of *What Is Man?*" *American Literature*, XXIX (March 1957), 1–17.

Kaplan, Justin. *Mr. Clemens and Mark Twain*. New York: Simon and Schuster, Inc., 1966.

Kaul, A. N. *The American Vision: Actual and Ideal Society in Nineteenth-Century Fiction*. New Haven: Yale University Press, 1963. Pp. 282–291.

Laing, Nita. "The Later Satire of Mark Twain." *Midwest Quarterly*, II (Autumn 1960), 35–48.

Laverty, Carroll D. "The Genesis of *The Mysterious Stranger*." *Mark Twain Quarterly*, VIII (Spring–Summer 1947), 15–19.

Leary, Lewis, ed. *Mark Twain's Wound*. New York: Thomas Y. Crowell Company, 1962. Pp. 3–32.

———. *Mark Twain*. University of Minnesota Pamphlets on American Writers Series, No. 5. Minneapolis: University of Minnesota Press, 1960. Pp. 42–45.

Lederer, Max. "Mark Twain in Vienna." *Mark Twain Quarterly*, VII (Summer–Fall 1945), 1–12.

Lewisohn, Ludwig. *Expression in America*. New York: Harper & Row, Publishers, Inc., 1932. Pp. 225–227.

Lorch, Fred W. "Mark Twain's 'Morals' Lecture During the American Phase of His World Tour in 1895–1896." *American Literature*, XXVI (March 1954), 52–66.

Lynn, Kenneth S. *Mark Twain and Southwestern Humor*. Boston: Little, Brown and Company, 1959. Pp. 204–207, 280–285.

Morris, Wright. *The Territory Ahead*. New York: Harcourt, Brace, & World, Inc., 1957. Pp. 79–90.

Paine, Albert Bigelow. "Introduction." *Mark Twain: The Mysterious Stranger and Other Stories*. New York: Gabriel Wells, 1923. Pp. ix–xiii.

———. *Mark Twain: A Biography*. 4 vols. New York: Gabriel Wells, 1923.

———. "Mark Twain at Stormfield." *Harper's Monthly Magazine*, CXVIII (May 1909), 955–958.

Parrington, Vernon Louis. *Main Currents in American Thought*, Vol. III: *The Beginnings of Critical Realism in America*. New York: Harcourt, Brace, & World, Inc., 1927. Pp. 90–100.

Parsons, Coleman O. "The Background of *The Mysterious Stranger*." *American Literature*, XXXII (March 1960), 55–74.

———. "The Devil and Samuel Clemens." *Virginia Quarterly Review*, XXIII (Autumn 1947), 582–606.

Reiss, Edmund. Foreword to Mark Twain, *The Mysterious Stranger and Other Stories*. New York: New American Library of World Literature, 1962. Pp. xiii–xv.

Salomon, Roger B. *Twain and the Image of History*. New Haven: Yale University Press, 1961. Pp. 191–210.

Salsbury, Edith Colgate. *Susy and Mark Twain: Family Dialogues*. New York: Harper & Row, Publishers, Inc., 1965. Pp. 362–400.

Schönemann, Friedrich. "Mark Twain and Adolf Wilbrandt." *Modern Language Notes*, XXXIV (June 1919), 372–374.

Scott, Arthur L., *"The Innocents Adrift.* Edited by Mark Twain's Official Biographer." *PMLA*, LXXVIII (June 1963), 230–237.

––––––, ed. *Mark Twain: Selected Criticism*. Dallas: Southern Methodist University Press, 1955.

Sherman, Stuart P. "The Misanthropy of Mark Twain." *The Nation*, CIII (December 21, 1916), 588–589.

Smith, Annella. "Mark Twain–Occultist." *Rosicrucian Magazine*, XXVI (1934), 65–68.

Smith, Henry Nash. "Can 'American Studies' Develop a Method?" in *Studies in American Culture: Dominant Ideas and Images*, ed. Joseph J. Kwist and Mary C. Trupie. Minneapolis: University of Minnesota Press, 1960. Pp. 7–8.

––––––, ed. *Mark Twain: A Collection of Critical Essays*. Englewood Cliffs: Prentice-Hall, Inc., 1963.

––––––. *Mark Twain: The Development of a Writer*. Cambridge, Mass.: Harvard University Press, 1962. Pp. 171–188.

––––––. "Mark Twain's Images of Hannibal: From St. Petersburg to Eseldorf." *Texas Studies in English*, XXVII (1958), 3–23.

––––––. *"Pudd'nhead Wilson* and After." *Massachusetts Review*, III (Winter 1962), 233–253.

Soule, George. "Mark Twain Protests." *The New Republic*, IX (November 18, 1916), 8.

Spiller, Robert E. *The Cycle of American Literature*. New York: The Macmillan Company, 1955. Pp. 158–162.

Sprague, Julian K. "Mark Twain's 'Things Not Generally Known' as Background for His Writings." *Twainian*, XVII (July–August 1959), 1–4.

Stone, Albert E., Jr. *The Innocent Eye: Childhood in Mark Twain's Imagination*. New Haven: Yale University Press, 1961. Pp. 231–250.

Stone, Edward. *Voices of Despair: Four Motifs in American Literature*. Athens: Ohio University Press, 1966. Pp. 64–69.

Tanner, Tony. "The Lost America–The Despair of Henry Adams and Mark Twain." *Modern Age*, V (Summer 1961), 299–310.

Taylor, Walter Fuller. *The Story of American Letters*. Chicago: Henry Regnery Company, 1956. Pp. 244–249.

Tuckey, John S. *Mark Twain and Little Satan: The Writing of "The Mysterious Stranger."* Lafayette: Purdue University Studies, 1963.

———, ed. *Mark Twain's "Which Was the Dream?" and Other Symbolic Writings of the Later Years*. Berkeley: University of California Press, 1967.

Wagenknecht, Edward. *Mark Twain: The Man and His Work*. Revised edition. Norman: University of Oklahoma Press, 1961. Pp. 201–219, 240–241 *et passim*.

Waggoner, Hyatt Howe. "Science in the Thought of Mark Twain." *American Literature*, VIII (January 1937), 357–370.

Webster, Samuel C. *Mark Twain, Business Man*. Boston: Little, Brown and Company, 1946.

Wecter, Dixon. "Mark Twain," in Robert E. Spiller *et al.*, eds., *Literary History of the United States*. Rev. ed. New York: The Macmillan Company, 1953. Pp. 917–939.

———. *Sam Clemens of Hannibal*. Boston: Houghton Mifflin Company, 1952. Pp. 204–222.

Wiggins, Robert A. *Mark Twain: Jackleg Novelist*. Seattle: University of Washington Press, 1964. Pp. 114–123.